Airbus 330 The Ultimate Guide for Pilots

Captain John A. Moktadier

Zeta Publishing

Ocala, FL

Copyright © 2017 Captain John A. Moktadier

All rights reserved. No part of this publication may be reproduced, distributed, or transmitted in any form or by any means, including photocopying, recording, or other electronic or mechanical methods, without the prior written permission of the publisher, except in the case of brief quotations embodied in critical reviews and certain other noncommercial uses permitted by copyright law. For permission requests, write to the publisher, addressed "Attention: Permissions Coordinator," at the address below.

Zeta Publishing, Inc
3850 SE 58th Ave
Ocala, FL 34480
www.zetapublishing.com

Advisory:
The information contained in this book is for informational purposes only and the author or publisher is not liable for any events resulting from the sole reliance of any information contained in this book or omission of any information. The information contained in this book should never be contradictory to any FAA Regulations of Air Traffic Control Clearances or be a substitution for any Company's Flight Manual.

Ordering Information:
Quantity sales. Special discounts are available on quantity purchases by corporations, associations, and others. For details, contact the publisher at the address above.
Orders by U.S. trade bookstores and wholesalers. Please contact Zeta Publishing: Tel: (352) 694-2553; Fax: (352) 694-1791 or visit www.zetapublishing.com

ISBN: 978-1-947191-41-9 (sc)
ISBN: 978-1-947191-47-1 (hc)
ISBN: 978-1-947191-42-6 (e)

Library of Congress: 2017956379
Printed in the United States of America

About The Book

In this book I have provided you with lots of useful information that I have learned from some of the best pilots and TREs along with my own personal observations during my 35 year career in professional aviation as a captain and TRE. I have also included Pilot Tips, Rules of Thumb, and Simplified A330 systems which will improve your understanding of the Airbus 330 system knowledge, increase your situation awareness and enhance your safety margin for each flight. Included are actual accident scenarios related to pilot mistakes, due to various misunderstandings and misinterpretations of ATC clearance during all phases of flight, especially during instrument approaches.

If you have any questions or comments, please feel free to contact me at: a330ultimate@bellsouth.net.

I would like to thank my wife Sheri for standing beside me throughout my entire career. She has always been my inspiration to reach my dream of becoming the best pilot I could be and help other pilots reach their goals.

AIRBUS 330

The Airbus A330 fly-by-wire is an economical mid-size long-range wide body twin-engine jetliner and is currently in commercial service around the globe. This aircraft continues to please pilots, passengers and airlines alike. A twin-engine twin-aisle wide body that can carry from between 270 to 440 passengers, the A330-300 is flexible enough to offer a range of seating options while consistently delivering high quality comfort to all on board. Benefitting from continuous investment over the last 20 years, it incorporates the most modern features in comfort and in-flight experience. The spacious and inviting cabin features elegant ambient lighting, comfortable seats that are wider than its rivals and the latest-generation entertainment systems. Its cabin is also one of the quietest in the skies creating a calm environment for the entire flight. Movies on-demand allow passengers to suit their own personal tastes while satellite connectivity options can let passengers use mobile phones, internet and email in the air – allowing them to stay up-to-date with their social media, business emails or whatever's happening on the ground. Airbus continues to build a very sophisticated airplane, especially the Airbus 350 and 380, with state of the art automation and system backups making it much easier to fly.

Table of Contents

Chapter One
AIR CONDITIONING/PRESSURIZATION/
VENTILATION 1

Chapter Two
COMMUNICATIONS 10

Chapter Three
ELECTRICAL 18

Chapter Four
FIRE 29

Chapter Five
FLIGHT CONTROLS 37

Chapter Six
FUEL 49

Chapter Seven
HYDRAULICS 59

Chapter Eight
ICE AND RAIN PROTECTION 67

Chapter Nine
LIGHTS 73

Chapter Ten
NAVIGATION 79

Chapter Eleven
LANDING GEAR 89

Chapter Twelve
OXYGEN 97

Chapter Thirteen
PNEUMATIC 106

Chapter Fourteen
APU 113

Chapter Fifteen
POWERPLANT 119

Chapter Sixteen
LIMITATIONS 125

Chapter Seventeen
INTERPRETATION OF GREEN DOT SPEED
AND SOME MISCONCEPTIONS ABOUT
FLYING BELOW GREEN DOT
SPEED 142

Chapter Eighteen
GROUND SPEED MINI (GS-MINI) 148

Chapter Nineteen
A330 QUESTIONS 159

Chapter Twenty
EXPERIENCE IN THE COCKPIT DOES
MATTER 201

Chapter Twenty-One
RISK MANAGEMENT 256

Chapter Twenty-Two
PILOT INCAPACITATION 260

Chapter Twenty-Three
TAKEOFF DEFINITIONS 276

Chapter Twenty-Four
NOISE ABATEMENT 290

Chapter Twenty-Five
REJECTED TAKEOFF 295

Chapter Twenty-Six
FLYING IN AND OUT OF HIGH ALTITUDE
AIRPORTS 312

Chapter Twenty-Seven
HOW TO MAKE AN A330 GO DOWN
AND SLOW DOWN 321

Chapter Twenty-Eight
HOW TO PREVENT A HARD LANDING 327

Chapter Twenty-Nine
NIGHT LANDING 333

Chapter Thirty
JET PERFORMANCE TERMS 338

Chapter Thirty-One
SUMMER AND WINTER OPERATIONS 351

Chapter Thirty-Two
OPTIMUM USE OF WEATHER RADAR 400

Chapter Thirty-Three
INTERCEPTION PROCEDURES 413

Chapter Thirty-Four
TIPS AND PROCEDURES FOR
PILOTS 428

Chapter Thirty-Five
AIRBUS ABBREVIATIONS 461

CHAPTER ONE

Air Conditioning
Pressurization
Ventilation

Brief System Explanation for Pilots

Air conditioning system operation is fully automatic. It provides a continuous flow of air, and maintains a constant selected temperature in the following four zones: Cockpit, Forward cabin, Mid cabin and Aft cabin, which are independently controlled.

Air is supplied by pneumatic system through:

* Two pack flow control valves
* Two packs
* Mixing unit which mixes the air that comes from the cabin and both packs. It is then distributed to the cabin in the cockpit. Temperature regulation adjust through the two hot air pressure regulating valves and the trim air valves, which add hot air tapped at the stream of the packs to the mixing unit air via two hot air manifolds. In case of emergency, a ram air inlet can provide ambient air to the mixing unit. Temperature regulation is controlled by a zone controller and two packs controllers. Flight deck and cabin temperature can be selected from the air panel in the cockpit. A control panel is provided on the forward attendant panel. It can modify each cabin zone temperature demand from the cockpit, during cruise with a limited authority of plus and -3°C.

PACK BAY VENTILATION

Ventilation of the pack bay ensures air circulation in order to maintain, on ground and in flight, a mean temperature compatible with the structure constraints in the relevant area. During flight, air from outside flows into the pack bay through a NACA air inlet. On the ground, a turbofan provides a sufficient air flow. The turbofan is driven by air from the bleed system.

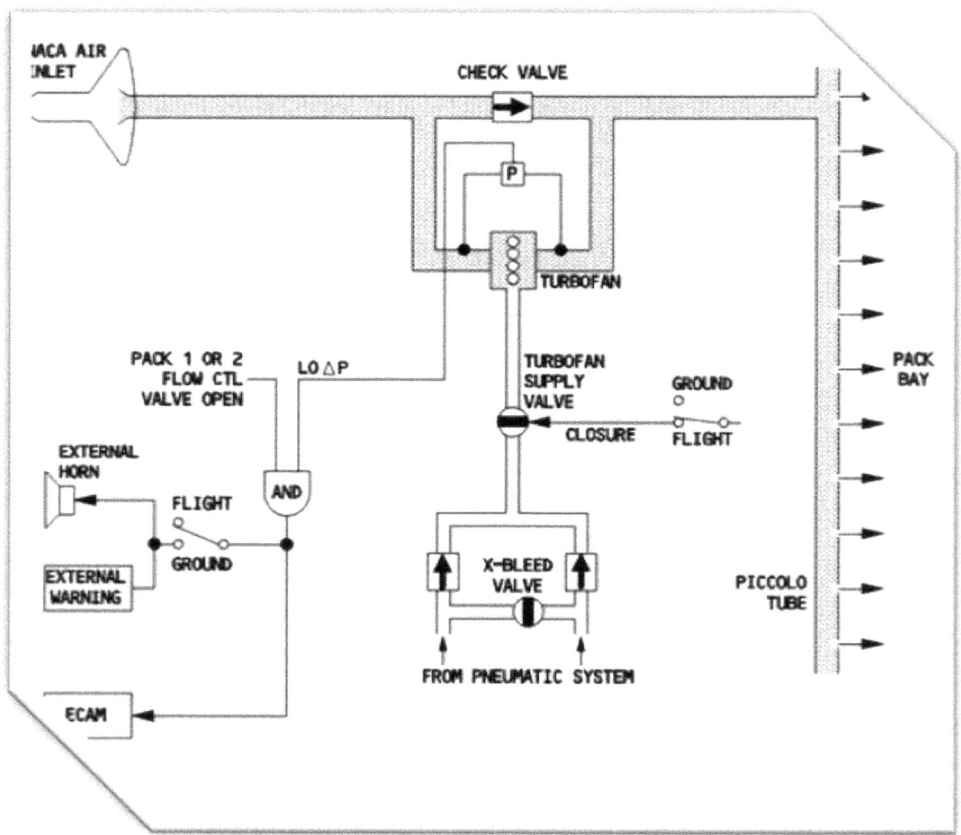

Overhead Panel Explanation

PRESSURIZATION / VENTILATION

Pack 1

On – Pack flow control valve opens automatically, closes when:
*Low Air Pressure below min.
*compressor outlet overheat
* During engine start sequence (Mode selector IGN, reopen after 30s if no eng start.)
*Any door is not closed and locked, a/c on gnd, with engine running.
*On side engine fire Pb pressed
*ditching selected.
If there is no electrical power, the flow valves remain open and permit NORM flow.
Off – Valve closes provided it is electrically supplied

Fault - Valve position disagree with Selector position

- Compressor outlet overheat and Pack outlet overheat

PACK FLOW SELECTOR KNOB

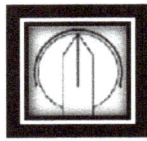
LO- 80% (Less than 160 passengers.
NORM – 100% when 200 passengers or more.
HI – 120% (abnormally hot and humid conditions) one bleed fail, then HI limited to 112%
Note: When single pack ops or APU supply – auto HI

COCKPIT (CABIN)

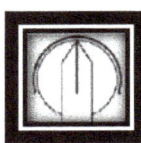
12 O'clock position- 24° C .The actual temp is measured by sensors inside of the aircraft in the Cockpit, Gally and Lavatorys
COLD- 18° C
HOT- 30° C

CAB FANS

On – The 2 cabin fans (recirculation fans) run.
- cabin air blown to avionics comp. And mixer unit.
Off – The 2 cabin fans stop

HOT AIR 1

On – hot air pressure is regulated by the hot air regulating valve
Off – Valve closes
    *Fault circuit is reset
*If HOT AIR 1 Fwd cargo heat is lost
Fault– duct overheat detected (88° C)
*Valve, associated trim air valve close automatically
*AULT Lt goes out automatically when temp dropped below 70° C, or OFF.

RAM AIR

On – Illuminates white
If DITCHING Pb is in normal position RAM air inlet opens
If Δp below 1 psi: each outflow valve remains opens partially as long as they are not under manual control. With a pressure differential above or equal to 1 psi: each outflow valve remains normally controlled.

Off – Ram air inlet closes and outflow valves return to work normal.

LDG ELEV

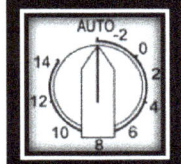
AUTO – System uses FMGS data to construct pressure schedule.
Other Positions – Doesn't use FMGS data.   Uses selected elevation. Elevation can be set between 2000 feet and 14,000 feet.

MODE SEL

AUTO – outflow valve is controlled by a pressure controller and pressurization is fully automatic.
*2 outflow valves.
   *Each operated by 1 of 3 motors, 1 man 2 auto.
   *Transfer between the 2 sys occurs 80s after ldg or if one fails. Can select stby sys by switching to MAN for > 3s then AUTO.
*Uses Ldg elev and QNH from FMGC, and press alt. from ADIRS. If FMGC data n/a the uses Capt. Baro Reference from ADIRS, and LDG ELEV selection.

MAN – Use MAN V/S CTL to control system.
FAULT lt – Amber with ECAM when both automatic systems faulty or failed.

V/S CTL

 Controls the position of the selected outflow as determined by the valve SEL switch when in MAN mode.
UP – The valve(s) move toward the open position. And cabin altitude increases.

DN – The valve(s) move toward the closed position and cabin altitude decreases.

 AFT – The aft valve MAN controlled, FWD outflow valve remains an automatic position.
BOTH – Both outflow valve manually controlled
FWD – The fwd outflow valve MAN controlled, but aft outflow valves remains automatic position.

DITCHING

 Normal – The system function normally.
ON (White) – The following valve closes; (Lt White)

*pack flow control valve
* RAM air inlet valve
*avionics ventilation overboard valve
*cargo compartment isolation valves
*pack flow control valves
*cabin fan stops
*outflow valves. Will not close automatically if under MAN control.

Note: If the ditching pb is put ON, on ground, with low pressure ground cart
connected and all doors closed, a differential press will build up.

EXTRACT

 AUTO – On ground, both Eng not running
* the under floor extract valve is closed
* OVBD valve is open
provided DITCHING is not selected.
* In flt, or on gnd, Eng 1 or 2 running
* Underfloor extract valve open
* OVBD extract valve closed

OVRD – underfloor extract valve closes
OVBD extract valve partially opens
provided Ditching is not selected.

FAULT Lt – Amber with ECAM low extract valve has been detected in the avionic compartment. Light goes out when OVERD is selected.

BULK
ISOL VALVES

ON – The inlet and outlet isolation valves open. Extraction fan runs.
-valves close and fan stops if DITCHING sel.
- valves close and fan stops if smoke in cargo compt
OFF – inlet and outlet isolation valves close, fan stops
FAULT Lt – Amber with ECAM when either valve not in selected position.

HOT AIR

ON– Fan heater operates the bulk cargo compartment temperature drop below selected value and the bulk cargo door is closed (fan blows onto electric element on provided:

OFF – Fan heater operation is stopped. Inlet air not heated.
FAULT -Amber associated with ECAM message in case of:
*fan heater failure
*temp sensor failure
*BULK cargo door not fully closed
*Ventilation system failure
*Duct overheat (above 88° C) Fault goes off when temp<70° and OFF is sel.

AIR OVHT COND
FANS RESET (Overhead Maintenance Panel)

FAULT Lt – Overheat
* Fan stopped
* Press Push button to reset.

CHAPTER TWO

COMMUNICATIONS

Brief System Explanation for Pilots

Communications system consists of the following subsystems:

Audio integrating systems (Audio Management Unit and Audio Control Panels)

Radio Tuning Systems (Radio Management Panels)

SATCOM system

The satellite communication system allows the exchange of information between aircraft and ground network.

VHF/HF transceivers

The aircraft has three identical VHF communication systems. Only VHF1 operates an emergency electrical configuration. The VHF1 ranges from 118.0 to 136.975 MHz. VHF has an alarm to indicate that the microphone is stuck. If a microphone is in the open position for more than 30 seconds an interrupted tone sounds for five seconds and the emission is turned off automatically. To activate the microphone, the crew must release the push to talk button and press it again. Two identical

HF communication systems are installed. Only HF1 is operating in emergency electrical configuration. HF ranges from 2.8 to 24.0 MHz

Note: HF1 will become inoperative when LAND RECOVERY is selected ON. HF must not be used during refueling. When in data mode, the digital information is transmitted between HF1 and ATSU (Air Traffic Service Unit). When receiving a call code corresponding to that particular SELCAL the aircraft SELCAL system aurally and visually lets the flight deck crew know that ground station is calling the aircraft. This aural signal is inhibited during takeoff and landing.

Cabin Intercommunication Data System (CIDS)

Provides signal transmissions, control and processing for the following cabin systems:

Cabin and service interphone
Passenger address
Passenger signs
Reading lights
Cabin illumination

Audio Control Panel

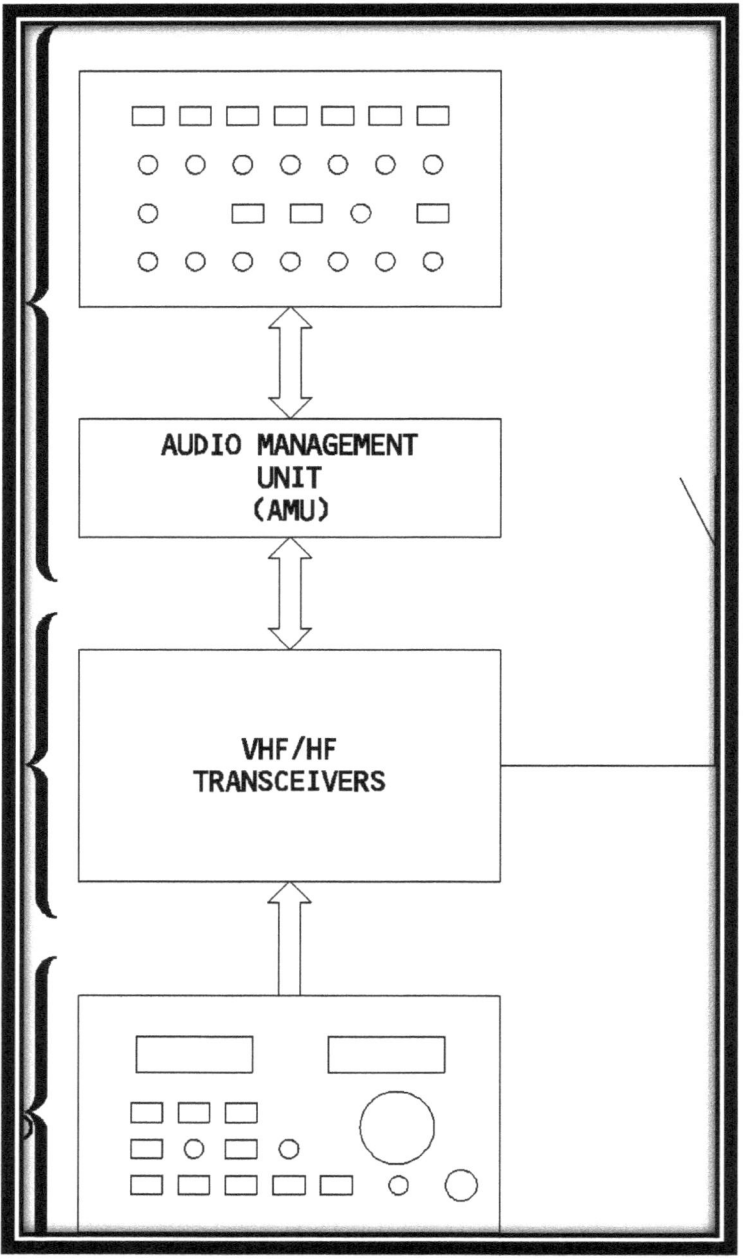

SVC INT
OVRD (Maintenance panel)

 AUTO – If ldg gear compressed, ground crew can use service interphone jacks to communicate with the cockpit.
ON – Comms possible with ldg gear not compressed
* ON light white

MECH

Pressed – COCKPIT CALL lights up Blue on external power panel.
* External horn sounds.
Released – COCKPIT CALL remains lighted
* external horn stops sounding however the blue cockpit call lights remains illuminates until it is reset.

ALL

Pressed – All stations respond as above.
- CALL ALL CAPT appears on AIP's.

EMER

ON – Pink light at all area control panels
* CALL PRIO CAPT message on all AIP's- Red light and 3 x Hi-Lo chimes.
* Hi-Lo Chime x 3 through all loudspeakers
* ATT Amber light flashes on Audio Control Panels
ON Lt – Flashes white for emergency call from cockpit to cabin.
CALL Lt – Flashes Amber for emergency call from Cockpit or Cabin
If call from Cabin to Cockpit:
  *White ON light & Amber CALL light flash
  *Amber ATT lights on ACP's flash
  *3 long buzzers sound in cockpit
  System resets when attendant hangs up.

EVAC

COMMAND

ON – Activates evacuation alert In the cockpit: - EVAV light flashes Red.
* In the cabin: - EVAC lights flash at all AIPS's
* "EVACUATION ALERT" appears on all AIP's and a Red light flashes
* specific evacuation tone sounds.

OFF – The alert is stopped
The EVAC light flashes Red when alert is activated

HORN SHUT OFF

Pressed – silences cockpit horn (generated when EVAC activated from cabin)

CAPT & PURS

CAPT & PURS – Alert may be activated from Cockpit or Cabin
CAPT– Alert may only be activated from Cockpit

RCDR
GND CTL

ON – CVR, DFDR, QAR are automatically energized for one of the following.
*On light Blue
AUTO-System automatically energized
*during first 5 min a/c elec network energized
*on gnd with 1 eng running (system auto switches from ON to AUTO at first eng start and in case of an electrical transient)
*in flight
System automatically de-energized 5 min after last eng shutdown.

CVR
TEST

* a/c on gnd
* parking brake on.

ERASE

Pressed (for 2 sec) – Erases tape completely if a/c on ground and parking brake on.

CHAPTER THREE

ELECTRICAL

Brief System Explanation for Pilots

A330 electrical power system consists of the following:

*Two engine-driven AC generators normal power 115 kVA.

*One auxiliary power unit (APU)

*One emergency generator (Constant Speed Motor or CSM/G), nominal power 8.68 Kva, hydraulically driven by green hydraulic system.

*One static inverter feed connected to two batteries and working either on the ground or when CSM/G inoperative.

*Two ground connectors, power 90 kVA

*DC system provided via two main transformer rectifier units (200A) and one essential (100A)

*A fourth TR (100A) is devoted to APU start or for APU battery charging.

*Three batteries normal capacity 37 Ah, 28V each.

*Two batteries used in emergency configuration to feed some equipment during RAT deployment or when CSM/G not operating.

*One battery dedicated to APU start. Each battery has an associated battery charge limiter (BCL). The BCL monitors by recharging uncontrolled battery contactor.

Note: In case of total loss of all main generators:

The EMER GEN will produce 8.6 kVA because the green hydraulic system is still powered by engine-driven pumps.

Note: In case of loss of both engines the EMER GEN will provide 3.5 kVA because the green hydraulic system is then powered by the RAT. In this case the batteries take over when slats are extended.

CIRCUIT BREAKERS

All circuit breakers are in the electronic equipment bay.

A circuit breaker monitoring unit (CBMU) monitor the circuit breakers status. It sends this information to the (ECAM) system for further investigation by the cockpit crew.

Airbus 330 The Ultimate Guide for Pilots

NORMAL ELECTRICAL CONFIGURATION IN FLIGHT

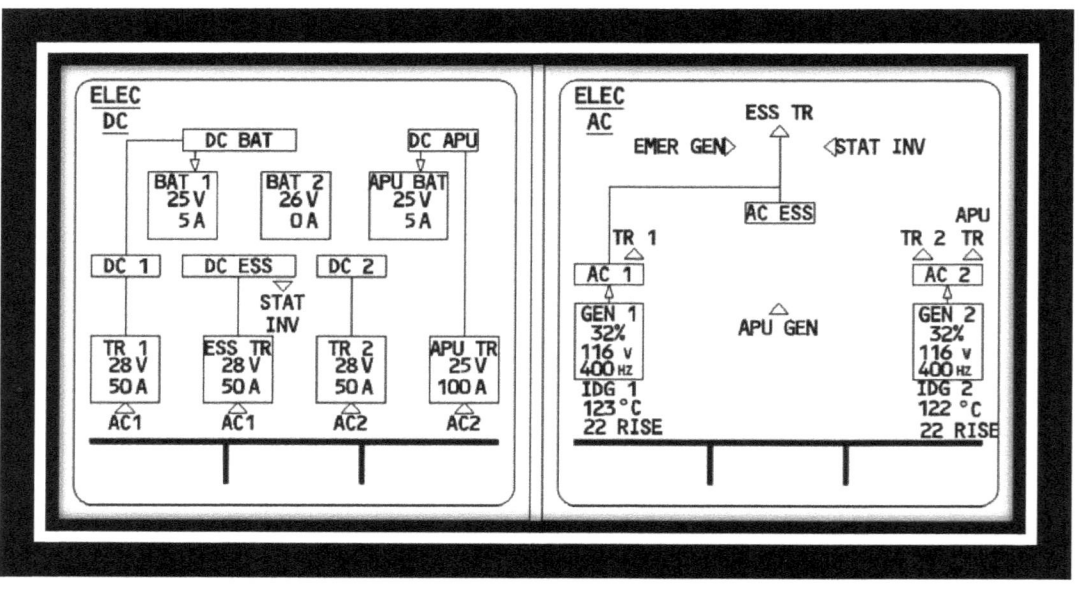

```
BAT
1
2
APU
```

NOTE: Selects the battery for voltage indication.
Voltage indicator Minimum battery voltage 25.5v
Normal 26.8v.

BAT 1(2)

Controls operation of corresponding Battery Charge Limiter (BCL)
AUTO – Automatically controls connect/disconnect of battery to DC BAT BUS by open/closing battery contactor.
Batteries connected to DC BAT BUS when:
*batteries voltage below 26.5V on the ground when only the berries are supplying power to the aircraft and aircraft the speed is below 50 knots. End of charge cycle when bat current below 4A for 10sec on ground & 30min in flight.
*In flt DC generation lost (limited to 7 seconds)

Batteries connected to DC ESS BUS when batteries only are supplying:
*In flight

Note: Batteries are normally disconnected
Auto cutoff logic prevents bat from completely discharging on gnd.

Logic – a/c on gnd
* main power off
* bat <23V for 16 sec or longer

OFF – BCL not operating & DC ESS BUS not connected to bat.
   *HOT buses remain supplied
FAULT - Amber with ECAM when charging current abnormal. Bat contactor opens

APU BAT

Controls the operation of APU BCL (battery charge limiter)
AUTO – APU BCL automatically controls closure/opening of line APU contactor.
Battery connected when:
* charging as per bat 1(2)
*When APU start sequence initiated
OFF / FAULT Lt – As for Bat 1(2)

AC ESS FEED

Normal – AC ESS BUS supplied by AC BUS 1.
*Automatically supplied by AC BUS 2 when AC BUS 1 is lost.
ALTN – AC ESS BUS supplied by AC BUS 2
FAULT. Illuminates Amber to indicate that the AC ESS Bus is and unpowered.

Note: If main generators are lost AC ESS BUS auto supplied by EMERG GEN or by static inverter if EMERG GEN not avail.

GALLEY

 AUTO – ECMU (Electrical Contactor & Management Unit) auto controls shedding of galleys if GEN failure or overload detected.
　　*On gnd APU gen or external pwr supplies galleys provided no overload detected.
　OFF – All galleys are shed and water/water ice protection lost.
FAULT Lt – Amber with ECAM if overload is detected and auto shedding is not occurred.
Note: OFF then AUTO resets galleys that have been shed due overload. If lost due to loss of gen, no reset.

COMMERCIAL

 OFF – Following equipment is shed:
　*Galleys
　　*passenger entertain system (music & video)
　　　*cargo loading system
　*electrical service
　*escape slide lock mechanism ice protection
　*water/waste (drain mast) ice protection
　*lav & cabin lights
　*water heater

IDG 1 (2) (Integrated Drive Generator)

 Pressed to disconnect IDG from drive shaft. Can only reconnect on gnd.
Caution: do not hold down for more than 3sec due damage to disconnection mechanism.
Caution: IDG disconnect inhibited when engine N2 is below the low speed threshold.

FAULT Lt – Amber with ECAM:
  *IDG oil outlet overheat (above 185° C) or
  *IDG oil press low. Inhibited if N2 <14% (N3 <52%)
  *Light extinguishes when IDG disconnected.

GEN 1 (2)

Each GEN can supply up to 75KVA 3 phase 115/200V 400 hertz power.
ON – Gen field is energized & line contactor closes only if generator parameters are within limits.
OFF/R – Gen field is de-energized & line contactor opens, also resetting circuit.
FAULT Lt – Amber with ECAM if protection trip initiated by Generator Control Unit (GCU). Line contactor opens.

Note: If protection trip initiated by a differential fault the reset action has no effect after 2 attempts.

APU GEN

Can supply up to 115KVA which is enough to power entire a/c.
ON – APU gen field is energized & contactor closes.
  * Each bus tie contactor 1,2,3 and/or 4 auto close if associated gen not operative.
OFF/R – Gen field de-energized & contactor opens, resetting circuit.
FAULT Lt – Same as GEN 1 FAULT. APU GEN FAULT Lt inhibited when APU slow

BUS TIE

AUTO   The 3 BUST TIE contactors open/close to provide power to all AC buses. All 3 are closed when a/c is supplied by only one eng generator or by only APU or single external power unit.
OFF – All BUS TIE contactors open.

EXT A (Momentary Action pb)

AVAIL Lt – Green if all external pwr parameters are normal.
* pressing when "AVAIL" ext pwr line contactor closes
- pressing when "ON" ext pwr line contactor opens

EXT B (Momentary Action pb)

AVAIL Lt – Green if all external power parameters are normal.
* if APU gen off, pressing when "AVAIL" ext pwr line contactor closes.
* pressing when "AUTO" ext pwr line contactor opens

Note 1:
* APU GEN has priority over EXT A & B for AC BUS 1
* APU GEN has priority over EXT B for AC BUS 2
* EXT A has priority over APU for AC BUS 2.
* ENG gens have priority over both EXT A&B
*External Power B has priority over EXT A for AC Bus1

Note 2: When EXT B is AUTO, AUTO Lt remains illuminated even when APU has taken over.

EMER ELEC PWR PANEL

EMER GEN TEST

Pressed – Activates the emergency generator and connects gen to ESS network provided that green hydraulic system is pressurized
*This test is inhibited when slats are extended.
*Deactivation only occurs on gnd when eng (1& 2) shutdown with N2 <50%.
*If pressed in flight LAND RECOVERY pb will need to be ON to recover LAND RECOVERY AC and DC BUSES.

EMER GEN MAN ON

When Green HYD sys powered by eng driven pump the EMERG GEN supplies:
*AC ESS BUS
    *AC ESS SHED
*through ESS TR:
    *DC ESS BUS
    *DC ESS SHED
When Green HYD sys powered by RAT the EMERG GEN supplies:
    *AC ESS BUS
    *DC ESS BUS through the ESS TR.
If buses (1 & 2) are lost and eng (1 & 2) are lost the RAT extends automatically to power EMERG GEN.
AUTO – In flight EMEG GEN auto starts if normal AC is lost.
Pressed – EMERG GEN runs.
EMERG GEN FAULT Lt – Red when not supplying and normal AC is lost.

Pushing the emergency generator MAN ON pushbutton will cause the emergency generator to run and connect to the aircraft electrical system

LAND RECOVERY

 ON – In EMERG GEN config. AC LAND RECOVERY & DC LAND RECOVERY bases are restored to power –

1. LGCIU 1
2. SFCC 1 (no flap if powered by RAT or batteries)
3. ILS 1
4. BSCU channel 1
5. LH windshield anti ice (not if powered by RAT or batteries)
6. LH LANDING light

Remaining fuel pump (if any) is lost. Pump may already be lost if below 260kt and Emerg gen is powered by the RAT.

CHAPTER FOUR

FIRE

Brief System Explanation for Pilots

Fire Protection and Description for Engine and APU

Each engine and the APU are equipped with a fire and overheat detection system consisting of:

— Two identical gas detection loops (A and B) mounted in parallel.

— A Fire Detection Unit (FDU).

Each detection loop consists of:

— Five sensing elements for the engine, located in the pylon nacelle and engine core, compressor and fan sections.

— One for the APU, located in the APU compartment.

When a sensing element is subject to heat, a signal is transmitted to the fire detection unit. As soon as a preset level of temperature is detected by loop A and B, the fire warning system is triggered.

A fault in one loop (break or electrical supply loss) will not affect the warning system. Fire detection is provided by the unaffected loop.

If an APU fire is detected on ground an APU automatic shut down and agent discharge will occur.

Avionics Smoke Detection

— Is provided by two smoke detectors (optical type) installed in the air extraction duct of the avionics ventilation system. Each detector is linked to one of the two detection loops of the system (dual loop principle).

— The Smoke Detection Control Unit (SDCU), receives signals from the two detectors, and transmits them to the ECAM, which displays a warning in the cockpit.

Smoke activates the avionics smoke warning if:

— Both detectors detect it for more than 5 seconds, or

— One smoke detector detects it for more than 5 seconds, and the other is inoperative.

When smoke is detected:

— The Repetitive Chime sounds.

— The MASTER WARNING light, on the Glareshield, comes on.

— The ECAM displays a caution on the E/WD.

— The SMOKE light, on the VENTILATION panel, comes on. (if installed):

Affected compartment closes automatically and the extraction fan stops.

Cargo Compartment Smoke Detection

The cargo compartments have a smoke detection system.

— Cavities in the cargo compartment ceiling panels hold smoke detectors (ionization type).

Each cavity has two smoke detectors, and each detector is linked to one of the two detection loops (dual loop principle)

— The forward cargo compartment has two cavities.

— The bulk cargo compartment has one cavity.

— The aft cargo compartment has two cavities.

The Smoke Detection Control Unit (SDCU) receives signals from the detectors and transmits them to ECAM, which displays a warning in the cockpit. The SDCU has two identical channels. Smoke in one cavity activates the cargo smoke warning if both smoke detectors detect it, or one smoke detector detects it and the other is inoperative. When the cargo smoke warning is activated, the isolation valves of the affected compartment close automatically and the extraction fan stops.

FWD CARGO
AFT/BULK CARGO

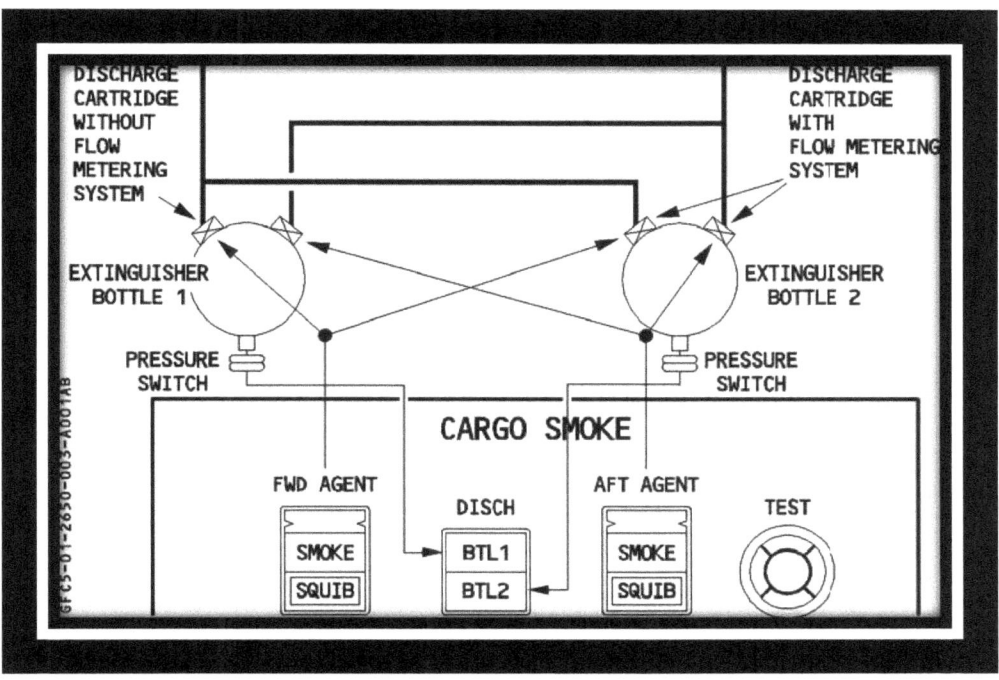

ENG 1 (2) FIRE

When LIFT CAP, PUSHING & RELEASING
* aural warning cancelled
*squib armed
* fuel LP valve closed
* eng return valve closed
* hyd fire valve closed
* eng bleed valve close
* pack flow control valve closed
* FADEC pw supply cut
FIRE Lt – Red whenever fire detected

AGENT 1   AGENT 2

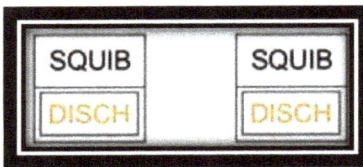

Both become active when ENG FIRE pb is released. Discharge when pushed.
SQUIB Lt – when ENG FIRE pb released
DISCH Lt – Amber when bottle lost pressure

TEST

When pushed – continuous repetitive chime
* MASTER WARNING Lt flashes
* ECAM ENG FIRE activated
On fire panel – all ENG FIRE pb Red
*all SQUIB Lts white (provided charged)
*all DISCH Lts Amber
Fire lights come on, Eng pedestal fire lights also come on.

APU FIRE

When released out –
* APU shuts down
* aural warning cancelled
* squib armed
* LP fuel valve closes
* APU fuel pumps shut off (fwd & aft)
* APU bleed valve and X bleed valve close
* APU gen de-activated
FIRE Lt – Red whenever fire detected

AGENT

Becomes active when ENG FIRE pb is released. Discharges when pushed.
SQUIB Lt – when ENG FIRE pb released
DISCH Lt – Amber when bottle lost pressure

Note: A thermal discharge of the APU fire bottle is indicated by missing red blowout disk located at the rear of fuselage.

TEST

Push to test the APU FIRE detection and extinguishing system.

VENTILATION

AVNCS

Detection by 2 smoke detectors (ionization type) in the air extraction duct of avionics ventilation system. Each detector is linked to one of two detection loops.
SMOKE Lt – Red with ECAM when smoke detected in avionics ventilation duct.

CARGO HEAT/SMOKE PANEL

FWD AGENT (AFT AGENT)

Pressing – Squib is ignited and extinguishing agent can be discharged into either cargo compartment.
*2 bottles ignite at once
* BTL 1 discharges into comp over 60 seconds
* BTL 2, slow flow metering system ensures concentration for 280 minutes.

The SDCU (Smoke Detection Control Unit) monitors squib integrity and bottle pressure.
SQUIB Lt - White in case of positive test.

BTL1 or BTL 2 – White light when bottle is discharged.

TEST

Pressing - smoke detectors in FWD, AFT, & BULK are tested by SDCU in sequence.
*BTL 1(2) Lts white
* isolation valves of ventilation system close
* SQUIB Lt white provided 1 of 2 filaments serviceable

* SMOKE Lt (AFT,FWD CARGO, AVNCS) Red with ECAM & chimes

Note: Each SDCU channel sounds its own warning which lasts about 25 seconds with a delay of about 30 seconds between them.

CHAPTER FIVE

FLIGHT CONTROLS

Brief System Explanation for Pilots

Airbus 330 fly-by-wire system was developed to increase safety and reduce cost. It is very comfortable and easier to fly than conventional aircraft. The flight control surfaces are completely electrically controlled, and hydraulically-activated. The stabilizer and rudder can be mechanically-controlled. Pilots use sidesticks to fly the aircraft in pitch and roll (and in yaw indirectly, through turn coordination). Computers interpreted by EFCS (electronic flight control system) or pilot input move the flight control surfaces, as necessary, to achieve the desired pilot commands. However, when in normal law, regardless of the pilot's input, the computers will prevent excessive maneuvers and exceedance of the safe envelope in pitch and roll axis. But, as on conventional aircraft, the rudder has no such protection. And the stabilizer can also be mechanically controlled.

Flight control surfaces

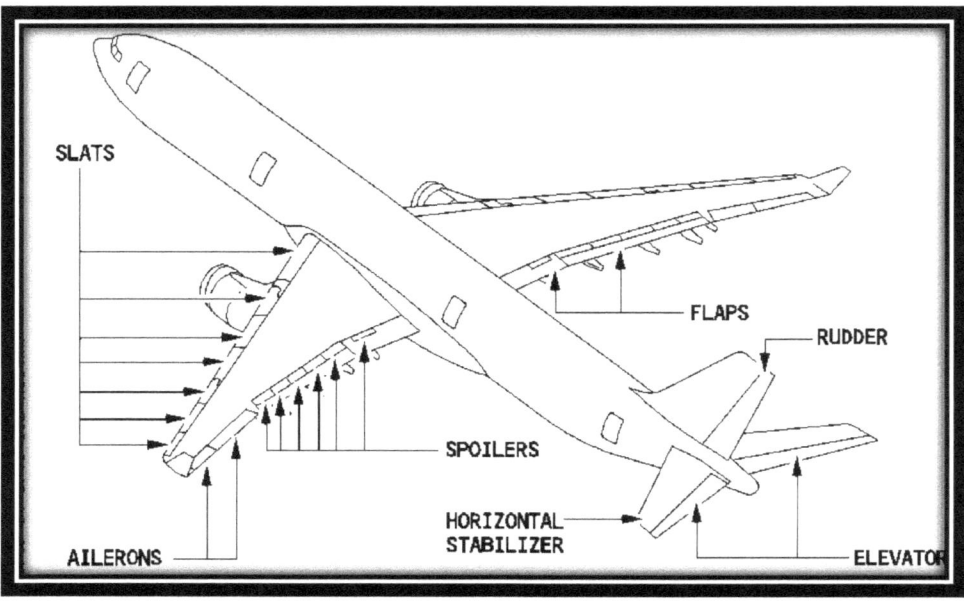

All flight controls are electrically or mechanically controlled.
Pitch axis
Elevator control   Electrical
Stabilizer control   Electrical for normal or alternate control.
Mechanical for manual
Trim control
Roll axis
Aileron control Electrical
Spoiler control Electrical
Yaw axis
Rudder control Mechanical, however control for yaw damping, turn coordination and trim is electrical.
Speed brakes   Electrical
All surfaces are hydraulically actuated.

Five flight control computers process pilot and autopilot inputs according to normal,
Alternate or direct flight control laws.

These computers are 3 PRIM (primary computers) and 2SEC (secondary computers)
Flight Control Primary Computer (FCPC). Each of which is used for.
*Normal, alternate and direct control laws.
*Speed brake and ground spoiler control.
 Protection speed computation.

2 SEC Computers

(Flight Control Secondary Computer — FCSC)
Direct control laws, including yaw damper function. Rudder trim, rudder travel limit, and pedal travel limit.

One computer of any type is capable of controlling the aircraft and of assuring safe flight and landing. In normal operation, one PRIM computer is declared to be the master (P1). It processes the orders and sends them to the other computers (P1 / P2 / P3 / S1 / S2).

High left devices are recommended by two slats flaps control computers (SFCC). In order to provide all required monitoring information to the crew and the central maintenance system (CMS) to flight control data, Concentrators (FCDC) obtain the outputs from the several computers to be sent to the ECAM and flight data interface unit(FDIU). These two FCDC ensure the electrical isolation of the flight control computer from the other systems.

Three hydraulic circuits (green, yellow and blue) power the flight controls. The distribution of the many control surfaces is designed to cover multiple failures cases.

Flight Controls Laws

Normal law
Alternate law
Direct law
Mechanical law
Abnormal low

Normal Law

Offer complete flight envelope protection as follows:

Maneuver Load Protection

Load factor is automatically limited to +2.5 G to minus 1G for flaps up and 2 G for flaps down.

Pitch Attitude Protection

The pitch attitude limits changes between 30° to 25° depending on the aircraft the speed and flaps setting. Pitch rate is controlled by G load and angle of attack. Maximum pitch down is limited to -15° nose down.

High Angle of Attack Protection

Three angles are related with this protection.

Alpha Protection

At this angle, the autopilot disconnects, the speed brake retracts and the angle of attack is relative to sidestick deflection.

Alpha floor protection becomes active at a predetermined angle of attack which then engages the auto throttle system and the auto thrust system will go to TOGA thrust regardless of the thrust lever position.

Alpha max the highest item of attack of the aircraft will fly with full aft stick input.

High-Speed Protection

The autopilot will be disconnected automatically and the aircraft pitches is up.

Bank Angle Protection

Up to 33° of bank, the aircraft attitude is maintained with a side stick at neutral position and bank angle up to 67° can be maintained with full sidestick deflection. At any bank angle above 33° when released, the sidestick aircraft were rolled back to a 33° bank angle.

Alternate Law

This is the first level of degraded flight control law and there are two categories of alternate law: (ALT1 and ALT2).

ALT 1

PITCH CONTROL. This mode is very similar to normal pitch law but no protection except for load factor protection.

High-Speed Stability - which will prevent the aircraft from accelerating any further by introducing a nose up command. This action can be overridden by the pilot at any time.

Low Speed Stability

This law replaces angle of attack protection and will activate between 5 to 10 knots above the stall warning. When activated, a nose down command tries to prevent the airspeed from decreasing any further; however the aircraft can be stalled. When Alpha floor is inoperative you will get an aural warning **"STALL, STALL"** in the event of a stall.

ALT 2

PITCH CONTROL is identical to the ALT1 law.

PROTECTIONS

Identical to protections in ALT 1, except that,
1. There is no bank angle protection in ALT 2 law. In alternate law, the PFD airspeed display replaces Alpha prot and Alpha max speed with red black Barbara poles.
2. In case of failure of 2 ADRs, there is no low speed stability.
3. In case of failure of 3 ADRs, there is no high speed stability.

Abnormal Attitude Law

Abnormal attitude law happens when aircraft is in extreme attitude or one of the following parameters is exceeded:

1. Angle of attack greater than 30° or less than 10 degree.
2. Pitch attitude more than 50° nose up or 30° nose down.
3. Bank angle greater than 125°
4. Airspeed over 440 knots or less than 60 knots.

Mechanical Backup

This will occur in the event of complete loss of an electrical flight control system. In this mode you are left with only two means to control the aircraft:

*Longitudinal (pitch) control of the aircraft achieved through manual trim as long as the hydraulics are still available.

*Lateral control from pedals. Roll damping is provided by the backup yaw damper unit (**BYDU**).

Message appears on PFD **MAN PITCH TRIM ONLY**

Ground Mode

Same as normal law ground mode.

Flight Mode

Flight law is a load factor demand law, comparable to normal law, with limited pitch rate depending on speed and configuration.

Note: When the yaw damper actuators are not available in case of (Hydraulic G + Y) failure the yaw damping function is achieved via the ailerons and the BYDU (Back up Yaw Damper Unit)

Flare Mode

Flare law is same as normal flare law

Direct Law (Lack of any Protection)

During specific multiple failures the aircraft returns to direct law. The pitch direct law is a direct stick to elevator relationship (elevator deflection is relative to side stick deflection).

In all configurations the maximum elevator deflection is varied as a function of CG.

It provides a compromise between enough controllability at forward CG and not too sensitive control at aft CG. There is no automatic trim and the pilot has to use manual trim. "**USE MAN PITCH TRIM**", amber message is displayed on the PFD. All protections are inoperative. The alpha floor function is inoperative. Over speed and stall warnings are available as for alternate law.

Mechanical

Pitch mechanical control is achieved through the THS using manual trim control. "**MAN PITCH TRIM ONLY**" will display in red on the PFDs.

PRIM 1(2, 3)

 Control the FCPC (Flight Control Primary Computers)
ON: The following functions are provided by each flight control primary computer.
*Normal pitch
*Normal lateral
*Maneuver Load Alleviation (MAL)
*Speed brakes, ground spoilers control logic
*Pitch alternate
*Pitch direct
*Roll direct
*Yaw alternate
*Ailerons droop
*Abnormal attitude law
*Autopilot orders
*Speed computation
OFF – computer off. Off then ON resets it.
FAULT Lt – Amber with ECAM when fault detected. Extinguished when OFF.

SEC 1(2)

Control the FCSC (Flight control Secondary Computers)
ON: The following functions are provided by each computer
   *Pitch direct
   *Roll direct
   *Yaw alternate
   *Rudder trim
   *Rudder travel

OFF – computer off. Switching off then ON resets computer.
FAULT Lt – Amber with ECAM when fault detected.
Extinguished when OFF.

TURB DAMP

ON – Command of Turbulence damping function is added to normal law elevator and yaw damper command.
OFF – Turbulence damping function inhibited.

CHAPTER SIX

FUEL

Brief System Explanation for Pilots

The fuel system consists of:

Fuel storage
Control refueling and defueling
Controls and monitors the correct quantity of fuel.
Delivers fuel to the engines and the Auxiliary Power Unit (APU).
Controls the transfer of fuel to maintain the Center of Gravity (CG) within it proper limits. And maintains fuel in the outer tanks for wing bending.

Fuel is stored in the following tanks:

Wings tanks
Center section
Trim tank in the Horizontal Stabilizer (THS)
The wings have inner and outer tanks. Each inner tank contains one collector cell that maintains a fuel reservoir for the fuel booster pumps and provide negative 'g' protection to feed the engines.
Is maintained full and contains about 1,000 kg (2,200 lbs) of fuel.

Each inner tank is divided into two parts via a SPLIT valve that normally remains open. The inner tank is used as a single tank and, if tank damage is suspected (i.e. FQI data is lost or there is a rapid FQI (Fuel Quantity Indicator) decreases following an engine failure), the SPLIT valve can be manually closed by using the dedicated pushbutton on the overhead panel.

In each wing, and on the right of the THS trim tank, there is a vent surge tank outboard of the outer tank.

After refueling to maximum tank capacity, fuel can expand by 2 % (20° temperature increase) without spillage.

There is an overpressure protector in each wing surge tank, in the trim surge tank, and between the center and the right inner tanks.

NORMAL FUEL FEED SEQUENCE OPERATION

Fuel is always fed to the engines from the inner tanks. The fuel transfer sequence is as follows:

1. Center tank fuel transfers to the inner tanks.
2. Each inner tank empties down to 4,000 kg (8,818 lbs).
3. Trim tank fuel transfers to the inner tanks.
4. Each inner tank empties down to 3,500 kg (7,716 lbs).
5. Outer tank fuel transfers to the inner tanks.

Note: If required for CG control, the trim tank may be emptied earlier.

AUTOMATIC FUEL TRANSFERS

CENTER TO INNER TANK TRANSFER

The center tank pumps run continuously whenever there is fuel in the center tank. Each inner tank inlet valve controls the transfer by cycling its inner tank contents between full and approximately 2,000 kg (4,415 lbs) below full. When the center tank is empty, both center tank pumps stop, and both inner tank inlet valves close.

OUTER TO INNER TANK TRANSFER

The outer tank transfers fuel to the inner tanks by gravity. Each outer tank transfer valve controls the transfer by cycling its inner tanks contents between 3,500 kg (7,716 lbs) and 4,000 kg (8,818 lbs). When each outer tank has been empty for five minutes, its outer tank transfer valves close.

AUTOMATIC FORWARD FUEL TRANSFER

The fuel system is controlled by two fuel control and monitoring computers (FCMC). It will trigger a forward fuel transfer, under one of the following conditions:

1. The calculated CG = Target. Forward fuel transfer stops, when the computed CG = the target CG - 0.5 %.

2. The fuel content of one of the two inner tanks decreases to 4,000 kg (8,818 lbs).

Forward fuel transfer stops automatically, when the fuel content reaches 5,000 kg (11,023 lbs). The FMGS sends a time-to-destination signal below the threshold, or the aircraft descends below FL 245. In this case, transfer is continuous, but is controlled by the inner tank high levels to prevent overflow.

MEMO DISPLAY

REFUEL IN PROCESS message is displayed in green, if the refuel panel is not set in the flight position.
REFUEL PNL message is displayed in amber, (after engine start), if the refuel panel and the cockpit refuel pushbutton are not set in the appropriate position for flight.
T TK XFRD message is displayed in flight when the trim tank has been emptied following a forward transfer.
TRIM TK XFR message is displayed in green, during a trim tank transfer.
OUTR TK XFRD message is displayed in green, when the outer tank has been transferred into the inner tank.
OUTR TK XFR message is displayed in green during an outer tank transfer.

L 1(Or R2) (Or2)

Supplies fuel from its own collector cell which it shares with a STBY pump. This collector cell is maintained full at 1,000 kg for negative "G" protection.
ON – Pump is on.
OFF – Pump is off.
Fault lt – Amber with ECAM when pressure drops. Inhibited when pump is switched to the OFF position.

L STBY 1(or R)

ON – The associated standby Pump is automatically energized when at least one associate main pump fails or is selected OFF.
OFF – Pump is off

Fault lt – Amber with ECAM when pressure drops. Inhibited when OFF is selected or main pump running.

L (or R) CTR TANK

ON – Pump is running fuel transfer is controlled by the appropriate valve. The FCMC stops the pump when the tank is empty.
OFF – Pump is off

FAULT LT – Amber with ECAM when:
- * delivery press drops or
- * trim pipe isol valve is failed open or
- * man xfr from CTR tank is required, and INR tank qtys are > 17000kg or
- * one outer, inner inlet valve failed open and INR tank qtys are > 17000kg

Fault Lt is inhibited when sel OFF.

T.TANK MODE

AUTO – Forward transfer is stopped when the trim tank level is low. CG controlled by Fuel Control and Management Computer.
*Auto begins at L/G up and SLATS in – fwd XFR (failure case only). At FL 255 aft XFR to target CG -0.5%. In cruise, fwd XFR to target CG -0.5% (burn = Taft CG).
*Auto ends at FL 245 or <35min (FMGS) to dest. (<75min if trim fwd XFR pump failure)

Transfer from t.tank to inner tank occurs when <u>one of the two inner tanks decreases to 4,000kg and stops at 5,000kg.</u>

FWD – Manual FWD transfer to center tank using t.tank fwd transfer pump:

*t.tank isolation valve opens
* auxiliary fwd transfer valve opens
* trim pipe isolation valve closes
* aft transfer valves closes

Note: Centre tank overflow must be manually prevented.

FAULT Lt – Amber with ECAM if:
- excess aft CG based on THS
* FCMC unable to fwd transfer
*FUEL LO TEMP warning triggered

T.TANK FEED

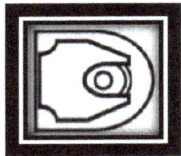 ISOL
AUTO
OPEN

AUTO – forward transfer is stopped when trim tank is low
ISOL – transfer line is isolated by closing:

* t.tank isolation valve
* t.tank inlet valve
* auxiliary forward transfer valve
* trim pipe isolation valve
* t.tank forward transfer pump stops

OPEN – Valves used for manual fwd transfer open & t.tank inlet valve open. Valves remain open for 3min after t.tank is low, to allow transfer pipe to drain.

Note: *APU supply is not possible when pipe is drained.*

X FEED

AUTO – the cross without is normally closed. The valve automatically opens in electrical emergency configuration.
ON – Valve opens

OPEN Lt – Green when fully open

CTR TK TXFR

AUTO – FCMC controls the all fuel from center to inner tank transfer using the inner tank inlet valve, cycling inner tank contents between <u>full and 2,000kg below full.</u>

MAN – transfer fuel from their center to inner tank transfer by opening the and energizing center tank pumps (provided the pumps are not selected to off position).

To avoid inner tank overflow, center tank pumps can be sel OFF.

FAULT Lt – Amber with ECAM when:
* inner tank L LEVEL and center tank not empty, or
* FCMC unable to carry out transfer to inner tanks

OUTR TK TXFR

AUTO – FCMC controls the transfer of fuel outer to inner tank by sing the outer tank transfer valves, cycling its inner tank contents between <u>3,500kg</u>

and 4,000kg. ON – Initiates outer to inner tank
transfer by:
* outer transfer valves open
* outer inlet valves open
* inner inlet valves open

FAULT Lt – Amber with ECAM when:

* inner tank L LEVEL and center tank not empty, or
* FCMC unable to carry out transfer to inner tanks
* FUEL LO TEMP is triggered

INR TK SPLIT L (or R)

 OFF – the emergency isolation valve is open Split valve open. Inner tank used as single tank.
ON – closes the emergency isolation valve and the split the inner tank into two parts. ON light white illminates.

* fwd part feeds inboard eng
* aft part feeds outboard eng and receives any XFRD fuel to the inner tank from the centre, outer or t.tank.

SHUT – Blue when valve shut

* During refueling, first inner tank high level sensor becomes wet, valve closes
* Valve reopens when fueling complete

CHAPTER SEVEN

HYDRAULICS

Brief System Explanation for Pilots

The Airbus 330 has three fully independent continuously operating systems - BLU, GREEN, and YELLOW. Each system is supplied from its own hydraulic reservoir. Normal system operating pressure is 3,000 psi (2,500 psi for RAT). There is no option to transfer hydraulic fluid from one system to another.

The system is monitored by a Hydraulic System Monitoring Unit (HSMU).

*For engine driven pumps, two of which are the green system.

*Three electrical pumps that can operate automatically as a backup.

They are managed by HSMU (hydraulic system monitoring unit) which ensures all automation (electric pumps, RAT, monitoring, etc.). Manual override is available on the overhead panel.

Note: There is one hand pump on the yellow hydraulic system for cargo door operation when there is no electrical power available.

GREEN SYSTEM HYDRAULIC PUMPS

There are two pumps individually driven by each engine pressurize the green system. In addition, an electric pump which can be manually or automatically operated can too pressurize the green system. The electric pump runs automatically in flight for 25 seconds in the event of failure of one engine, when landing gear lever is selected up (to ensure gear retraction in a proper time). A pump driven by a ram air turbine (RAT) pressurizes the green system in an emergency. When the green system hydraulic pressurized by the RAT, the aileron, elevator and spoiler servo control operating speeds are reduced.

BLUE HYDRAULIC SYSTEM PUMPS

One pump driven by engine 1 pressurizes the blue system.

A manually controlled electric pump can also pressurize the system.

YELLOW HYDRAULIC SYSTEM PUMPS

A pump driven by engine 2 which pressurizes yellow system.

In addition, an electric pump which can be manually or automatically controlled can also pressurize the yellow system. This enables ground operations when the engines are shut down. The electric pump runs automatically:

- In flight

- In the event of engine 2 failure

- If the flaps are not retracted (to ensure flap retraction after takeoff when you move the flaps lever to up position).

- On the ground during cargo door operation

Note: If engine 2 failure at takeoff, yellow electric pump is automatically controlled on if the green electric pump is not running for landing gear retraction.

ENG 1 (2) PUMP

Hydraulic systems have accumulators to maintain constant pressure. HP bleed air from Eng 2 (Eng 1) pressurize hydraulic reservoirs and if air press dropped too low, uses air from X-bleed duct.

ON – Pump pressurizes the system to 3000 psi when the respective engine running.
OFF – Pump is depressurized. Power generation stops.

FAULT Lt – Amber with ECAM if
* reservoir low level
* reservoir overheats
* reservoir low air pressure
* pump low pressure
*

Extinguish when OFF sel. Except in overheat case (light stays on until overheat gone)

ELECTRIC HYD PUMPS
GREEN ELEC PUMP (or YELLOW)

AUTO – Pump is auto controlled by HSMU (Hydraulic System Monitoring unit)

*Green hydraulic electric pump runs for 25sec in the event of eng 1 fails, when gear lever selected up and speed above 100kts

*Yellow hydraulic electric pump runs when (eng 2) fails and FLAPS lever not at zero position and the aircraft the speed is above 100kts, remains running until engine one las shutdown.

*Yellow runs when a/c on ground and cargo door manual selector in OPEN or CLOSE. (no flap movement)

OFF – The Yellow pump is de-energized

FAULT Lt – Amber light illuminates with ECAM IN THE EVENT OF:
* A low reservoir level
* Reservoir overheats
* Low reservoir air pressure

ENG 1 (2) <u>plus</u> pump overheat in which case the pump shuts down

GREEN ELEC PUMP ON (or YELLOW) (Spring-loaded-guarded)

AUTO – pump controlled according to ELEC PUMP push button switch.

ON – Blue light illuminates when supplied pump energized provided an ELEC PUMP is not in the off position. Will not start after elec power interruption

BLUE ELEC PUMP

STANDBY – pump controlled by BLUE ELEC PUMP ON pb

OFF – pump is off
FAULT Lt – Amber with ECAM illuminates in following cases.
* A low reservoir level
* Reservoir overheats
* Low reservoir air pressure
* low pump out put pressure
* Pump overheat in which case the pump shuts down

BLUE ELEC PUMP ON (Spring-loaded-guarded)

ON – pump on provided ELEC PUMP pb is not sel OFF.
- If elec power supply removed, pump remain off till power is restored.

STBY – pump is off

RAT MAN ON

The RAT may extend the anytime by pressing RAT MAN ON pushbutton. This will provide 2500 psi to green hydraulic system
Auto extends when:
or * Both engines fail
or * GREEN & BLUE LO LVL
or * GREEN & YELLOW LO LVL .

Note: whenever the RAT extended it can only be stowed on the ground only

LEAK MEASUREMENT VALVES

OFF – valve closes and HYD supply to primary flight controls is shut off.
- * inhibited if speed above 100kts
- * OFF light illuminates

Note: Yellow valve auto closed on ground when cargo door is operated

CHAPTER EIGHT

ICE AND RAIN PROTECTION

Brief System Explanation for Pilots

DESCRIPTION

The ice and rain protection system allows unrestricted operation of the aircraft in icing conditions and heavy rain.

ANTI ICE

Hot air or electrical heating protects critical areas of the aircraft as follows:

HOT AIR

*Provides to anti ice the four outboard leading-edge slats of each wing and engine air intakes.

See shaded area in the diagram below.

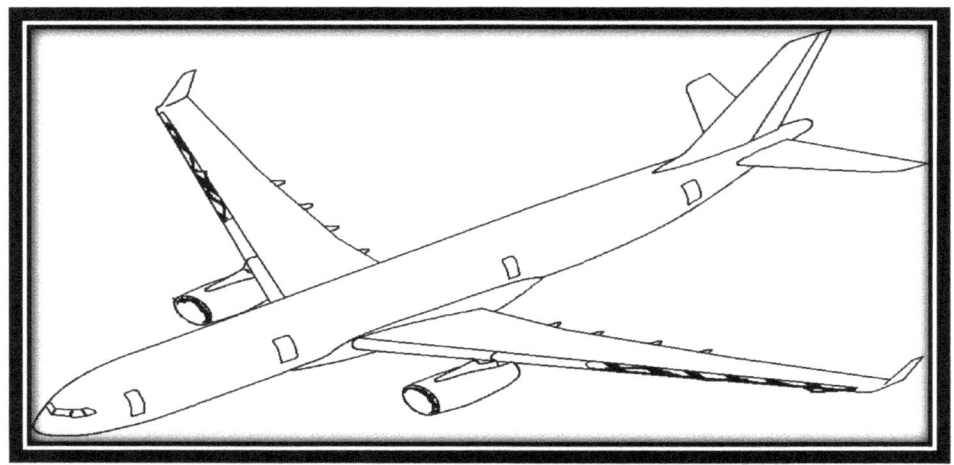

ELECTRICAL HEATING protects the following:

Pitots

Static ports

Angle Of Attack (AOA) probes

Total Air Temperature (TAT) probes

Three independent Probe Heat Computers (PHC) automatically control and monitor:

Captain probes

F/O probes

STBY probes

Waste, water drain mast

They provide overheat protection and fault indication.

The probes are heated:
Automatically when at least one engine is running, or in flight manually by switching ON the PROBE/WINDOW HEAT pushbutton.

On the ground, TAT probes are not heated and pitot heating operates at low level.

RAIN REMOVAL

Fluid rain repellent during moderate to heavy rain may be sprayed on the windshield to improve visibility.
The window is covered by spray after about 30 seconds.
Application of rain repellent is controlled by a pushbutton.
Wipers remove rain from the front windshield panel.

ANTI-ICE
WING

Hot air is supplied from pneumatic system and heats the four outboard slats (4,5,6,7). If a leak is detected, valves auto close. Elec pwr supply failure, valves close.

ON – Blue light with WING A.ICE indication on ECAM MEMO
* Wing a.ice control valves open if pneumatic supply avail.
* On gnd valves open for 30 sec only for test.
* N1 (EPR) limit Reduced
* Idle N1 (EPR) increased

OFF – valves close, ON light goes out

FAULT Lt – Amber with ECAM if
* position disagrees with selection (valve and switch this agreement)
* low pressure detected

ENG 1 (2)

Hot air supplied by independent bleed from HP compressor thru open/close valve.
Elec pwr supply failure, valves open.
ON – Blue light with ENG A.ICE indication on ECAM MEMO
* valve opens and continuous ignition activated
* If EIU (engine interface unit) inop, cont. ign is automatically activated

OFF – valves close, ON light goes out

FAULT Lt – Amber with ECAM if anti ice valve disagrees with ENG pb selection.
Or low air pressure

PROBE/WINDOW HEAT

AUTO – Heated automatically:
*in flight
*on gnd (except TAT probes) with one eng running.
*(Both) on gnd pitot heat at low level

ON Lt – Blue light indicates probes and windows are heated.

Note: on the ground TAT probes are not heated. On takeoff, windshield switches from low to normal.

WIPERS

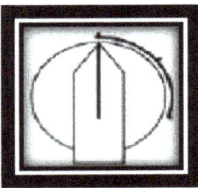

Max speed 230 kts

Wiper has three positions:
OFF – wipers out of view
SLOW
FAST

RAIN RPLNT

One button per side, when pressed once timer applies measured amount of liquid.
Inhibited when on ground & engines stopped.

CHAPTER NINE

LIGHTS

Brief System Explanation for Pilots

LIGHTING DESCRIPTION

Instrument and Panel Integral Lighting

All instruments and panels installed in the cockpit (other than DU) are integrally lit.

The brightness of all instruments and panels can be adjusted.

Annunciator Light Test and Dimming

The brightness of all the annunciator lights in the flight deck can be changed, depending

*On the ANN LT TEST / BRT / DIM sw position on the overhead panel. The lights are dimmed to a fixed level.

An annunciator light test is provided to verify cockpit annunciator lamp operation.

The test is done by selecting TEST position on ANN LT «TEST / BRT / DIM» switch and by visually checking that all lights illuminate.

Dome Lights and Lighting Strips

Two dome lights and lighting strips supply general cockpit illumination providing shadow free lighting.

Map Holder Lighting

Map chart holder is provided at the CAPT and F/O stations.

Console and Floor Lighting

Briefcase stowage, side console and floor lighting are provided at the CAPT and F/O stations.

Center Instrument and Standby Compass

The center instrument is lighted by a set of lights located below the glare shield.

The standby compass is provided with integral illumination.

Reading Lights

Individual reading lights and supplementary reading lights are provided at the CAPT and F/O stations.

Pedestal Lighting

Located in the middle of the overhead panel, a flood light provides illumination of the center pedestal.

External Lights Include:

The beacon
The navigation lights
The landing lights
The runway turns off lights
The TO and TAXI lights
The logo lights
The anti-collision lights
The wing and engine scan lights.

External lighting is controlled by means of switches located on the overhead panel.

Note: For location and operation of each light switch refer to overhead panel in the following pages.

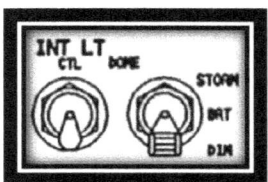

There are two 2-way switches to control the dome light.
* one located on rear panel near cockpit door
* one on overhead panel

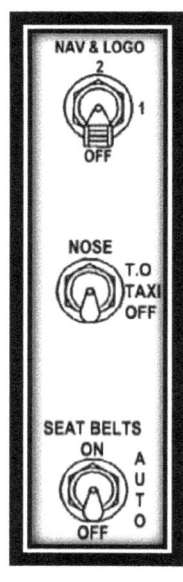

POS'N 1 & 2 – NAV & LOGO lights are ON when main gear struts are compressed or the flaps are extended 15° or more.
Lights attached to nose gear strut go out when gear is retracted RWY TURN OFF – Same as nose lights
SEAT BELTS
AUTO – ON when all engines running and either slats or main gear is extended.

* Gives low tone chime
* On ground, signs remain on after slats retracted

STROBE

Control light on each wingtip and one on the tail cone.
AUTO – Strobes on when struts not compressed. If you turn off strobe light in flight a message will appear in ECAM "STROBE   LT OFF"

 AUTO – Signs (NO SMOKING & EXIT) on when gear extended - Signs off when gear retracted

Note: When cabin alt is excessive (14,350ft) cabin lights come on. NO SMOKING, FASTEN SEAT BELT, EXIT signs come on regardless of their switch pos'n.

EMER EXIT LT

ARM – Cabin emerg lighting illuminates if:

* DC ESS BUSS fails or
* normal a/c elec pwr fails
* The overhead emerg lights auto illuminate if AC BUS 1 fails.

This will provide min cabin lighting

Emergency exit light has three positions –
ON, ARM and OFF.
ON: Emergency light, exit signs and proximity emergency escape path marking come on
EMER EXIT LT-OFF Lt - Amber when EMER EXIT LT switch is selected OFF

Note: the overhead emergency light automatically comes on in case of partial loss of the normal AC power supply. This will provide minimum cabin lighting.

CHAPTER TEN

NAVIGATION

Brief System Explanation for Pilots

DESCRIPTION

Airbus 330 navigation system consists of three identical ADIRU's (Air Data and Inertial Reference Units). Each ADIRU is divided in 2 parts, either of which can work separately in case of failure:

*ADR which supplies barometric altitude, speed, Mach, angle of attack, temperature and over speed warnings. It also supplies temperature, anemometric barometric and inertial parameters to the EFIS system (ND and PFD) and to other user systems (FMGC, PRIM, SEC, FWC, FADEC, SFCC, GPWS, CMC, CPC, ATC).

*the IR (Inertial Reference) which supplies attitude, flight path vector, track, heading, accelerations, angular rates, ground speed, vertical speed and aircraft position.

Note: The ADIRU gives the true heading instead of magnetic heading
Above 82° North

Above 73° North between 90° and 120° West (magnetic polar region)

Above 60° South.

One ADIRS control panel located on the overhead panel for modes selection (NAV, ATT, OFF) and failure indications referred to in Figure 1.

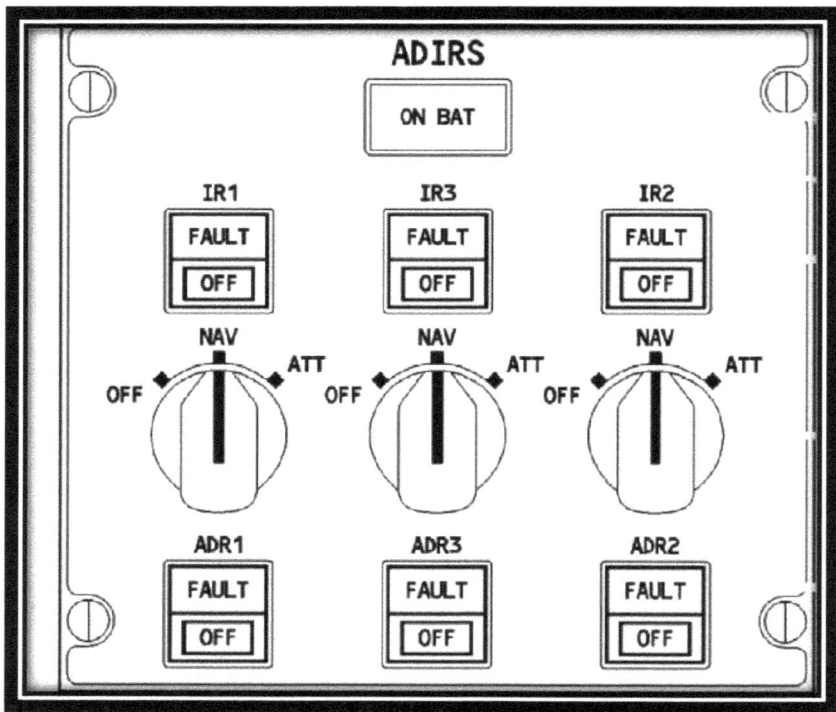

Figure 1

2 GPS receivers, which are connected to the IR part of the ADIRU's for GP/IR hybrid position calculation.

Four Types of Sensors:

Three pitot probes

Six static pressure probes (STAT)

Three angle of attack sensors (AOA)

Two total air temperature probes (TAT)

These sensors are electrically heated to prevent from icing up.

Eight ADMs (Air Data Modules) which convert pneumatic data from pitot and static probes into numerical data for the ADIRUs. A switching capability for selecting ADR3 or IR3 for instrument displays in case of ADIRU1or2 failure.

A (MAG / TRUE) pushbutton switch for polar navigation.

AC BUS provides to normal electrical supply. DC BUS provides as a backup.

TCAS DESCRIPTION

TCAS (Traffic alert and Collision Avoidance System):
Detects any aircraft equipped with an ATC transponder flying in its vicinity.
Displays possibility and calculates collision targets and issues vertical orders to avoid conflict.

TCAS is normally independent of the ground-based air traffic control system. The TCAS detection capability is limited to the intruders flying within a maximum range of 30-40 NM (depending on aircraft configuration and external conditions), and within a maximum vertical separation of 9,900 feet above and below the threatened aircraft.

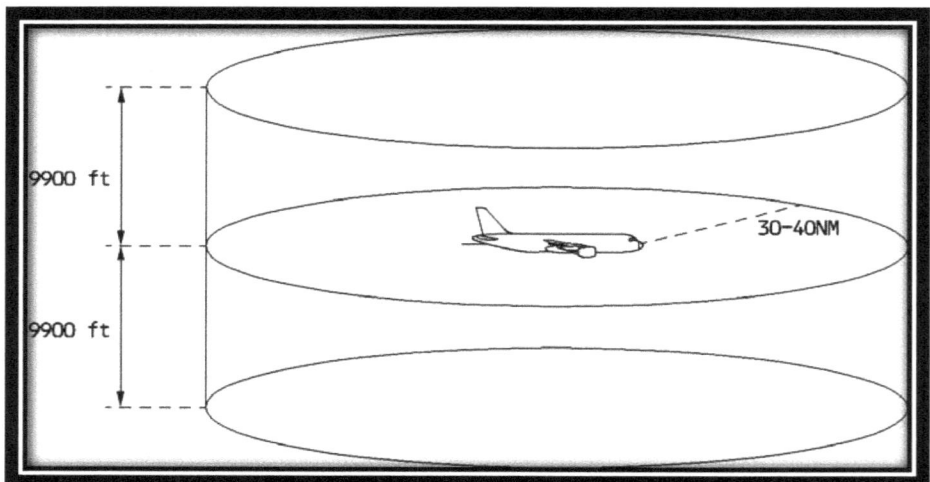

TERRAIN AWARENESS

The Terrain Awareness and Display (TAD) function calculates a caution and a warning ahead of the aircraft, according to the aircraft altitude, the nearest runway altitude, the range to the nearest runway threshold, the ground speed, and the turn rate. When the boundary of these envelopes conflicts with the terrain memorized in the database, the system generates the relevant alert.

*Any time when the TERR ON ND switch is selected ON, the ND displays the terrain memorized in the database according to the aircraft's position, when ARC or ROSE mode is selected. The terrain is displayed in various densities of green, yellow, red, or magenta, depending on the threat (INDICATIONS ON ND). When an alert is generated (either caution or warning) and the TERR ON ND is not selected, the terrain is automatically displayed, and the ON light, of the TERR ON ND pushbutton, comes on.

Note: 1. When TERR ON ND is selected, the weather radar display image is not displayed, even if the weather radar is ON.

2. The relative height of the aircraft is computed using the Captain's BARO setting. Thus, the Terrain Awareness Display (TAD) does not protect against BARO setting errors.

3. The TAD and Terrain Clearance Floor (TCF) functions operate using the FMS 1 position. Thus, in case of an FMS 1 position error, the system gives erroneous information.

ADR 1 (2, 3,)

 OFF – Air data output disconnected ADR information is not available.

FAULT Lt – Amber with ECAM if fault detected in the Air Data Ref. or system failure.

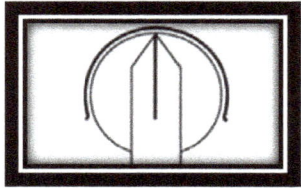 OFF – ADIRU not energized, ADR and IR information not available.
NAV – Normal mode of operation.
ATT – A backup IR mode which only provides attitude & heading. ADR information still available.

* no nav capability
* hdg must be entered thru MCDU regularly (approx 10 mins)

Complete realign – sel OFF for more than 5 secs. Takes approx. 10 min

* recommend before long range flight

Fast realign – cycle OFF then ON within 5 secs. Takes approx. 3 min.

IR 1(2, 3)

OFF – inertial data output disconnected
FAULT LT – Amber with ECAM if fault detected.

* steady light = respective IR is lost
* flashing light = attitude & heading may be recovered in ATT mode

Light Only
Amber when 1 or more IRS supplied by aircraft batteries.
If Amber on ground – external horn sounds
- ADIRU Lt on SERVICE INTERPHONE BAY panel comes on.

GPWS
Mode 1: Excessive Rate –"SINK RATE" & "PULL UP"
Mode 2: Excessive Terrain Closure – "TERRAIN" & "PULL UP"
Mode 3: Altitude Loss After T/O – "DON'T SINK"
Mode 4: Unsafe Terrain Clearance – "TOO LOW-GEAR (FLAPS, TERRAIN)"
Mode 5: Descent Below Glide Slope – "GLIDE SLOPE"
EGPWS: "TERRAIN AHEAD" "PULL UP"

SYS

OFF – All GPWS alerts (1 to 5) inhibited
FAULT LT – Amber with ECAM when GPWS fault detected
Note: *ILS 1 fails, only mode 5 inhibited. No Fault Lt or warning.*

G/S MODE

OFF – Glide slope mode (mode 5) inhibited "GLIDE SLOPE" message during excessive deviation below the glide slope. This mode use only for localizer and back course approaches.

FLAP MODE

OFF – Flap mode ("TOO LOW-FLAPS) inhibited.

* Avoids warnings with landing less than normal landing flaps setting. This function usually use when landing with abnormal flaps setting.
* CONF 3 sel in MCDU auto inhibits warning when Flap 3 is reached

FAULT Lt – Amber with ECAM if TAD or TCF made fails.

TERRAIN

 OFF - inhibits Terrain Awareness Display (TAD) & Terrain Clearance Floor (TCF) modes.
Does not affect the basic GPWS modes 1 to 5.
Fault lt – Amber with ECAM if TAD or TCF mode fails.

CHAPTER ELEVEN

LANDING GEAR

Brief System Explanation for Pilots

Landing Gear Features

Conventional landing gear with a single bogie nose gear and double bogie main landing gear with direct action shock absorbers.

The main landing gear retracted laterally and the nose gear retracted forward into the fuselage.

Hydraulically actuated by green system with alternative freefall and electrically controlled by two landing gear interface unit (LGCIU). The LGCIUs process gears and doors positions, sequencing control and gear lever selection. They also provide landing gear information on ECAM, and ground/flight signals for other aircraft systems.
MAIN GEAR Main landing gear is also provided with a shock absorber extension and retraction system.

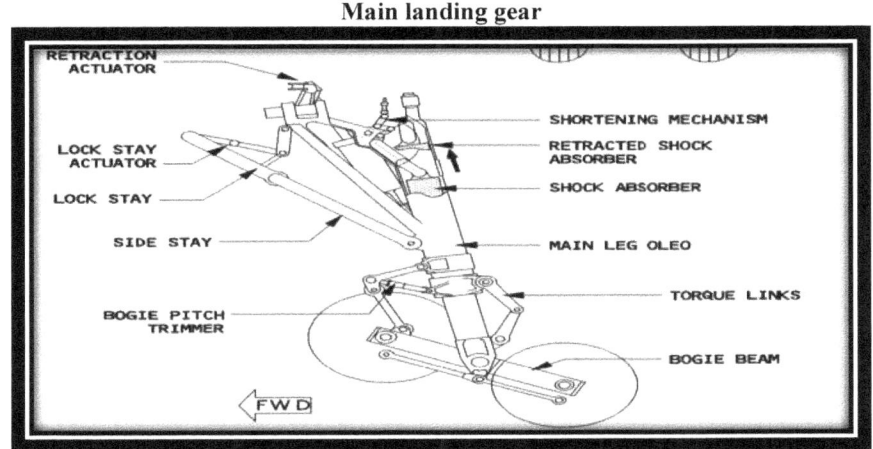
Main landing gear

GRAVITY EXTENSION

The gravity extension system is an electromechanical system controlled through two selectors located on the center instrument panel. It permits the main and nose landing gear extension in case of normal extension system failure.

When the related electrical selector are set to DOWN:

The landing gear hydraulic system is isolated from green hydraulic system

The main landing gear and nose landing gear doors and gears electrically unlock

Main landing gear and nose landing gear extend by gravity

Locking springs assist the down locking

The main and nose landing gear doors remain open.

After a free fall extension, it is possible to restore normal operation provided the green

Hydraulic pressure is available.

Landing gear gravity extension panel

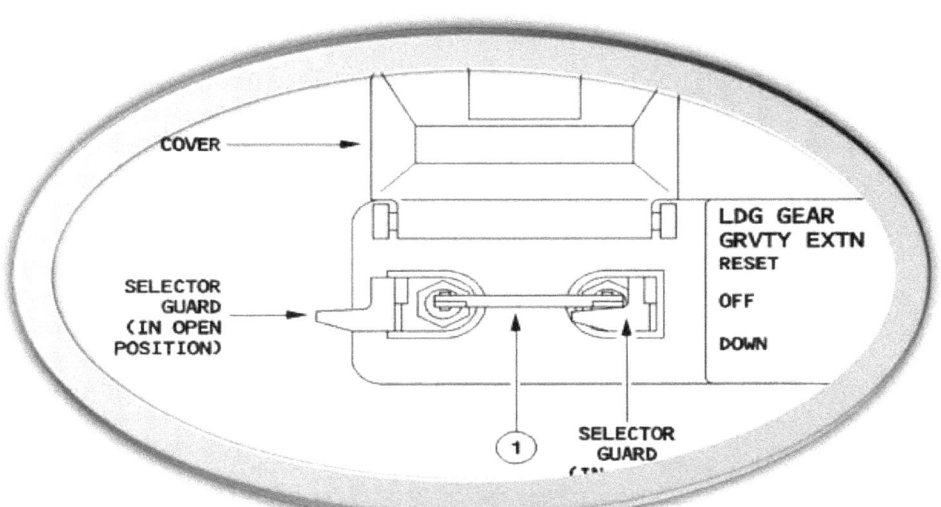

1. Landing gear gravity extension selector

BRAKING SYSTEM

Main wheels are equipped with carbon multidisc brake which can be actuated by either of two independent brake systems. The normal system uses green hydraulic pressure whilst the alternate system uses the blue hydraulic system backed up by hydraulic accumulator. An antiskid and autobrake system is also provided. These are four modes of breaking.

1. Normal braking.
2. Alternate braking with antiskid.
3. Alternate braking without antiskid.
4. Parking brake.

AUTOBRAKE

0 MAX, MED, LO pushbutton switch (spring-loaded)
The pb controls the arming of the required deceleration rate.
MAX mode is normally selected for takeoff.
In the event of an aborted takeoff, maximum pressure is sent to the brakes as soon as ground spoiler deployment order is present.

MED or LO mode is normally selected for landing.
When LO is selected, progressive pressure is sent to the brakes starting 1 second after ground spoiler deployment order to provide a 1.8 m/s, (5.9 fit/s) deceleration. When MED is selected, progressive pressure is sent to the brakes starting at ground spoiler deployment order to provide a 3 m/s (9.8 ft/s) deceleration.
ON: The ON light illuminates blue to indicate positive arming.

The DECEL light illuminates green only if the autobrake function is active and when actual aircraft deceleration reaches to predetermined rate. (In LO or MED, 80% of the selected rate this occurs approximately 5 to 8 seconds after activation for LO (MED) using brakes alone.

Predetermined rates could be achieved also by reversers alone or a combination of both reversers and brakes.

Note: On slippery runway, the predetermined deceleration may not be reached due to antiskid operation. In this case DECEL light will not come on.

This does not mean that autobrake is not working.

Off: The corresponding autobrake mode is deactivated.

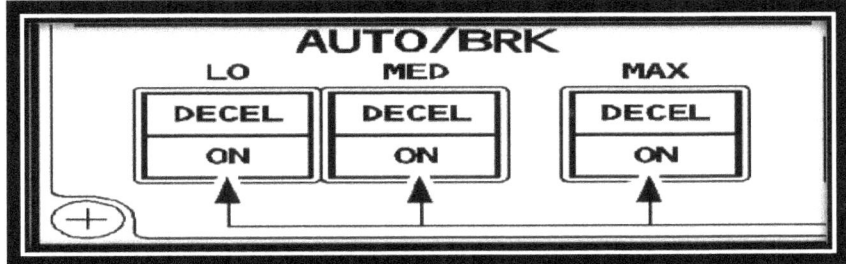

PARK BRK Handle

Pull the handle, and then turn it clockwise to apply the parking brake.

PARK BRK message is displayed on the ECAM memo page.

CAUTION:

If the handle is not in the ON position, the parking brake is not applied.

BRAKE and ACCU PRESS indicator

ACCU PRESS indication green band allowed pressure area in the brake Accumulators Provides full pressure to the brakes.

Amber band: forbidden pressure area requires a repressurization of the accumulators.

BRAKE pressure indication Indicates blue pressure delivered to left and right brakes.

NWS TOWING FAULT LIGHT

FAULT – Red on gnd when NWS has exceeded 93°. It is associated with illumination of the red over steering warning light, located on the nose landing gear. When pressed, the light out.

CHAPTER TWELVE

OXYGEN

Brief System Explanation for Pilots

The cockpit's fixed oxygen system consists of the following,

*One high-pressure cylinder in the left-hand lower fuselage.

*One pressure regulator, connected directly to the cylinder that delivers oxygen, at a pressure suitable for users.

*Two overpressure safety systems to vent oxygen overboard, through a safety port, if the pressure gets too high.

*A supply solenoid valve that allows the crew to shut off the distribution system.

*Four full-face quick-donning masks, stowed in readily-accessible boxes adjacent to the crewmembers' seats (one at each seat).

*One filling port for external oxygen replenishment (as installed).

OXYGEN MASK OPERATION

The pilots needs to squeeze the red grips to pull the mask out of its box, and this action will cause the mask harness to inflate. Each mask-mounted regulator supplies a mixture of air and oxygen, 100% oxygen, or performs emergency pressure control. With the regulator set to NORMAL, the user breathes a mixture of cabin air and oxygen up to the cabin altitude at which the regulator supplies 100 % oxygen. The user can select 100 %, in which case the regulator supplies pure oxygen at all cabin altitudes.

If the situation calls for it, the user can use the emergency overpressure rotating knob and receive pure oxygen at positive pressure.

The storage box contains a microphone lead, with a quick-disconnect, for connection to the appropriate mask microphone cable.

Note: Each mask may have a removable film that protects the visor against scratches. This strip is optional and may be removed from the mask at any time.

DESCRIPTION

The fixed oxygen system in the cabin supplies oxygen to the occupants in case of cabin depressurization. The system stores its oxygen in interconnected cylinders (5, plus up to 5 additional) behind the right hand sidewall lining in the forward cargo compartment. The oxygen goes to the mask containers in the cabin via two main supply lines and a network of pipes. The containers are above the passenger seats, in the lavatories, in each galley and at each cabin crew station. Each container has between 2 to 5 masks. An altimetric flow regulation device in each mask container controls the flow rate. The Quantity Calculation and Control Unit (QCCU) supply the value of the average, temperature-compensated pressure for indication on the ECAM system page.

CABIN OXYGEN OPERATION

Normally the system is unpressurized. A pneumatically controlled ventilation valve releases any residual pressure. Each container has an electrical latching mechanism that opens automatically to allow the masks to drop. If the cabin pressure altitude exceeds 14,000 feet, the system pressurizes, the masks drop and (if installed) prerecorded instructions sound automatically over the passenger address system. The cockpit crew may operate the system manually. The generation of oxygen begins when the passenger pulls the mask toward the passenger seat. The mask receives pure oxygen under positive pressure at a rate governed by the cabin pressure altitude and a flow regulating device in each container. The length of time that the oxygen supply will last after the cabin suffers decompression depends on the number of bottles installed, the number of masks in use and the flight attitude profile flown.

At a cabin pressure altitude of less than 10,000 feet, there will be no oxygen flow. A reset is available for the rearming of the system when the cabin altitude is below 14,000 Feet and the masks have been returned to their containers.

A manual release tool allows the Crew to deploy the masks if the pneumatic door latch release fails it is stored at the cabin attendants' station.

Note: If oxygen system supply lines sustain damage from an engine burst, the supply to cabin oxygen system could be partially lost without any indication of the loss appearing in the cockpit.

ECAM DOOR/OXY PAGE

OXY high pressure indication

Green (steady) when pressure is 1200 psi

Green (pulsing) when pressure is 200 psi and < 1200 psi

Amber when pressure is < 200 psi

An amber half frame appears when oxygen pressure is < 1600 psi

REGUL LO PR indication appears amber if one of the low pressure switches fails or one of the systems shut off valves is not fully closed and the system has not been activated.

One of the main supply line shut off valves is not fully open and the system has not been activated. Both main supply line shut off valves are closed when the system has been activated.

PAX OXY Indication

Normally white becomes amber when pressure goes below 200 psi.

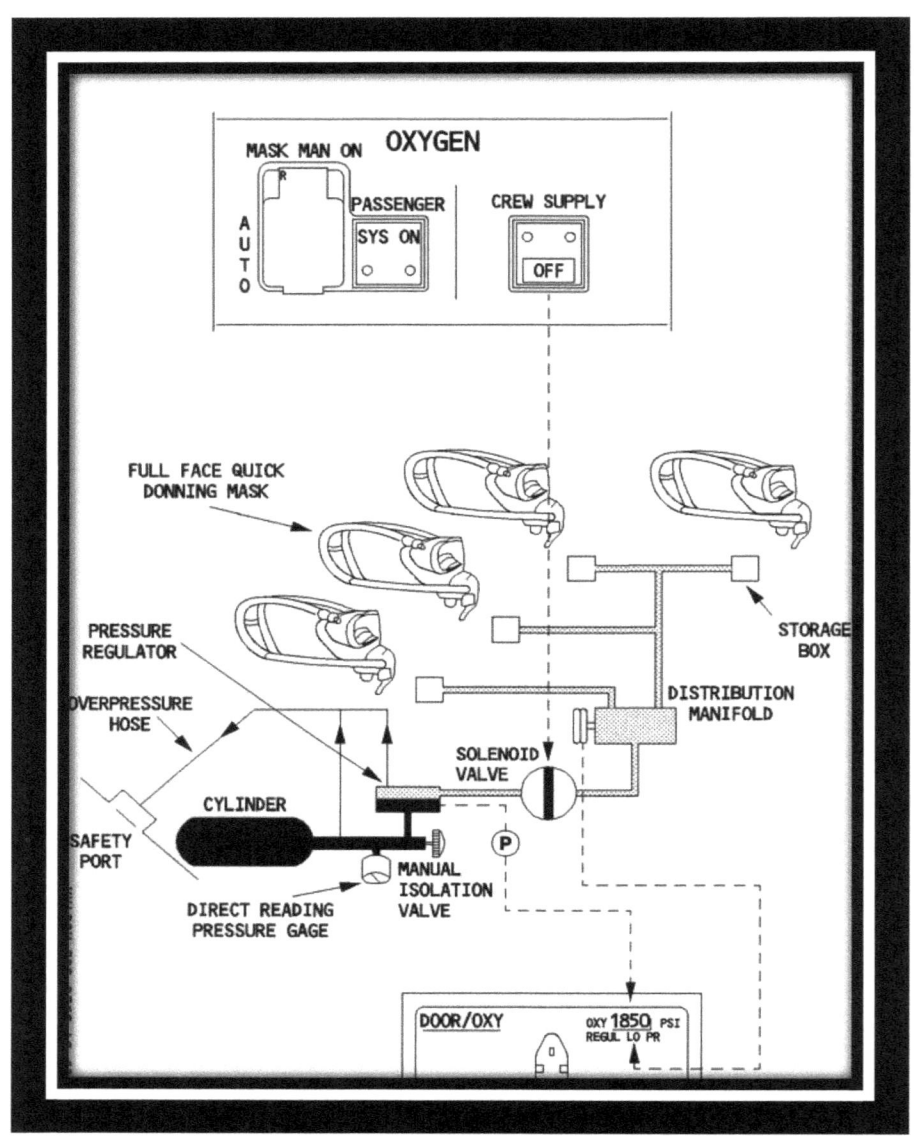

Schematic of Oxygen System

CREW SUPPLY

High pressure cylinders in LH lower fuselage.
Over pressure auto supplied above 30,000 ft cab alt to help prevent condensation, etc.
Mix of cabin air and oxy up to 35,000 ft cab alt. 100% oxy above 35,000ft cab alt.
ON – Valve is open, supplying low pressure oxy.
　* is normal position in flight
OFF – Valve closed. White light on.

Electric latching system allows masks to fall when cab alt exceeds 14,000ft (+0, -500ft). Oxygen delivered at constant pressure by oxygen generator which lasts about 22 min. Oxygen generation may emit heat and smoke.

PASSENGER SYS ON

White light when system on. Remains on until RESET on maint panel is pressed.

MASK MAN ON

PA automatically broadcasts instruction whether MAN or AUTO Deployment

AUTO - Passenger oxygen masks automatically drops when cabin altitude reaches 14,000 ft or by lifting the red cover and pressing the button will deploy the passengers' oxygen masks in the cabin.

RESET

Maintenance crew use this pb to reset after the system has operated.
ON – White light comes on, PASS SYS ON light goes off
FAULT Lt – Amber when door latch solenoids are energized for more than 30 secs

CHAPTER THIRTEEN

PNEUMATIC

Brief System Explanation for Pilots

A330 pneumatic system supplies high pressure air for:
Air conditioning
Engine starting
Wing anti icing
Hydraulic reservoir pressurization
Water pressurization
Pack bay ventilation turbofan actuation

High pressure air is provided from three sources:

Engines bleed systems
APU load compressor
Two HP (high pressure) ground connections

Each engine bleed systems are interconnected by a cross bleed duct to the same one that the APU and ground sources are connected. Pneumatic system operation is controlled and monitored by two Bleed Monitoring Computers BMC (bleed monitoring computers 1 and 2). Each BMC is provided with bleed pressure, temperature and valve position information, and is interconnected to other systems involved with bleed system. The other BMC provides indications and warnings to the ECAM and CMC (central maintenance computer). In case of failure of one BMC, the other one takes over most of the monitoring functions.

Each bleed valve is electrically controlled by its associated BMC and pneumatically operated.

The APU bleed supply is controlled by the APU Electronic Control Box (ECB). Also a leak detection system is provided to detect any overheat in the vicinity of hot air ducts system.

APU BLEED AIR SUPPLY

Air is supplied by the APU on ground and in flight. APU bleed air is controlled by the APU bleed valve which operates as a shut off valve. It is electrically controlled and pneumatically operated. The APU bleed valve is controlled by the APU BLEED push button. When the pushbutton is selected to ON position, APU bleed air supplies the pneumatic system provided that the APU N > 95%. This causes the X-BLEED valve to open and the engine bleed valves to close.

AUTO POSITION X-bleed valve is open if APU bleed valve is open X-bleed valve is closed if APU bleed valve is closed.

OPEN positon   X-bleed valve is open.

CLOSE position X-bleed valve is closed.

ENGINE BLEED VALVES Indications

In line — Green: The bleed valve is normally open.
Crossline — Green: The bleed valve is fully closed (by manual or automatic control).
In line — Amber: The bleed valve disagrees in the open position.
Crossline — Amber: The bleed valve disagrees in the closed position or the bleed valve is fully closed and the respective engine is not running.

Note: In certain circumstances (such as a different engine setting, or minor bleed valve regulation drift), it is possible that one bleed valve on one side closes and will be indicated closed and green on the ECAM BLEED page. There is no operational impact on the bleed system, provided there is no associated "AIR ENG X BLEED FAULT" ECAM warning.

Pneumatic System Schematic

ENG 1 BLEED (2)

 ON – Bleed valve opens provided:

* Upstream pressure is above 8psi
* APU BLEED pb is at OFF or APU bleed valve closed
* No onside wing or pylon leak, overpressure or overtemp.
* ENG FIRE pb is not out or released
* Eng start valve closed

FAULT Lt – Amber with ECAM if:

* Overpressure, over temperature, bleed valve-positioned disagreement for example.
* Bleed valve not closed during eng start
* Bleed valve not closed with APU bleed ON and for RH eng X-bleed open) Also with auto closure of bleed and HP valves
* Overpressure downstream of bleed valve
* Bleed overheat
* Wing or eng leak on related side
* Extinguishes when ENG BLEED pb is at OFF provided failure disappeared
* OFF light (white) – Bleed valve and high pressure valve are close.
* FAULT Lt & auto closure signal reset

APU BLEED

 ON: (Blue) APU bleed valve opens provided:

* APU speed is above 95%

* Altitude below 25,000ft climbing or below 23,000ft during descending
* No leak detected on APU. At any time when debut valve opens, the cross bleed valve opens an engine bleed valve close automatically

OFF – APU bleed valve closes
FAULT Lt – (Amber with ECAM) when APU bleed air leak detected

X-BLEED

 AUTO valve opens anytime APU bleed air is used.
X-bleed valve closed APU valve closed.
APU bleed valve is closed when bleed air leak detected or APU fire pushbutton is pushed.
OPEN – X-bleed valve is open.
CLOSE – X-bleed valve is closed

CHAPTER FOURTEEN

APU

Brief System Explanation for Pilots

APU General Description

The Auxiliary Power Unit (APU) is a self-contained unit which makes the aircraft independent of external pneumatic and electrical power supply.

On Ground:

— It supplies bleed air for starting the engines and for the air conditioning system.
— It supplies electrical power to the electrical system.

During Take-Off:

It supplies bleed air for air conditioning, thus avoiding a reduction in engine thrust caused by the use of engine bleed air for this purpose when optimum aircraft performance is required.

In Flight:

— It backs up the Electrical system
— It backs up the Air conditioning
— It can be used to start the engines

The APU may obtain power for starting from the aircraft's batteries or in combination with the external power or from ground service, or normal aircraft supply. APU starting is permitted throughout the normal flight envelope except when APU battery only is supplying. The ECAM displays APU parameters.

A330 APU ENGINE

The basic element of the APU is a single shaft gas turbine which delivers mechanical shaft power for driving the accessory gearbox (electrical generator) and produces bleed air (engine starting and pneumatic supply).

ELECTRONIC CONTROL BOX

The Electronic Control Box (ECB) is primarily a full authority digital electronic controller that performs the APU system logic for all modes of APU operation such as:

— Sequence and monitoring of start
— Speed and temperature monitoring
— Monitoring of bleed air (IGV)
— Sequence of shut down (manual, protective or inhibited)

AIR INTAKE SYSTEM

The air intake and an electrically operated flap allow external air to reach the compressor inlet.

STARTER

The ECB controls the electric starter. The starter engages if the air intake is fully open and the MASTER SW and the START pushbutton are ON.

FUEL SYSTEM

The APU is supplied from the trim tank transfer line. The ECB controls the fuel flow.

OIL SYSTEM

The APU has an integral independent lubrication system (for lubrication and cooling).

INLET GUIDE VANES (IGV)

The IGVs control bleed air flow, and a fuel-pressure-powered actuator positions the IGVs. The ECB controls the actuator in response to aircraft demand.

AIR BLEED SYSTEM

The ECB controls the APU BLEED valve. It is automatically closed above 25,000 ft. (climbing) or 23,000 ft. (descending).

MASTER SW

 ON/R – Blue light

- * Elec power supplied to APU system, ECB (electronic control box) performs power up test.
- * Opens the APU air intake door
- * APU fuel isolation valve and APU low pressure valve open

Fuel pumps operate (FWD & AFT)
APU page appears on ECAM

OFF – Manual shutdown sequence:
- * ON light goes off
- * APU keeps running for 105 sec at 100% for cooling
- * After further 15 sec (NBPT (No Break Power Transfer) APU shuts down and AVAIL Lt goes off
- * AT 7% air inlet flap closes

Note: Switching OFF then ON the MASTER SW resets the ECB

FAULT Lt – Amber with ECAM when automatic APU shutdown occurs, due to :

1. Fire (on ground only)
2. Air inlet flap not open
3. Overspeed - High oil temp
4. No acceleration
5. Slow start - ECB failure
6. EGT over temp - No flame
7. Loss of over speed protection

8. Low oil pressure
9. under speed
10. DC power loss (when aircraft on Battery) only.

START

 ON – Blue light comes on.

When flap is fully open APU starter is energized
* N = 7%, ignition turned on
* N = 50%, APU starter de-energized
* N = 95%, ignition turned off ON light on START pb goes out AVAIL Lt comes on

APU may now supply bleed air and elec pwr to a/c.
10 sec later the APU page on ECAM disappears
AVAIL Lt – Green when N reaches 95%

CHAPTER FIFTEEN

POWERPLANT

Brief System Explanation for Pilots

ENGINE

Each engine is a high bypass ratio turbofan.

DESCRIPTION

Low-Pressure (LP) Compressor/Turbine

The low-speed rotor (N1) consists of single stage LP compressor (front fan) connected to a four stage LP turbine.

Intermediate Pressure Compressor/Turbine

The intermediate speed rotor (N2) consists of an eight-stage intermediate pressure compressor connected to a single-stage IP turbine.

High-Pressure (HP) Compressor/Turbine

The high-speed rotor (N3) consists of a six-stage HP compressor connected to a single-stage HP turbine.

— **Combustion Chamber**

The annular combustion chamber is fitted with 24 fuel nozzles and 2 igniters.

— **Accessory Gearbox**

The accessory gearbox, located at the bottom of the fan case, receives torque from horizontal HP rotor drive shaft and drives gearbox mounted accessories:

LP COMPRESSOR (FAN)

IP COMPRESSOR

HP COMPRESSOR

FADEC

GENERAL

Each power plant has a FADEC (Full Authority Digital Engine Control) system. FADEC, also called the electronic engine control (EEC), is a digital control system that performs complete engine management. FADEC has two-channel redundancy, with one channel active and one in standby. If one channel fails, the other automatically takes control. The system has a magnetic alternator for an internal power source.

FADEC is mounted on the fan case. The engine interface unit (EIU) transmits to FADEC the data it uses for engine management.

AUTOMATIC MODE

In the auto thrust mode (A/THR function active), the thrust is computed by the FMGC and is limited to the value corresponding to the thrust lever position (except if the alpha-floor mode is activated).

INDICATIONS ON FMA

The FADECs monitor the positions of the thrust levers, and trigger appropriate indications on the FMA.

LVR ASYM: appears in amber (third line on the FMA) if, with A/THR active and both engines running, one thrust lever is set out of CLB detent.

LVR CLB: flashes white (3rd line on the FMA) if the thrust levers are not in CL Position while the aircraft is above the altitude of thrust reduction with both engines running.

LVR MCT: flashes white (3rd line on the FMA) if the thrust levers are not in MCT position after an engine failure (with speed above green dot).

Airbus 330 The Ultimate Guide for Pilots

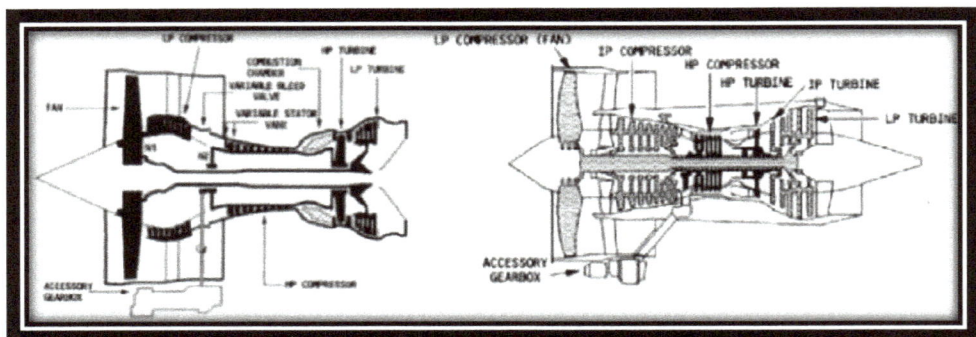

ENG MAN START (1,2)

ON (Blue) Start valve opens if ENG START sel is CRANK or IGN/START

* both pack valves close during start
* start valve closes automatically when N2 reaches about 50%.
* On light Blue

OFF – When ENG MAN START pb is set OFF during manual start, start valve closes provided eng master switch is OFF

N1 MODE 1

ON – Thrust control reverts from EPR mode to N1 rated mode.

* Following an automatic reversion to N1, rated or unrated mode, pressing the pb confirms the mode.
* ON light Blue.

OFF – The FADEC controls the eng in EPR mode if available.

Note: If in N1 mode: No auto thrust, ALPHA FLOOR prot lost & FLEX T/O lost.

<u>Rated N1 mode</u> - FADEC computes an EPR COMMAND depending on TLA, then convert it into a N1 COMMAND as a function of mach

<u>Unrated N1 mode</u> - N1 is defined as a function of TLA and altitude and is limited by FADEC to smaller of N1 max or N1 Redline (if eng data T2, total air temperature, is avail) or N1 Redline (if T2 not avail) TA

CHAPTER SIXTEEN

LIMITATIONS

WGTS	MTaxiW	MTOW	MLW
A332	233,900kg	233,000kg	182,000kg
	MZFW 170,000 kg	**MinWeight** 116,000 kg	
	MinAutoInd 123,000 kg	**Max Fuel** 109,186 kg	
A333	**MTaxiW** 233,900 kg	**MTOW** 233,000 kg	**MLW** 187,000kg
	MZFW 175,000 kg	**MinWeight** 121,000 kg	
	Min AutoInd 123,000kg	**Max Fuel** 76,561kg	

DIMEN A332	RANGE 13,400 km	WINGSPAN 60.3m
LENGTH 58.82 m	**HEIGHT** 17.39 m	**PAYLOAD max** 36.4T

MAX –SEATS
375 / 406

DIMEN A333	RANGE 10,800km	WINGSPAN 60.3m
LENGTH 63.69 m	**HEIGHT** 16.83 m	**PAYLOAD max** 45.9T

MAX-SEATS
440

T.O/LAND CONFIG   **T.O CONFIG**
(appears 2 mins after engs start)

-Rudder Trim & Pitch Trim
-Flap/Slat position
-Speed brake not retracted
-L/R sidestick fault
-Doors
-Brakes hot
-Eng ½ Oil Lo temp
-FWS OEB/FWC discrepancy

LAND CONFIG (appears below 2000ft)

T.O INHIBIT: Most of the less critical warning are inhibits from **80kt** to **1500ft AGL**, (or **2 min**) after the take off.

LAND INHIBIT: Most of the less critical warnings are inhibits below **800ft AGL**.

T/O SIDESTICK   Xwind > 20kt or tailwind: N1 to 50% then 70% then FLX/TOGA to reach TO thrust by 40kt g/s.
Push ½ fwd stick (xwind: full fwd) until 80kt, then reduce fully by 100kt. Use yaw bar after rotate to assist.

V SPEEDS   VFE: Flap speed limit. Climbing: Red & Black strip, Descent: Orange double dash.

Flap VFE: 1, 1+F, 2, 3, Full: **1:** 240kt, **1+F:** 215, **2:** 196kt, **3:** 186kt, **Full:** 180kt.
L/G: **VLE/VLO:** 250kt/M0.55. **Gravity Ext:** 200kt.
VMCL: **A333:** 123kt
          A332 200: 118kt
Best angle (Vx):   Green Dot
Best rate (Vy):   Turbulence Speed. Between Green Dot and Econ speed. M0.82 at high alt
Vat: Threshold Speed: 1.3 Vso
Green Dot: Best climb speed/best lift-drag ration speed in clean config.
Max tyre speed: 204kt.
Max wiper/window: 230kt.
Climb/Descent speed limit: 250kt below 5000ft or MSA. 80kt max is approved below 5000ft not below MSA.
Best diversion speed/alt: VMO/MMO between 30000ft – 31000ft at M0.86/330kt.

WEATHER
Wind direction: **True:** TAF / METAR / ND wind arrow.

Magnetic: ATIS / Tower / ND winds.

Min/Max operating TAT/SAT°:**Min: TAT**: -53°/**SAT**: -78°**Max: TAT**: +55° *If TAT inop, no go item.*

WIND	**Head Tail Cross**
Dry (15kt-F.O)	40 kt
	Passenger/Cargo Doors Operation if: Max Wind
	40kt/*50kt

*if nose into wind, cargo door on leeward side

WIND	**Head Tail Cross**
Wet (15kt-F.O)	30 kt

Turbulence **Below FL200**: **A332**: 240kt
             A333: 240kt
             Above & FL200: A332:260/M0.80
             A333: 260/M0.78(use lowest)

T/O in turbulence: Retracting flap/slat, wait for target speed +20kt to VFE-5kt.

WINDSHEAR

Reactive: Active from **3s** after lift-off up to **1300ft.** Max pitch to 22.5°
Predictive: Below **2300ft:** Active, no alerts, scanning **5NM** ahead.
Below **1500ft:** Warnings & cautions active.
T/O: Alerts inhibited above **100kt**& up to **50ft**.
Warnings: from liftoff to **1300ft**.
Appch: Warnings: from **1300ft** down to **50ft.**

INSTRUMENTS Altimeter – On ground: PFD1 & PFD2: +/- 25ft.

Flight Instrument Tolerances

Altimeter on the ground: Within 75ft.
Altimeter – FL100 ADR 1,2,3 check on PFD: 60ft.
ISIS & any ADR: 130ft.
HDG difference – NDs: 4°
SPEED difference – PFDs: 6kt on ground – between ADR1&2 / ADR1&3 / ADR2&3 / ISIS & ADR1,2,3

FDs disappear: Above 25° & Below 13°, bank of 45°

PERFORMANCE
Pressure altitude:
Indicated altitude + ((1013 – QNH) x 30ft)
Density altitude: Pressure altitude + (OAT – ISA) x 120).
This is the actual performance of a/c.

ALTITUDES
Opt alt in crz: GW – 570 or TOW – 580
Max gear ext alt: 21000ft / Dispatch with L/G down: FL350
Max flap / slat use: 20000ft
REC MAX based on: 0.3g buffet margin, fly V/S of 300ft/min at Max CLB thrust, fly above GD.
OPT FL based on: Min of FL100, min crz time is 5 min.
Updated automatically until 15NM before TOD.

FLT control	F(1+F) auto flap retract: 200kt Aileron droop 5° when flaps are at F(1+F), F2,3, and with full flaps: 10° Slats Alpha/Speed lock: Inhibit slat retraction if speed < 148kt (200) < 168kt (300) or AOA > 8.5° - 9°

<u>LPC DATA:</u>
TAKE OFF Min turn after take-off: **IMC:** At THR RED.
VMC: At 400ft
Straight out departure: After T/O, turns are < 15°
ASDA / TODA:nASDA measured from nose gear / TODA measured from main gear.

EFATO
Min terrain clearance: 35ft level flight / 50ft during a turn
Turn reqd before G.D: Based on 15° bank, thereafter 25° bank is used
Turning speed exc hold: Max G.S of 215kt in still air (2.5NM radius of turn)

Holding / Hold MSA: 5NM leg, 2NM radius, 3NM protected buffer zone each side, MSA is for All engines
EOSID: Climb straight ahead on rwy trk until at acc alt, then level off, clean up & climb MSA
Special EOSID: Climb straight ahead until specified to turn, at acc alt it's the same as EOSID.

LANDING Actual landing dist **(ALD):** Distance from 50ft above threshold to full stop at Vapp (1.3Vs)
Reqd landing distance **(RLD): DRY RLD** = ALD x 1.67.
WET RLD = DRY RLD 1.15 or **ALD** x 1.92

GO AROUND   Min app climb gradient:

Single Engine: G/A at DA:

CAT1: 2.1%   **CAT2:** 2.5%
Min landing climb gradient:
2 Engines TOGA: G/A at 50ft: 3.2% with flaps, gear down

All Jepp G/A climb gradients: 2.5%
Min T/O climb gradient: 2.4%. Only required for 2nd segment.
If overweight with flaps 3: Retract flaps to 1 for G/A.

ELECTRICS
Bat charge cycle: 20mins
Bat 1 or 2 voltage / current: 25.5 to 31V / > 5A
A/C on bat only (gnd): Ground horn triggers, vent Extract Fault on ECAM after 5min.
APU start on bat only: Bat 1, 2, APU bat > 23.5V, or APU may abort start.
Bats loaded correctly: When Off to ON, current drops < 60A after 10s.

Gen load (amber if): > 108% for over 10sec.
Emergency gen supplies: AC 8.5 Kva. If RAT supplying G system then supplies: AC 3.5kva.
TR current: 2 Main: 200A / 1 Ess: 100A.

HYDRAULICS
Normal PSI: 3000psi +/- 200. Amber < 1450psi.
Electric pump can supply: 18% of an engine driven pump if failed.
G electric pump runs: Automatically if eng failure for 25s when L/G is selected up. Prim1or3 must be avail.
ECAM pg – horizontal line: On G System: Above that quantity its safe level to use L/G.
RAT provides: 15% - 45% of engine driven pump depends on a/c speed. Operates above 100RPM.

FADEC
Assumes engine failure: If
1. Eng sw is off
2. N2 below idle
3. TLA < 5° & other is > 5° 4.

ENGINES
EGT max: Start: **Ground:** 750° **In Air:** 975°
TOGA time: T/O & G/A: **2 Eng:** 5min **1 Eng**: 10min
MCT max: 940° / No time limit.
Nacelle overheat: 260° - White Dash.

Max start attempt: 5min. If no start on 1st attempt, wait 30s for each minute of start attempt (for cooling)

After two 5min cycles: Wait 10min after 2 consecutive stat attempts before starting again.

No start engagement: N2 < 30%

FADECS when A/C powered: Online for 15min
N1 max (low speed rotor): 115.5% - Depends on ambient cond. & eng bleed config. May be lower.
N2 max (high speed rotor): 113%
"Check EWD": If a discrepancy between N1, N2, EGT, FF displayed and the real value.
Derate climb: **D1:** GW between 205 – 220 T. **D2:** GW < 205
Flex temp: **Max:** ISA + 72°
Min: OAT or ISA + 15° - *Whichever is **lower***
Flex temp restriction: Reported friction coefficient < 0.4mu or windshear suspected. Must use TOGA
Max reverse achieved: N1 between 70% & 85%, controlled by FADEC.
Start sequence: **N2: 10%:** Ign powered. **15%:** Fuel flow. **50%:** Start valve closes. **54%:** Ign off.
Sea level reading: N1 = 23% EGT = 360°   N2 = 63% FF = 550 kg/h

APU
N usage: 95%
Max: 107%
EGT max: 650°
Start: 1250°

Start attempts: After 3 attempts without cooling, allow 60s cooling before next attempt.

Start APU with Gnd power: -15°
Bleed psi on ECAM: Up to 12psi in cold weather, below 10°
Max bleed operation: 22,500ft

Max APU use: **Engine Start:** 20,000ft   **Pack Use:** 1 Pack: 22,500ft / 2 Packs: 17,500ft

OIL	Oil quantity: >= 12 qt + consumption (est. 0.56 qt/h, range 0.56 – 0.78 qt/h) Max Cont. temp: 160° Max transient temp: **15min** 175° Min start temp: -40° Oil Hi temp: 160° – 175° > 15min, or above 175°. Pulses above 160° Min oil quantity: 12qt + est. consumption (max avg: 0.56 qt/hr, max: 0.87 qt/hr) Min oil pressure: 10 psi IDG oil temp (amber): > 185° Flashes if between: 142° - 185°
LDG GEAR	Max brake temp – fans off: **T/O:** 300° (Maint reqd if > 800°, difference between L/G: 200°) **Land:** 150° Max brake temp – fans on: **If >150°:** delay T/O. **If <150°:** turn brake fans off. Hot wx operation: >100°: fans on Brake temp warnings: Green arc > 100° / Amber arc or HOT on brake fan > 300° (possible hyd fluid ignite) Brake pressure test: 2200–2700psi VMO/MMO L/G down: 255kt/M0.60 Max auto braking: Speed > 72kt Anti-skid deactivates: Below 10kt. Can only reset on ground with parking brake on Accumulator pressure: Below 1500°, PB is much less effective, turn off NWS & use triple indicator to brake.

TAXI	A330 Aerodrome ref code: Code E: Wingspan: (Outer main L/G wheel span) 52m (9m) up to not inc 65m (14m) NWS control: Below 100kt & up to 72° Rudder steering control: Up to 150kt for T/O & below 100kt for landing. NWS taxi / towing & push 72° / 65 Nose gear behind cockpit: 6.67m Main gear located behind cockpit: 32.04m (25.37 + 6.67) 180° Turn min width: With symmetric thr & no braking: **A332** 46m and for **A333** 50m require. Taxi speed: **Straight:** 30kt / 10kt (LVP, Icing Cond.) **90° Turn:**< 10kt N1 max for taxi: 40% Deflated tyre taxi speed: **1 tyre:** 7kt, **2 tyres:** 3kt, **NWS turn:** 30° Rapid exit taxiways: 60kt limit and at least 75m long with 30° turn off Flap selection in snow: Delay until reaching holding point to avoid contamination of mechanical movement. Delay retraction when taxiing in until stopped and visually inspected at gate.
ICING	Engine anti-ice should turn on: when OAT (on ground) or (TAT in flight) = **10°C** or less, including temp < -40° with visible moisture (clouds, fog vis of 1SM/1600m or less) Wing anti-ice: any indication of ice buildup on ice detector, windscreen or wipers. Ice detectors: 2 on fwd lower fuselage.

Clean:	No ice detected: After 130s & "ICE NOT DET" on EWD. Severe icing: 5mm of ice accretion on airframe + Severe Icing on ECAM. If ice accretion: **Clean:** VLS + 15kt. **Not** VLS + 5kt, and landing distance x 1.1. If ice on de-iced areas: **Clean:** VLS + 15kt. **Not Clean:** VLS + 10kt, Rain repellent: Use for moderate to heavy rain only.
FUEL	Min T/O fuel: 5200kg & WING TK LO LVL warning must not be on ECAM Min landing fuel: ALTN + FINL Avg fuel burn: **Taxi:** 25kg/min or 1500kg/hr. **In Flight:** 5500kg/hr Collector cell: 1000kg Fuel temp: **Min:** Jet A: -40° **Jet A1:** -47° **Max:** Jet A: +55° **Jet A1:** +55° Fuel temp Inner tanks: -54° or Freezing point + 3°, whichever is higher. Aft Tx occurs: Above FL255 & above 6250kg (inner tanks) & target CG reached. Fwd Tx occurs: Thru FL245 or 35min to land (75min if trim fwd pump fails, gravity fed then) or, inner tanks are below 4000kg, until reaches 5000kg, or in emer elec config. Fuel flow: Center to Inner. (Inner < 4000kg) - Trim to Inner. (Inner < 3500kt) - Outer to Inner. Max fuel imbalance: 3000kg. Refuelling: Trim tank begins filling > 36500kg fuel. Takes 35min for all tanks at 35psi.

Coupled both sides takes: **A332:** 25min, **A333:** 33min.
ECAM STS – Fuel imbalance: 3000kg or greater between wing tanks
FINL fuel based on: **FMGS FINL:** S Speed (Flap 1) / **OFP FINL:** G.D (Clean)
ALT fuel based on: **FMGS ALT:** Max RC   **OFP ALT**: LRC

AIR   Ram Air Inlet: Opens if: ΔP < 1psi
Cabin ΔP: Green (> 0.2 – 8.85) Green Pulse (> 1.5 below 800ft on appch) Amber (>10)
Cabin alt (Excess Cab alt): Normal (0 – 6600ft) Green Pulse (> 8800ft) Amber (>9950ft +/- 350ft)
Cabin V/S: Green (+1400 to -750 fpm) Green Pulse (> +/-1800 fpm)
Max Pos ΔP: 9.25psi
Max Neg ΔP: -1 or -0.73psi depends on a/c
Safety Relief Valve setting: 8.85psi / -0.26psi

Engine bleed psi: 44 – 52psi. If 85psi is reached, overpressure valve closes.
Zone controller fails: Pack delivers 20° temp only.
Cargo temp selectors: Cold: 5° / Mid: 15° / Hot: 25°
Cabin depressurizes: Before T/O & 80s after land. Fully Depressurized 3min after land.

FIRE PB

ENGINE	**APU**
- Silence aural warning	- Shuts down APU
- Arm squibs	- Silence aural warning
- Closes LP fuel valve	- Arms squibs (on gnd: fires squibs)
- Closes hyd fire shut off valve	- Closes LP fuel valve
- Closes both eng bleed	- Shuts off APU fuel valves pump
- Closes pack flow control	- Closes APU bleed valve valve & x-feed valve

FIRE PB

ENGINE	**APU**
- Cuts off FADEC power supply - Deactivates engine generator	- Deactivates APU - generator

OXYGEN

Oxygen HP ECAM ind: **Green**: >= 600psi / Pulse Green < 600psi **Amber:** < 300psi / Amber ½ box < 1000psi
REGUL LO PR (amber): If O2 psi on LP circuit is low (50psi)
CKPT OXY (amber): < 300psi or low o2 psi detected, or OXY Crew Supply pb OFF
CKPT oxygen duration: 98min
Cabin masks open: If Alt > 4000ft
Cabin masks supply: **22min** under 100% positive pressure
Smoke hoods supply:15min

SAFETY EQUIP

F: Fire Extinguisher
A: Axe
S: Smoke Hoods
T: Torches *(FAST GOEL)*
G: Gloves
O: Oxygen Masks
E: Escape Ropes
L: Life Jackets

RADAR
Max turbulence detection: 40NM on ND
Storm avoidance: Avoid yellow, red, magenta areas by 20NM min. or if cells higher then 28000ft.
Clearing cells: Min top clearance of 5000ft to avoid severe turbulence. Never fly under.
Top of clouds calculation: (Tilt x Range) x 100. Top of clouds are x ft above aircraft.

HOLDING SPEEDS

Altitude	Normal	Turbulence	Time
Up to 1400 ft:	230 kt	280 kt	1 min
14001-20000ft	240 kt	280kt/M0.80 (whichever is lower)	1 ½ min
20001-34000ft	265 kt	280 kt/M0.80 (whichever is lower)	
Above 34000ft	M0.83	M0.83	

TCAS
Intruder types: 4 types. (Hollow diamond, full diamond, (TA) circle, (RA) square)
Scans: Above: -2700/+9900ft. All: +/-2700ft.
Below: if cruise alt is +/-2000ft of FL410 or in

Descent: +2700/-9900ft.
TA / RA limits: TA: 8NM. RA: 5NM, 5sec to react.
RA command: "Climb" or "Descend" within 5sec at 1500ft/min. "Climb Now", "Increase Climb" within 2.5sec at 2500ft/min. on appch: G/A initiate.

GPWS

GPWS modes: 5 Modes
Audio/Visual warnings at: 10ft – 2450ft.

EGPWS

EGPWS additional modes:2
Modes: Terrain Clearance Floor, Terrain Awareness Display.
Accuracy: HIGH
Color Coding:
Amber Caution: 60s before impact. +1000ft ahead.
Red Warning: 30s before impact. +2000ft ahead.

Terrain on ND for T/O: Required when airport elevation is > 3000ft within 10NM.

RNAV

Accuracy: Enroute: 1.0 / Terminal Area: 0.5 / App: 0.3 / G/A: 1.0
FMGS approved for: B-RNAV, P-RNAV, RNP 4, RNP 10
RNAV types: B-RNAV: required to maintain track within 5NM for 95% of time.

MEL Repair Intervals:

Category **A:** No standard intervals
Category **B:** 3 consecutive days.
Category **C:** 10 consecutive days.
Category **D:** 120 consecutive days

Notes. Total interval check: 800 hours
Daily check:36 hrs, extended to 48hrs.
FMGS DB expire: 5 days expired allowed at outstation.

OTHER

Disregard PAPI: Below 200ft, if TCH threshold > 52" (332) 51" (331)

Noise abatements: NADP1 close, NADP2 far, NADP-A, NADP-B, NPR.

No FD for T/O: Pitch to 12.5°. At THR RED Alt: Set CLB SPD, levers to CL & activate A/THR.
         Side Slip Beta Target: Appears blue if thrust asymmetry > 30% and one engine is > 80%.

CHAPTER SEVENTEEN

INTERPRETATION OF GREEN DOT SPEED AND SOME MISCONCEPTIONS ABOUT FLYING BELOW GREEN DOT SPEED

Interpretation of Green Dot Speed and Some Misconceptions about Flying Below Green Dot Speed

Holding is all about killing as much time as possible for the fuel you have and that differs from "flying the most miles for the fuel you have". Best time per fuel is called max endurance, while best mileage per fuel is called max range. For the max endurance you'd want to fly close to the minimum drag speed. This requires you to pump the least amount of fuel into the engines per minute and that makes the airline's shareholders and Greenpeace the happiest. In practice you also have to make turns in a holding pattern and while turning, the drag increases, with an associated increase in the minimum drag speed. Therefore, pilots generally fly a few knots above that minimum drag speed anyway. That also increases the speed stability of the airplane: it's easier to maintain a speed a few knots higher to the knot. Flying below the minimum drag speed is not stable: pilots call that "flying the back of the curve" because if the plane slows down there, it increases the drag and slows it down even more. Pilots must be very alert when they fly at the back of the curve and most airlines don't allow it for that reason. Airbus indicates a speed close to this minimum drag speed with a green circle on the airspeed indicator. It's therefore very poetically called "green dot speed"(**Optimum Engines Out Glide Speed**). Green dot speed takes into account speed stability and is very close to minimum drag speed and best lift to drag speed. This speed depends a lot on the weight of the airplane, but is always visible to the pilots. Heavy airplanes have a high optimal holding speed and light ones have a lower one. Usually at the end of a flight, when only enough fuel weight remains for the approach and landing plus some reserves, that speed is around 200 to 230 knots.

Flying below the green dot speed would be of no operational benefit <u>at all</u> in fuel savings.

Why would some TREs and captains of a major airline deliberately fly below F, S and Green Dot speeds in selected speed thinking they will save fuel? This careless action is more about the pilot's ego and not understanding the consequences of such an action. Ninety-nine percent of the time managed speed does not go below the green dot speed, so why take away the protection; all the pilots need is a distraction (ATC, Cabin...) or some turbulence to find themselves close to VLS and possibly triggering Alpha Floor and shortly after be called into the fleet office to explain their actions.

For those of us who really want to save fuel - please do not fly below F, S and green dot speeds during approach; just follow these recommendations to maximize fuel savings:

Good airmanship

Experience and knowledge

An aerodynamically clean aircraft

Well maintained engines

Good flight planning

Good flight procedures

Take-off Flap

Lowest flap/slat setting will give lowest fuel burn and best flight profile. Other priorities such as maximizing TOW, maximizing flextemp, etc. may require other flap settings

Take-off Acceleration Altitude

The minimum acceleration altitude required by regulations will optimize fuel consumption

Climb

Optimum climb law is dependent on the Aircraft, on selected modes and cost indices. In general, it is not profitable to climb at high-speed or climb at very slow climb speeds.

Cruise

Cruise is the most important phase in terms of fuel savings. Fuel efficiency during cruise can be optimized by cruise with stepped climb, cruise with an economic speed.

Descent

Avoid using the speed brake as much as possible.

Fuel consumption increases significantly with airspeed and also in the case of a premature descent. Descent performance depends on A/C, weight and cost index. The lower the cost index, the lower the speed. The less steep the descent path and the longer the descent distance, the greater the descent time. The earlier the top of descent (TOD) point is reached, the lower the fuel consumption. The FMS computes the TOD as a function of cost index.

Holding

Green dot speed is the one or 2 engine out operating speed in clean configuration; being approximately the best lift to drag ratio speed, it provides in general the lowest fuel consumption. Green Dot Speed may not be appropriate at some airports. It is then advised to hold at a lower speed or in FLAP 1 at S speed.

Approach:

Keep in clean configuration as long as possible

Delay gear selection

A continuous descent approach saves fuel

Visual approach from downwind saves fuel

However, does not compromise the stabilized approach philosophy.

Landing Flap:

The lower flap setting will save fuel; however consider runway length, exit point, occupancy time, runway surface conditions, tailwind, brake cooling, no Cat 2 or 3 landings, etc.

After landing perform single engine taxi (if applicable).

CHAPTER EIGHTEEN

Ground Speed Mini

Understanding the Logic behind Ground Speed Mini (GS-MINI)

GS-MINI is, as the name implies, based on a minimum ground speed. Before the approach, once the crew can predict with reasonable confidence what the surface-wind is likely to be at the landing threshold, they enter the figure into the approach Performance page. The FMS works out the correct Vapp, which is a threshold IAS based on weight and headwind component.

Now: let's take the sea-level ISA case, where IAS=TAS; a Vapp of 130kts; and a predicted headwind of 10kts entered into the Performance page. On a conventional aero plane stabilized at Vapp (130kts) at a height of 500ft, if the headwind is 30 kts the GS will be 100kts. But when it comes over the threshold, where the headwind is only 10kts, it will need to have accelerated to a GS of 120kts to maintain the required Vapp of 130. This will require a lot of extra energy (from the engines), which may cause problems, particularly if the loss of headwind happens suddenly (like at night). It makes sense, therefore, to ensure that the GS remains at or above 120kts throughout the approach, even though this initially results in a higher IAS

(150kts at 500ft in this case). The "managed" speed (IAS) target on the ASI (used by the pilot and the auto throttle) goes up and down with the headwind, but never below Vapp. Reaching the threshold, provided the actual headwind equals the predicted figure, the speed target will be Vapp. If the wind is higher, the speed target will be above Vapp. This should not be a problem for stopping in the runway length, because the groundspeed (GS) will be no higher than originally planned. In practice! Works very well, particularly using manual throttle, provided the pilot uses the "managed" speed as a target speed; not a minimum speed. The power changes required in wind shear are far less than on a conventional aero plane, because the GS (kinetic energy) is steady. My subsequent experience tells me this is the least understood feature of the aircraft by the overwhelming majority of Airbus drivers. That is not in any way to be condescending, but that is my personal observation after thousands of hours on type. It is also possible to be flying the Airbus for many years and not really grasp what is going on in this department.

A sure sign of not grasping how it works is when someone thinks that it is dangerous to have a high approach speed generated by the GS mini function on a relatively short runway. If you think that then read on!

Question 1. Why do we have a groundspeed mini function in the first place?

Answer: To enable the aircraft to make an approach at the minimum safe approach speed.

Question 2. What is groundspeed mini anyway?

Answer: If you consider an approach in a conventional aircraft, we will all accept that the aircraft groundspeed is the difference between the TAS and the headwind component of wind. (For all practical purposes, TAS = IAS/CAS at the low levels and speeds associated with nearly every approach). If there is a gust of wind, due to the inertia of the aircraft, the ground speed stays constant (in an instantaneous sense) but there is an instantaneous drop/rise in IAS. Over a period of several seconds, the groundspeed eventually settles to a lower level (assuming an increase in headwind component) and the IAS settles back to its original level before the gust. If that gust then disappears completely, groundspeed instantaneously becomes IAS (i.e. TAS) until the same settling process occurs as described previously. If that original gust was substantial (say 25kts+) and the loss of gust is equally substantial, a situation can arise whereby the aircraft is encroaching into the stall regime and at the very least may experience a significant, and potentially dangerous, loss of speed/lift. In a conventional aircraft this potential problem is overcome by adding up to 15kts, typically, onto your approach speed in gusty or crosswind conditions. In an Airbus the problem is handled by working out the minimum groundspeed that is acceptable for a given wind condition and ensuring the aircraft never drops below that value. This ensures that regardless of gusts the aircraft is guaranteed a safe flying speed. This minimum groundspeed is known as 'groundspeed mini' or 'gs mini'. Easy!

Question 3: What do I need to know about gusts of wind?
Answer: What we conventionally think of as gusts and what Airbus calls a gust are 2 different things! A "conventional" pilot thinks about a gust of wind as being an unanticipated and rapid change in speed or direction of a volume of air. (There are no doubt better definitions but I think you get my drift!) The Airbus, being a dull machine, has a different way of assessing a "gust". On the PERF App Page, one of the programmable fields is for wind - that wind is known as the 'Tower Wind'. Although you do not see it, a computer takes that wind and resolves it into a headwind component relative to the programmed runway. The Tower Wind is used to provide a datum setting of guaranteed minimum wind that may be safely assumed to always be there (which is why Airbus insists on

entering the wind without the gust component). The IRS's are always calculating the wind direction and velocity. Which will be displayed to the pilot on the ND. That wind is resolved into a headwind component by one of the computers. Although that value is never formally displayed, it is easily calculated by taking the groundspeed from the TAS on the ND. The aircraft then takes that value and compares it to the headwind component of the Tower Wind (wind in the Perf App page) - known as the "Tower Head Wind Component" or THWC. The difference between the two values is taken as the "gust"- i.e. the "unanticipated" wind component. The calculation assumes that the THWC is a minimum of 10 kts so if the Tower wind is say 260/6 the calculation will assume it is 260/10.

Question 4: What does the Airbus do with that calculated gust of wind?

Answer: It simply adds the rest of that "gust" onto the calculated approach speed (VAPP) on the PERF App page. That is then displayed to the pilot as the VAPP TARGET, which is the magenta triangle approach speed we all know and love on the PFD.

Question 5. How many possible approach speeds does the Airbus calculate and what one does it use?

Answer: The Airbus actually calculates four possible approach speeds but only displays the highest one to the pilot as the magenta speed triangle (VAPP TARGET). That also becomes the auto thrust speed target. Two of those speeds do not consider groundspeed mini and two do use it. The first two are straightforward and are calculated from the following equation: VAPP = Max (VLS + 5, VLS + 1/3 THWC [to max of 15kt])

The important thing about VAPP is that it is known beforehand as it appears on the PERF App page. It is the highest of VLS + 5 or VLS +1/3 of the THWC (limited to a max of 15 knots). Say for example VLS is 125 kts, and the reported wind is 260/50 on runway 26 (ie all headwind) then VAPP would be 140 kts as the max value of the tower headwind component would be 15kts. VLS + 5 would only be 130 kts so the higher value would be displayed on both the PERF App page and on the magenta triangle speed bug on the PFD.

In equation terms, groundspeed mini is described as follows:
GS mini = VAPP – THWC or VAPP – 10 [If Tower tailwind or THWC < 10]

This leads us to the calculation of the next 2 possible speeds, both of which consider groundspeed mini. The equation is as follows:

VAPP TARGET = Max (VAPP, GS mini + Current HWC)
As an example:
VLS = 120kts Tower Wind 260/27
1/3THWC = 9.0 R/ wind direction 260
VAPP = 129 kts Current Wind 260/35
Current HWC = 35.0kts x-wind = 0
GS Mini 102kts

VAPP-derived speeds:
VLS + 5 = 125kts
VLS + 1/3 THWC (max of 15kt) = 129kts
Groundspeed mini-derived speeds:
VLS + 5 -max (THWC, 10) + Current HWC = 133kts
VLS +min (1/3THWC, 15) - max (THWC, 10) + Current HWC = 137kts
Therefore, VAPP TGT = 137 (which is displayed on the PFD)

Question 6: In general terms then, what is the rough rule of thumb about the expected approach speed?

Answer: The magenta bug speed will always be VAPP from the PERF App page, plus any "gust" along the runway axis.

Question 7: Does it matter what wind I write in the Perf App page?

Answer: If the wind is 10kts or less you can write anything you like and it will have no effect whatsoever on the final approach speed. So, for example, if landing on runway 26 you can write 080/10 and the approach speed will still be VLS + 5. Once the wind is greater than 10kts what you write does affect VAPP TGT (i.e. the magenta bug speed).

Question 8: What is the effect of increasing the Tower Wind on VAPP target?

Answer: It is the exact opposite effect many people imagine. If I am approaching runway 31 and the instantaneous wind is 310/35 but the Tower Wind in the PERF APP page is 310/8 the gust is taken as 25kts (the calculation always assumes a minimum headwind of 10kts). That would be added to the VAPP of say 135 knots to give 160kts magenta bug speed. If I now write 310/15 in the Perf App page as the Tower wind that will have the effect of reducing the approach speed because the gust is now only 20kts. That would be added onto VAPP of 135kts to make 160kts. You can try this for yourself and see it instantly work. So in general terms, reducing the Tower Wind increases the approach speed and vice versa. Therefore it is important to put in the steady state wind and not the max gust because by so doing you can weaken the protection the function is trying to provide. Putting in a very high wind at the last minute will instantaneously decrease the approach speed bug.

Question 9: When does the groundspeed mini function because problems and what can I do about it?

Answer: The function causes problems typically at 1500' above the runway on a very windy day when the wind can be enormous compared to the Tower Wind. If for example on RW 08 with a VAPP of 125kts and the Tower Wind is 080/15 but the instantaneous wind is 080/70 (as can happen) then 55 knots can be added to VAPP making VAPP TARGET 180kts. This can be above the flap limiting speed for Config Full (177kts) and give an enormously high approach speed. However as you approach the ground that speed will progressively decrease as the headwind component (and "gust") decreases. There are two ways to overcome this. One is to enter an artificially high Tower Wind and thereby reduce the gust and subsequent VAPP TARGET or the more common method is to immediately select a speed (say 160kts) and wait for the gust to die down. As soon as it has done so, you manage the speed again and the VAPP TARGET will be sensible. That easy!

Question 10. Why do we activate the secondary runway on a circling approach?

Answer: This is because the groundspeed mini calculation will see any wind over 10kts from the reciprocal direction as only 10kts. Therefore it will make the approach speed VLS + 5 which removes all the gust protection that should be there. If you activate the correct runway then the headwind components are resolved in the correct direction and any genuine 'gust' is taken into account during the VAPP TARGET calculation.

Question 11. Is GS Mini not potentially dangerous on short runways?

Answer: No! The whole point of GS Mini is to provide the lowest possible safe approach speed. It assumes that the "Tower Wind" is always there and is not a gust. By definition a gust is temporary and therefore if a gust appears it will be added onto the final approach speed but the groundspeed will still be the same as if the gust was not there. Therefore no extra landing distance will be required even if it is a high approach speed. The key thing is that the correct wind should be entered on the PERF App page – as long as you do that then you will not have any problem.

CHAPTER NINETEEN

A330 QUESTIONS

System Review Questionnaire

1. What does the green dot represent?

a. Green dot represents the maneuvering speeds in clean configuration.

2. If the FPV is above the horizon line, what is the aircraft actually doing?

a. Aircraft is climbing.

3. When will the glide slope half index flash continuously?

a. When the deviation value reaches 2 dots for two seconds.

4. What height while airborne are the TO INHIBIT and LOG INHIBIT function active?

a. T.O. till 1,500 feet AGL, and LND below 800 feet AGL respectively.

5. During the exterior pre-flight on a warm day, in what position would you expect to find the avionics ventilation EXTRACT Valve to be in?

a. OPEN.

6. What happens when a temperature selector rotary knob is adjusted?

a. A signal is sent to the zone controller requesting a different temperature.

7. What is the position of the engine bleed valves with APU running, APU bleed ON and engine BLEED switches ON with engines running?

a. CLOSED.

8. Are there any control surfaces with a mechanical backup?

a. Yes, the THS and the Rudder.

9. What controls are provided for the pitch axis?

a. Two independent elevators and a Trimmable Horizontal Stabilizer (THS).

10. What happens in the event of a single PRIM FAILURE?

a. The functions of the failed PRIM will be assumed by the other PRIM.

11. In normal law, if one stick is rapidly pulled fully back, can the aircraft's maximum allowed 'G' load be exceeded?

a. No. The load factor limitation overrides side stick commands to avoid excessive 'G' load.

12. What is the maximum spoiler deflection (AIR)?

a. 35 degrees.

13. What happens to the rudder trim inputs?

a. Yaw damping and turn coordination signals are not fed back to the rudder pedals.

14. When will the Side Stick Order indicator be displayed?

a. After first engine start and disappears after rotation.

15. When ground spoilers deploy automatically, how many deploy?

a. Six spoiler panels on each wing deploy.

16. What is the pitch nose up attitude limit?

a. 30 degrees progressively reduced to 25 degrees at low speed.

17. What's the pitch nose down attitude limit?

a. 15 degrees.

18. Which altitude limitation is associated with high lift devices?

a. Max altitude for extension is 20,000 ft.

19. What are the different types of flight guidance?

a. Managed and selected.

20. What powers the Emergency Generator?

a. The green hydraulic system when pressurized by engine driven pump(s) or the RAT.

21. What is the function of the ram air valve?

a. Emergency smoke removal and ventilation in the event of a Dual pack failure.

22. With regards to FCTL laws and protections, what is available below 100 feet AGL?

a. Only some damping by load factor and pitch rate feed backs.

23. What does a green SPEED BRK memo message mean on lower ECAM?

a. This is a normal indication whenever speed brakes are used.

24. Are there any approach restrictions with LOW ACCURACY message displayed?

a. Yes, NAV Accuracy check determines the AP/FD guidance mode to be used.

25. When high and low and speed stabilities are available in alternate law, what will be their function?

a. To warn the pilot when the limits of normal flight envelope are being approached.

26. When does the sideslip indicator change to a blue Beta target?

a. Any ENG N1 greater than 80% and difference between ENG N1 is > 30%.

27. Which control will apply in case of dual RA failure when landing gear is extended for landing?

a. Flare law is introduced when the landing gear is extended and both autopilots are disengaged.

28. What does the cost Index = 0 (zero) correspond to?

a. Minimum fuel consumption (max range).

29. When can managed vertical navigation be engaged?

a. Only after managed lateral navigation has been engaged.

30. What does pushing the APPR pushbutton do?

a. Arms the Flight Guidance system to capture a localizer and Glide slope if the information has been entered into the MCDU.

31. What is the function of Alpha floor protection?

a. It helps prevent the aircraft from stalling and protects against wind shear encounters during take-off and approach.

32. When does the CVR stop automatically after the last engine shutdown?

a. 5 minutes.

33. What is the flight deck handset on the center pedestal used for?

a. PA announcements.

34. What happens if the upper DU fails?

a. The lower ECAM will display the engine/warning display (E/WD).

35. Which lights are associated with the EMERGENCY EXIT LIGHT switch?

a. Exit signs, emergency lights, and escape path marking.

36. Which condition will automatically illuminate the EXIT signs?

a. Excessive cabin altitude.

37. What is the meaning of the green AVAIL light on External Power pushbutton?

a. External power is plugged in and parameters are normal. You must push the external power to connect it.

38. What does the blue EXT PWR ON light mean?

a. External power is supplying the aircraft's electrical system.

39. Is it possible to determine the source of power for aircraft busses?

a. Yes, press the ECAM ELEC push button and view the electrical scheme on the ECAM.

40. What would cause the GALLEY amber Fault light to illuminate?

a. An overload has been detected and the automatic shedding did not occur.

41. Can an IDG be reconnected in flight?

a. No, it is not possible.

42. What happens when the EMER GEN MAN ON pushbutton is pushed?

a. Emergency generator runs and is connected to the aircraft network.

43. What will occur if there is an APU fire in flight?

a. The APU must be shut down manually and the agent manually discharged.

44. Which components are included in the fire protection for the forward, aft and bulk cargo?

a. Two fire extinguishing bottles, which can be discharged into either compartment.

45. What happens to the Rudder Trim Limit if associated SEC's fail?

a. It freezes at its present position and a maximum rudder deflection is available when slats are extended.

46. What is the correct action when a cockpit oxygen pressure is displayed in a half amber box?

a. Quantity must be checked to ensure that it is not below the minimum (ref. FCOM LIMITATIONS).

47. Which systems are the pneumatics supplying high-pressure air for?

a. Air Conditioning, water pressurization and engine starting.

48. With both engines operating, when would an ENG BLEED pushbutton FAULT light illuminate?

a. The valve position disagrees from that of the pushbutton.

49. With the aircraft on ground with engines not running and no GPU, how will the APU be started?

a. With the APU battery.

50. While climbing, above what altitude would the APU BLEED Valve automatically close by the ECB?

a. 25,000 feet.

51. How is it determined that the cockpit-sliding window is closed and locked?

a. The locking handle is placed forward with its top flush.

52. Which system powers the cargo doors?

a. The yellow hydraulic system.

53. A few seconds after selecting reverse the amber REV Indication changes to green. What does this mean?

a. The reversers are now fully deployed.

54. What is the outcome if the instinctive disconnect pushbuttons on the thrust levers are depressed momentarily to disconnect auto thrust?

a. Auto thrust can be reengaged using the A/THR pushbutton on the FCU, Alpha Floor available if required.

55. What is the purpose of the safety valve?

a. To avoid excessive positive or negative pressure differential.

56. If the engine bleed switches are ON, the APU is running and the APU bleed is ON are the engine bleed valves open or closed?

a. Closed.

57. What happens to the pack flow control valves during engine start?

a. They close automatically.

58. By what means is the temperature of each aircraft zone optimized?

a. By a TRIM AIR valve.

59. When does normal pressurization commence?

a. Pressurization commences during the take-off roll.

60. What is controlled by the FADEC control during an automatic engine start?

a. The start valve, the HP fuel valve, fuel flow and the ignition.

61. What are the FADEC system electrical power requirements?

a. Aircraft power when IGN START or CRANK is selected until approximately 15% N2.

62. What are the two basic modes of the A/THR system?

a. Thrust and Speed (KIAS or M).

63. What does the left column, first line of the FMA indicate?

a. The mode of the A/THR in use when A/THR is armed or active.

64. How can changes from FLEX to MCT be achieved after take-off?

a. By setting the thrust levers to the TOGA or CLB detent and then back to FLX/MCT.

65. When the aircraft is in the Managed Guidance mode, which guidance orders is it following?

a. It is following vertical and speed profiles as determined by the FMGS.

66. The Captain's FMA indicates "-FD2" in column five, line two, what does this mean?

a. The Captain's FD pushbutton on the FCU has not been selected 'ON' and FD2 has automatically crossed over.

67. Can Alpha-Floor be disengaged while in Alpha Protection?

a. Yes, by manually disengaging the auto thrust.

68. What will occur if one A/P is engaged on the ground when the engines are not running?

a. This A/P will disengage when one engine is started.

69. What happens once the Wing Tip Brakes are activated?

a. The asymmetrical affected high lift system surfaces are locked in their current position.

70. What control modes for elevators control does each servo jack have?

a. 3 control modes: Active, Damping and Centering.

71. What will result in failure to retract the flaps after take-off when using CONF 1+F?

a. Automatic flap retraction.

72. What happens if when at 40 degrees of bank the sidestick is released to neutral?

a. The aircraft rolls back to 33° and resumes flight path stability.

73. When do you get FLARE Mode in Alternate Law?

a. The FLARE Mode begins from 100' RA.

74. How can the brake accumulator be pressurized when on ground with engines stopped?

a. By the Blue Electric pump.

75. What is the normal pressure in the hydraulic system?

a. 3,000 psi.

76. What is the purpose of the leak measurement valve pushbuttons on maintenance panel?

a. They are for maintenance purposes and ground operation only.

77. What does the RAT MAN ON switch do?

a. Extends the RAT, pressurizes GREEN system.

78. With the loss of the G HYD system due to LO LVL, which of the following equipment is lost?

a. Gear retraction, nose wheel steering, part spoilers, normal brakes and autobrakes.

79. What would amber OVHT next to the hydraulic quantity displayed on ECAM HYD page indicate?

a. The temperature of the returning hydraulic fluid, at the inlet to its reservoir is above normal.

80. With the loss of the YELLOW system, what equipment is lost?

a. Cargo doors (if LO LVL), part spoilers and yaw damper 2.

81. An electric pump can also pressurize the yellow hydraulic system. When will this pump run automatically?

a. In flight, in the event of engine 2 failure if the flap lever is not at 0.

82. Can the cargo doors be opened when aircraft electrical systems is not powered?

a. Yes, with the help of a hand pump to pressurize the yellow system.

83. When would the GREEN ELEC HYD pump run automatically?

a. In the air during a one-engine failure to ensure gear retraction in proper time.

84. Even if the HYD pushbutton is switched off, in which condition would amber FAULT light remain on?

a. HYD pump OVHT is present.

85. Which slats are anti-iced in flight?

a. The 4 outboard slats.

86. What is the meaning of '9000' in blue at the top of the altitude scale?

a. It marks the FCU selected altitude.

87. Once the crewmember has completed viewing a specific system, what is the correct procedure for clearing the screen and returning it to a normal presentation?

a. Press the respective system push button again.

88. If the ECAM control panel fails, which buttons remain operative?

a. CLR, RCL, STS, EMER CANC and ALL

89. After the engine shutdown, you observe a pulsing STS message. What does it mean?

a. It is a reminder that the Status page holds a maintenance message.

90. Which system page is automatically displayed on ECAM during TAXI as a default?

a. WHEEL.

91. The upper ECAM Display Unit (DU) has failed. How can the DOOR/OXY page be displayed?

a. The DOOR key on the ECP needs to be pressed and held momentarily.

92. Is it possible to get E/WD indications if both ECAM screens fail?

a. Yes, it must be manually transferred to one of the ND's with the ECAM/ND XFR switch.

93. What happens when a discrepancy between the signals sent to the E/WD and the signal are detected?

a. A 'CHECK EWD' message appears on the upper ECAM and on the ND.

94. What are the indications in a case of FWC1 fault?

a. A message "FWS FWC 1 FAULT' appears on the upper ECAM.

95. How can the ILS 1 FAULT be restored from being a CANCELLED CAUTION?

a. By pressing and holding the RCL key for more than 3 Seconds.

96. The Speed Trend Arrow is a dynamic information indication displaying the speed at which, if the acceleration remains, the aircraft reaches in how many seconds?

a. 10 seconds.

97. While on descent and approaching a selected altitude when does the altitude window start pulsing yellow?

a. When within 750 ft. of FCU altitude and stops when it is within 250 ft.

98. What specific indications are present when an EGT exceeds its maximum value?

a. A red strip appears on the EGT indicator.

99. When would the REACTIVE W/S warnings be provided during Take-off?

a. From 3 seconds after lift-off up to 1,300 feet.

100. When does the red arrow on the landing gear indicator panel illuminate?

a. If the landing gear is not down and locked in landing configuration.

101. When the gear is gravity extended, will nose wheel steering be available?

a. No.

102. Autobrakes, if selected will only be activated by which means?

a. The ground spoiler extension command.

103. There are two triangles for each gear on the ECAM WHEEL page. What do they represent?

a. Each triangle represents the position detected by one of the two computers systems.

104. The height provided by the Radio Altimeter refers to what?

a. The height of the main landing gear above the ground.

105. When are the predictive wind shear system alerts available?

a. During take-off roll, both warnings and cautions are available from 50 feet to a range of 3 NM.

106. How can an EGPWS "PULL UP" warning cancelled?

a. By leaving the warning envelope.

107. How can an EGPWS "TERRAIN" warning be cancelled?

a. By increasing either the barometric or inertial aircraft altitude by 300 feet.

108. What is the main difference between the crew and the passenger oxygen system?

a. Crew is supplied from an oxygen cylinder(s); passengers are supplied by chemical oxygen generators.

109. What happens when the mask is used with the selection at 100% position?

a. Mask is supplied with oxygen undiluted on demand.

110. What occurs when while engine and wing anti-ice are in use a BMC detects a pylon leak signal?

a. The wing and engine anti-ice on the associated side will be lost.

111. What sensors are the air leak monitoring based on?

a. Single loop for pylon and APU and double loop for the wings.

112. What would the APU AVAIL indication as the APU master is switched off?

a. The APU is running a cooling period of 120 seconds.

113. With the engines off, if the AVAIL light is illuminated on both APU pushbutton and the EXT PWR pushbutton, what is the source of electrical power for the aircraft busses?

a. The APU.

114. Can the flight compartment sliding windows be used as Emergency exits?

a. Yes and there are escape ropes mounted above each window behind an access panel.

115. What would illumination of the red panel/light on the main cabin door represent?

a. This indicates that the aircraft cabin is still pressurized and the cabin door should not be opened.

116. What is required for the FADEC to compute a reduced thrust setting?

a. A FLEX temperature must be entered on the TAKE-OFF page of the MCDU.

117. When manual thrust is used, does the thrust lever position determine the thrust setting for the engine?

a. Yes. They will operate like conventional throttles.

118. Is there any mechanical linkage between the thrust levers and the engines?

a. No, it is totally electrical.

119. In case of which condition does the air conditioning pack flow valve close automatically?

a. During Engine start.

120. During the exterior preflight on a warm day, in what position would the avionics ventilation EXTRACT valve be in?

a. Always open when on the ground.

121. What happens when a temperature selector rotary knob is adjusted?

a. A signal is sent to the zone controller requesting a different temperature.

122. When may APU BLEED air be used?

a. When below 23,000 feet, as the bleed valve opens when descending.

123. What does the LOW ACCURACY message mean?

a. The EPE (Estimated Position Error) exceeds the required navigation defined by airworthiness authorities for particular flight area.

124. The thrust delivered by A/THR is already at MAX CLB thrust. Is it possible to obtain some additional thrust?

a. Yes, by moving the thrust levers forward from the CL detent.

125. What information is supplied by the Air Data Modules (ADM'S?) and is displayed on the PFD's?

a. Airspeed, vertical speed, and altitude.

126. What occurs when the IR pushbutton is selected to OFF?

a. Inertial data information is disconnected.

127. Which statement is correct with regard to the takeoff phase and the SRS mode?

a. SRS provides guidance for a minimum climb slope of 0.5°

128. During an ILS approach with both autopilots ON, which FMGC is the Master?

a. FMGC1.

129. How can you get the mechanic's attention when he is outside the aircraft?

a. Use the MECH pushbutton on the CALLS panel, which sounds an external horn.

130. What would the VHF 3 transmission key illuminated amber showing the word \CALL\ indicate?

a. Indicates a SELCAL.

131. Which VHF radios can be tuned via RMP #1?

a. All radios.

132. How can the APU generator be connected to power the aircraft electrical system with the APU running?

a. The APU generator must be switched ON.

133. Are there any limitations associated with disconnecting an IDG?

a. Never disconnect an IDG unless the engine is running, nor Push the IDG disconnect pushbutton for more than 3 seconds.

134. What is the order of priority for the different generators?

a. Engines, APU or external A (if connected at the same time with priority for the right side), external B.

135. Where is the MAINT BUS switch located?

a. On the FWD Circuit Breaker Panel behind the cockpit.

136. What is the minimum voltage that will cause the batteries to connect the DC BAT BUS and the charging cycle to begin?

a. Less than 26.5 volts.

137. When will a battery fault light illuminate?

a. Battery charging current is outside normal limit.

138. If the battery voltages are below the minimum, how can they be charged?

a. Ensure that the BAT pushbuttons are AUT0 and switch the External power ON.

139. Is it possible to parallel generators?

a. The electrical system will not allow 'paralleling' of generators.

140. Where is the ground power receptacle located?

a. Near the nose wheel bay.

141. If an APU fire is detected on the ground, the APU shuts down automatically and the agent is discharged at which time after the warning is activated?

a. Immediately.

142. What fire monitoring warning systems are engine nacelle and pylon equipped with?

a. Two detection loops and a FDU.

143. Which pushbutton switch on ECAM cancels an aural warning, extinguishes the MASTER CAUTION lights, but does not affect the ECAM message display?

a. EMER CANC.

144. What would the presence of VOR1 in red on the ND indicate?

a. The #1 VOR receivers are inoperative.

145. Weather radar can be displayed in what modes on the ND?

a. All modes except PLAN.

146. Which hydraulic system(s) supply pressure to the landing gear system?

a. Green.

147. Which is the correct statement in case of green hydraulic system loss due to LO LVL?

a. Gear extension is done by gravity, nose wheel steering is lost and braking with anti-skid is available.

148. If the brake automatically transitions to alternate brakes with the A/SKID & NIW STRG switch in the ON position, what would be available?

a. Brakes with anti-skid.

149. What is indicated by the autobrake DECEL light?

a. Airplane deceleration is 80% of selected rate.

150. Which of the following is used in the FMGC computation of a radio position?

a. VOR/DME and DME/DME.

151. What does an amber box on the MCDU screen indicate?

a. A mandatory data entry.

152. How does the FMGS update its position at take-off when the thrust levers are moved to the take-off position?

a. By using the navigation database and the take-off runway entered into the MCDU by the pilot.

153. Where is the data derived from ADIRU 1 normally displayed?

a. PFD1, ND1, DDRMI (if fitted) and ATC 1.

154. On which ECAM page could the flight crew check the exact pressure of the oxygen cylinder?

a. The DOORS page.

155. Which controls should be used for routine APU shutdown?

a. The controls on the APU panel are used for routine shutdown.

156. How many thrust lever positions are there, and how are they labeled?

a. 4 thrust levers positions: TO/GA, FLX/MCT, CL, IDLE.

157. Can a take-off be executed without a FLEX temperature being inserted into to the MCDU PERF TO page?

a. Yes, but only using the TO/GA detent.

158. During an engine start sequence; the gray background on N2 disappears. What does this indicate?

a. That the start sequence is completed.

159. What does the FLEX represent in the FLX/MCT detent?

a. This is a reduced thrust setting used for take-off.

160. How many FADEC's are installed in the aircraft?

a. Two, one per engine.

161. OVERSPEED ECAM warning is provided at which speed?

a. VMO + 4 kt, and MMO + 0.006.

162. What precaution must be observed before opening a cabin door from the outside of the aircraft?

a. The cabin must be depressurized.

163. What will cause the auto thrust to disconnect?

a. Moving the thrust lever to idle, auto thrust button selected to off, loss of arming signal.

164. When would the Y (Yellow) ELEC HYD pump run automatically?

a. In the event of engine 2 failure at take-off and the flap lever is not at 0.

165. When does the aileron droop occur?

a. When the flaps are extended and the amount of the droop is dependent on the flap setting (two positions are available).

166. What happens in the sidestick neutral high-speed protection mode?

a. The autopilot disengages, bank angle limit is 45° and the aircraft rolls level and a nose-up order is applied to aid recovery to normal flight conditions.

167. What is the purpose of the electric hydraulic pump within the G HYD SYS?

a. It serves as an additional means for pressurization of the G HYD system.

168. When would the ram air turbine (RAT) extend automatically?

a. In the event of both engine failure.

169. What is the purpose of an accumulator attached to the green hydraulic system?

a. To help maintain a constant pressure by covering transient demands during normal operations.

170. Which situation would cause a Hydraulic Shutoff Valve closure in flight?

a. Both engine green HYD shutoff valves are automatically closed in the event of low green reservoir level.

171. When would the Yellow HYD electric pump run?

a. Until the last engine shutdown, when started automatically in flight.

172. Which parts of the aircraft will be heated on ground when SAT is +3 degrees C, icing conditions exist and the wing anti-ice is selected ON?

a. The pneumatic system provides hot air for the four outboard slats and a 30-second test sequence is run by the wing anti-ice system only.

173. Which is the correct procedure in case of ICE NOT DET ECAM message?

a. Ice is no longer detected; normal procedures for use of engine Anti-ice system still applies.

174. When should WING ANT ICE system be used?

a. Whenever there is an indication that the airframe is icing up; an accumulation of the ice on the ice detector or on the windshield wipers.

175. Which DMC supplies data to the upper ECAM DU?

a. DMC 3 supplies data to the upper and the lower ECAM DU's.

176. How can the engine/warning page be viewed by the crew in case the upper ECAM display is turned OFF (the CTL/Brightness Knob turned to OFF)?

a. The engine/warning page automatically replaces the system/status page on the lower ECAM DU.

177. What would a message "CHECK ALT" on the First Officer's PFD indicate?

a. There is a discrepancy between the altitude values greater than 250 feet (QNH selected) between both PFD's; the Captain's PFD displays the same message.

178. Which component is fitted with the cockpit sliding windows that serves as the crew emergency exits?

a. A small compartment, located above each window contains an escape rope that is long enough to reach the ground.

179. What information is displayed as MEMO's (in the lower part of the E/WD)?

a. Functions or systems that are temporarily used in normal operations.

180. When will "TO INHIBIT" memo be displayed?

a. As the aircraft enters phase 3 (1st engine to take-off power), the computer inhibits some warnings and cautions to avoid alerting the pilots unnecessarily.

181. When does the T.O memo appear?

a. 2 minutes after the second engine start.

182. Which landing gear doors are mechanically operated?

a. The doors, which are fitted to the landing struts.

183. What happens to the main landing gear during retraction?

a. The shortening mechanism reduces the main gear length by retracting the absorber into the main leg.

184. When can the landing gear be lowered in flight by normal means?

a. The speed must be below 280 kt.

185. When do the Logo lights come ON?

a. When the NAV & LOGO light switch is ON and flaps are extended at 15° degrees or more.

186. When are the nose T.O and TAXI lights ON?

a. When the NOSE light switch is in T.O position and the main gear is down.

187. What will cause the amber FAULT light for the G ELEC HYD to stay illuminated?

a. G reservoir overheat (as long as overheat is present)

188. Which failure would be indicated by a steady amber FAULT light on the ADR pushbutton switch?

a. A fault is detected in the air data reference part.

189. What is indicated by a flashing green "IRS IN ALIGN" MEMO message?

a. IRS alignment is faulty.

190. Does an APU fire in flight automatically shut down the APU?

a. No.

CHAPTER TWENTY

EXPERIENCE IN THE COCKPIT DOES MATTER

Experience in the Cockpit Does Matter

The number of less-experienced pilots in the cockpit of some major airlines is growing and this trend will increase the risk of having a major incident or an accident. Don't let anyone tell you otherwise. Numerous studies have proven that experience enhances safety and inexperienced airline pilots are almost twice as likely to get into an accident than those with more experience, according to an FAA report that analyzes multiple studies. For pilots of commercial jetliners - experience is crucial! A commercial jet carrying between 150 to 600 passengers at speeds of over 500 miles per hour, must have pilots that are experienced, knowledgeable and confident to be able to handle any situation they might encounter during a particular flight (for example: bad weather, turbulence or mechanical problems). All passengers must feel safe and assume the flight they are on have experienced pilots that have flown many hours and grappled with many things that could go wrong in the air. As another example, if you were having brain surgery, do you go with the surgeon who has been doing it for 20 years or the guy who has just graduated from medical school? The same principle applies to pilots operating a flight. Would someone prefer flying in an airplane with experienced pilots or with those with very limited experience? Remember wisdom is gained by experience. There is no text book or a simulator in the world that can teach experience and this is a fact.

To further prove the value and importance of having an experienced pilot in the cockpit of a commercial jetliner, the following pages detail two such accidents - US Air Flight 1549 and Air Florida Flight 90. The final results speak for themselves.

USAir Flight 1549 Accident Report (Miracle on the Hudson River)

The plane had just taken off from La Guardia Airport when it suffered bird strikes in both engines. Thrust was lost in both engines and the crew was able to ditch the plane in the Hudson River. All 107 aboard survived.

LGA - La Guardia ATC

L116 - New York TRACON LaGuardia Departure

TEB - Teterboro ATC

3:24:54: [Flight 1549 cleared for takeoff]
3:24:58 (LGA): Cactus 1549.
3:25:51 (AWE1549): Cactus 1549 - 700 climbing 5,000.
3:26:00 (L116): Cactus 1549, New York departure radar contact. Climb and maintain 15,000.
3:26:04 (AWE1549): Maintain 15,000, 1549.
3:27:32 (L116): Cactus 1549, turn left heading 270.
3:27:36 (AWE1549): Ah, this is, uh, Cactus 1539. Hit birds, we lost thrust in both engines. We're turning back toward LaGuardia.
3:27:42 (L116): Okay, yea, you need to return to LaGuardia. Turn left heading of, uh, 220.
3:27:46 (AWE1549): 220.
3:27:49 (L116): Tower, stop your departures. We got an emergency landing.
3:27:53 (LGA): Who is it?
3:27:54 (L116): It's 1529. He, ah, bird strike. He lost all engines. He lost the thrust in the engines. He is returning immediately.
3:27:59 (LGA): Cactus 1529, which engines?

3:28:01 (L116): He lost thrust in both engines, he said.
3:28:03 (LGA): Got it.
3:28:05 (L116) Cactus 1529, if we can get it, do you want to try to land Runway 13?
3:28:11 (AWE1549): We're unable. We may end up in the Hudson.
3:28:31 (L116): Alright, Cactus 1549, it's going to be left traffic to Runway 31.
3:28:34 (AWE154): Unable.
3:28:36 (L116): Okay, what do you need to land?
3:28:46 (L116): Cactus 1549, Runway 49-- Runway 4 is available if you want to make left traffic to Runway 4.
3:28:50 (AWE1549): I'm not sure if we can make any runway. Oh, what's over to our right? Anything in New Jersey? Maybe Teterboro?
3:28:55 (L116): Okay, yea, off to your right side is Teterboro Airport.
3:29:02 (L116): Do you want to try and go to Teterboro?
3:29:03 (AWE1549): Yes.
3:29:05 (L116): Teterboro, Empire-- actually LaGuardia Departure got an emergency inbound.
3:29:10 (TEB): Okay, go ahead.
3:29:11 (L116): Cactus 1529 over the George Washington Bridge, wants to go to the airport right now.
3:29:14 (TEB): He wants to go to our airport, check. Does he need any assistance?
3:29:17 (L116): Ah, yes. He, ah, he was a bird strike. Can I get him in for Runway 1?
3:29:19 (TEB): Runway 1, that's good.
3:29:21 (L116): Cactus 1529, turn right 280. You can land Runway 1 at Teterboro.
3:29:25 (AWE1549): We can't do it.
3:29:26 (L116): Okay, which runway would you like at Teterboro?
3:29:28 (AWE1549): We're gonna be in the Hudson.

3:29:33 (L116): I'm sorry, say again, Cactus.

3:29:51 (L116): Cactus, ah, Cactus 1549, radar contact is lost. You also got Newark Airport off your two o'clock and about 7 miles.

3:30:14 (L116): Cactus 1529, uh, you still on?

3:30:22 (L116): Cactus 1529, if you can, ah, you got, ah, Runway 29 available at Newark off your two o'clock and 7 miles.

3:30:30: [Splashdown. Radar and tower notify Coast Guard, which responds, "We launched the fleet."]

3:31:30 (unknown): Was that Cactus up by the Tappan Zee?

3:31:32 (L116): Uh, yeah, it was Cactus. He was just north of the, uh, George Washington Bridge when they had the bird strike.

3:33:38 (L116): Alright, alright. Departure, we're stopped on departure Runway 4 - 360s runway.

3:33:44 (L116): Okay.

3:33:45 (L116): You know about the Cactus?

3:33:46 (L116): Right.

3:33:47 (L116): I guess it was a double bird strike and he lost all thrust, so...

3:33:52 (L116): (Unintelligible) what do you want to do as far as departures?

3:33:55 (L116): Okay, I'll figure it out.

Back to Last Words

Summary of USAir Flight 1549

US Airways Flight 1549 was an Airbus A320-214 which, three minutes after takeoff from New York City's LaGuardia Airport on January 15, 2009, struck a flock of Canada geese just northeast of the George Washington Bridge and consequently lost all engine power. Unable to reach any airport, pilots Chesley Sullenberger and Jeffrey Skiles glided the plane to a ditching in the Hudson River off Midtown Manhattan. All 155 people aboard were rescued by nearby boats and there were few serious injuries. The incident came to be known as the "Miracle on the Hudson", and a National Transportation Safety Board official described it as "the most successful ditching in aviation history." The pilots and flight attendants were awarded the Master's Medal of the Guild of Air Pilots and Air Navigators in recognition of their "heroic and unique aviation achievement". Landing on the Hudson River, Sullenberger's years of experience and wisdom paid off on January 15, 2009, when the US Airways plane he was piloting struck a large flock of Canada geese during liftoff from New York's LaGuardia Airport. Both engines were damaged, and suddenly neither was providing any thrust. With air traffic control, Sullenberger discussed his options: either return to LaGuardia or land at

Teterboro Airport in New Jersey. Sullenberger quickly considered the situation too inacceptable for the plane to stay in the air long enough for either plan to be successful, so he decided that ditching (performing an emergency water landing) the jet in the Hudson River was the best option.

He announced over the intercom, "Brace for impact," and took the plane down onto the water's surface. The maneuver was a success, and all 155 people onboard flight 1549 survived, and all but a few uninjured. The crew evacuated the passengers; Captain Sullenberger left the plane last.

Airbus 330 The Ultimate Guide for Pilots

USAir Flight 1549 Pictures

USAir Flight 1549 in the Hudson River

NATIONAL TRANSPORTATION SAFETY BOARD
AIRCRAFT ACCIDENT REPORT
AIR FLORIDA, INC.
FLIGHT 90
BOEING 737-222, N62AF
NEAR WASHINGTON NATIONAL AIRPORT

SYNOPSIS

On January 13, 1982, Air Florida Flight 90, a Boeing 737-222 (N62AF) was a scheduled flight to Fort Lauderdale, Florida, from Washington National Airport, Washington, D.C. There were 74 passengers, including 3 infants, and 5 crewmembers on board. The flight's scheduled departure time was delayed about 1 hour 45 minutes due to a moderate to heavy snowfall which necessitated the temporary closing of the airport. Following takeoff from Runway 36, which was made with snow and/or ice adhering to the aircraft, the aircraft crashed at 1601 e.s.t. into the barrier wall of the northbound span of the 14th Street Bridge, which connects the District of Columbia with Arlington County, Virginia, and plunged into the ice-covered Potomac River. It came to rest on the west side of the bridge 0.75 nm from the departure end of Runway 36. Four passengers and one crewmember survived the crash. When the aircraft hit the bridge, it struck seven occupied vehicles and then tore away a section of the bridge wall and bridge railing. Four persons in the vehicles were killed; four were injured.

The National Transportation Safety Board determined that the probable cause of this accident was the flight crew's failure to use engine anti-ice during ground operation and takeoff, their decision to take off with snow/ice on the airfoil surfaces of the aircraft, and the captain's failure to reject the takeoff during the early stage when his attention was called to anomalous engine instrument readings.

Contributing to the accident were the prolonged ground delay between deicing and the receipt of ATC takeoff clearance during which the airplane was exposed to continual precipitation, the known inherent pitch up characteristics of the B-737 aircraft when the leading edge is contaminated with even small amounts of snow or ice, and the limited experience of the flight crew in jet transport winter operations.

HISTORY OF THE FLIGHT

On January 13, 1982, Air Florida, Inc., Flight 90, a Boeing 737-222 (N62AF), was a scheduled passenger flight from Washington National Airport, Washington, D.C., to the Fort Lauderdale international Airport, Fort Lauderdale, Florida, with an intermediate stop at the Tampa International Airport, Tampa, Florida. Flight 90 was scheduled to depart Washington National Airport at 1415 E.S.T.* The Boeing-737 had arrived at Gate 12, Washington National Airport, as Flight 95 from Miami, Florida, at 1329. Snow was falling in Washington, D.C., in the morning and in various intensities when Flight 95 landed and continued to fall throughout the early afternoon. Because of the snowfall, Washington National Airport was closed for snow removal from 1338 to 1453 and Flight 90's scheduled departure was delayed. At 1359:21, Flight 90 requested and received an instrument flight rules (IFR) clearance from clearance delivery.

Seventy-one passengers and three infants were boarded on the aircraft between 1400 and 1430; there were five crewmembers - captain, first officer, and three flight attendants. About 1420, American Airlines **maintenance personnel began deicing the left side of the fuselage using a model D40D Trump vehicle

(No.5058) containing Union Carbide Aircraft Deicing Fluid II PM 5178. The deicing truck operator stated that the captain told him that he would like to start deicing just before the airport was scheduled to reopen at 1430 so that he could get in line for departure. American maintenance personnel stated that they observed about one-half inch of wet snow on the aircraft before the deicing fluid was applied. Fluid had been applied to an area of about 10 feet when the captain terminated the operation because the airport was not going to reopen at 1430. At that time, the flight crew also informed the Air Florida maintenance representative that 11 other aircraft had departure priority and that there were 5 or 6 aircraft which had departure priority before Flight 90 could push back from the gate.

*Note: All times herein are eastern standard time, based on the 24-hour clock.

** American Airlines Inc., provided, certain services to Air Florida, Inc., under a contractual agreement.

Between 1445 and 1450, the captain requested that the deicing operation be resumed. The left side of the aircraft was deiced first. According to the operator of the deicing vehicle, the wing, the fuselage, the tail section, the top part of the engine pylon, and the cowling were deiced with a heated solution consisting of 30 to 40 percent glycol and 60 to 70 percent water. No final overspray was applied. The operator based the proportions of the solution on guidance material from the American Airlines maintenance manual and his knowledge that the ambient temperature was 24 degrees F, which he had obtained from current weather data received at the American Airlines line maintenance room. The operator also stated that he started spraying at the front section of the aircraft and progressed toward the tail using caution in the areas of the hinge points and control surfaces to assure that no ice or snow remained at these critical points. He also stated that it was snowing heavily as the deicing/anti-icing substance was applied to the left side of the aircraft.

Between 1445 and 1500, the operator of the deicing vehicle was relieved from his deicing task, and he told his relief operator, a mechanic, that the left side of the aircraft had been deiced. The relief operator proceeded to deice the right side of the aircraft with heated water followed by a finish anti-ice coat of 20 to 30 percent glycol and 70 to 80 percent water, also heated. He based these proportions on information that the ambient temperature was 28 degrees F. (The actual temperature was 24 degrees F) The operator stated that he deiced/anti-iced the right side of the aircraft in the following sequence: the rudder, the stabilizer and elevator, the aft fuselage section, the upper forward fuselage, the wing section (leading edge to trailing edge), the top of the engine, the wingtip, and the nose. Afterwards, he inspected both engine intakes and the landing gear for snow and/or ice accumulation; he stated that none was found. The deicing/anti-icing of Flight 90 was completed at 1510. At this time about 2 or 3 inches of wet snow was on the ground around the aircraft. Maintenance personnel involved in deicing/anti-icing the aircraft stated that they believed that the aircraft's trailing and leading edge devices were retracted. American Airlines personnel stated that no covers or plugs were installed over the engines or airframe openings during deicing operations.

At 1515, the aircraft was closed up and the jet way was retracted. Just before the jet way was retracted, the captain, who was sitting in the left cockpit seat, asked the Air Florida station manager, who was standing near the main cabin door, how much snow was on the aircraft. The station manager responded that there was a light dusting of snow on the left wing from the engine to the wingtip and that the area from the engine to the fuselage was clean. Snow continued to fall heavily.

A tug was standing by to push Flight 90 back from Gate 12. The operator of the tug stated that a flight crewmember told him that the tower would call and advise them when pushback could start. At 1516:45, Flight 90 transmitted, "Ground, Palm Ninety, like to get in sequence, we're ready." Ground control replied, "Are you ready to push?" Flight 90 replied, "Affirmative," at 1516:37. At 1517:01, Ground control transmitted, "Okay, push approved for Palm Ninety-- better still, just hold it right where you are Palm Ninety, I'll call you back." At 1523:37, Ground control transmitted, "Okay Palm Ninety, push approved."

At 1525, the tug attempted to push Flight 90 back. However, a combination of ice, snow, and glycol on the ramp and a slight incline prevented the tug, which was not equipped with chains, from moving the aircraft. When a flight crewmember suggested to the tug operator that the aircraft's engine reverse thrust be used to push the aircraft back, the operator advised the crewmember that this was contrary to the policy of American Airlines. According to the tug operator, the aircraft's engines were started and both reversers were deployed. He then advised the flight crew to use only "idle power."

Witnesses estimated that both engines were operated in reverse thrust for a period of 30 to 90 seconds. During this time, several Air Florida and American Airlines personnel observed snow and/or slush being blown toward the front of the aircraft. One witness stated that he saw water swirling at the base of the left (No.1) engine inlet. Several Air Florida personnel stated that they saw an area of snow on the ground melted around the left engine for a radius ranging from 6 to 15 feet. No one observed a similar melted area under the right (No.2) engine.

When the use of reverse thrust proved unsuccessful in moving the aircraft back, the engines were shut down with the reversers deployed. The same American Airlines mechanic that had inspected both engine in-takes upon completion of the deicing/anti-icing operation performed another general examination of both engines. He stated that he saw no ice or snow at that time. Air Florida and American Airlines personnel standing near the aircraft after the aircraft's engines were shut down stated that they did not see any water, slush, snow, or ice on the wings.

At 1533, while the first tug was being disconnected from the towbar and a second tug was being brought into position, an assistant station manager for Air Florida, who was inside the passenger terminal between gates 11 and 12, stated that he could see the upper fuselage and about 75 percent of the left wing inboard of the tip from his vantage point, which was about 25 feet from the aircraft. Although he observed snow on top of the fuselage, he said it did not appear to be heavy or thick. He saw snow on the nose and radome up to the bottom of the windshield and a light dusting of snow on the left wing.

At 1535, Flight 90 was pushed back without further difficulty. After the tug was disconnected, both engines were restarted and the thrust reversers were stowed. The aircraft was ready to taxi away from the gate at 1538.

At 1538:16 while accomplishing after-start checklist items, the captain responded "off" to the first officer's callout of checklist item "anti-ice." At 1538:22 the ground controller said, "Okay and the American that's towing there...let's... six twenty four can you get around that...Palm on a pushback?" Flight 90 replied, "Ground, Palm Ninety, we're ready to taxi out of his way." Ground control then transmitted, "Okay Palm Ninety, Roger, just pull up over behind that TWA and hold right there. You'll be falling in line behind a...Apple ** ...DC Nine." Flight 90 acknowledged this transmission at 1538:47. Flight 90 then fell in behind the New York Air DC-9. Nine air carrier aircraft and seven general aviation aircraft were awaiting departure when Flight 90 pushed back.

**Note Air traffic control designation for New York Air.

At 1540:15, the cockpit voice recorder (CVR) recorded a comment by the captain, "...go over to the hangar and get deiced," to which the first officer replied "yeah, definitely". The captain then made some additional comment which was not clear but contained the word "deiced," to which the first officer again replied "yeah - that's about it." At 1540:42, the first officer continued to say, "it's been a while since we've been deiced." At 1546:21, the captain said, "Tell you what, my windshield will be deiced, don't know about my wings." The first officer then commented, "well - all we need is the inside of the wings anyway, the wingtips are gonna speed up on eighty anyway, they'll shuck all that other stuff." At 1547:32, the captain commented, "(Gonna) get your wing now." Five seconds later, the first officer asked, "D'they get yours? Did they get your wingtip over'er?" The captain replied, "I got a little on mine." The first officer then said. "A little, this one's got about a quarter to half an inch on it all the way."

At 1548:59, the first officer asked, "See this difference in that left engine and right one?" The captain replied, "Yeah." The first officer then commented, "I don't know why that's different - less it's hot air going into that right one, that must be it - from his exhaust - it was doing that at the chocks awhile ago ah." At

1551:54, the captain said, "Don't do that - Apple, I need to get the other wing done."

At 1553:21, the first officer said, "Boy...this is a losing battle here on trying to deice those things, it (gives) you a false feeling of security that's all that does." Conversation between the captain and the first officer regarding the general topic of deicing continued until 1554:04. At 1557:42, after the New York Air aircraft was cleared for takeoff, the captain and first officer proceeded to accomplish the pre-takeoff checklist, including verification of the takeoff engine pressure ratio (EPR) setting of 12.04 and indicated airspeed bug settings of 138 kts (V1); 140 kts (Vr) and 144 kts (V2). Between 1558:26 and 1558:37, the first officer asked, "Slush (sic) runway, do you want me to do anything special for this or just go for it." (The first officer was the pilot flying the aircraft.) The captain responded, "Unless you got anything special you'd like to do." The first officer replied, "Unless just take off the nose wheel early like a soft field takeoff or something; I'll take the nose wheel off and then we'll let it fly off."

At 1558:55, Flight 90 was cleared by local control to "taxi into position and hold" on Runway 36 and to "be ready for an immediate [takeoff]." Before Flight 90 started to taxi, the flight crew replied, "... position and hold," at 1558:58. As the aircraft was taxied, the tower transmitted the takeoff clearance and the pilot acknowledged, "Palm 90 cleared for takeoff." Also, at 1559:28, Flight 90 was told not to delay the departure since landing traffic was 2 1/2 miles out for Runway 36; the last radio transmission from Flight 90 was the reply, "Okay" at 1559:46.

The CVR indicated that the pre-takeoff checklist was completed at 1559:22. At 1559:45, as the aircraft was turning to the runway heading, the captain said, "Your throttles". At 1559:46, the sound of engine spool up was recorded, and the captain stated, "Holler if you need the wipers..." At 1559:56, the captain commented, "Real cold, real cold," and at 1559:58, the first officer remarked, "God, look at that thing, that don't seem right, does it?" Between 1600:05 and 1600:10, the first officer stated, ".that's not right...," to which the captain responded, Yes it is, there's eighty." The first officer reiterated, "Naw, I don't think that's right." About 9 seconds later the first officer, added, ".maybe it is," but then 2 seconds later, after the captain called, "hundred and twenty," the first officer said, "I don't know."

Eight seconds after the captain called "Vee one" and 2 seconds after he called "Vee two," the sound of the stickshaker (stall warning) was recorded. At 1600:45, the captain said, "Forward, forward," and at 1600:48, "We only want five hundred." At 1600:50, the captain continued, "Come on, forward, just barely climb." At 1601:00, the first officer said, "Larry, we're going down, Larry," to which the captain responded, "I know it".

About 1601, the aircraft struck the heavily congested northbound span of the 14th Street Bridge, which connects the District of Columbia with Arlington County, Virginia, and plunged into the ice-covered Potomac River. It came to rest on the west end of the bridge 0.75 nm from the departure end of Runway 36. Heavy snow continued to fall and visibility at the airport was varying between 1/4 mile and 5/8 mile.

When the aircraft struck the bridge, it struck six occupied automobiles and a boom truck before tearing away a 41-foot section of the bridge wall and 97 feet of the bridge railings. As a result of the crash, 70 passengers, including 3 infants, and 4 crewmembers were killed. Four passengers and one crewmember were injured seriously. Four persons in vehicles on the bridge were killed; four were injured, one seriously.
At 1603, the duty officer at the airport fire station notified crash/fire/rescue (CFR) equipment based on his monitoring of a radio transmission between Washington National Tower and

the operations officer that an aircraft was possibly off the end of Runway 36.

Safety Board investigators interviewed more than 200 witnesses to establish the sequence of events from the start of the takeoff until impact, and more than 100 written statements were obtained. Ground witnesses generally agreed that the aircraft was flying at an unusually low altitude with the wings level and attained a nose-high attitude of 30 to 40 degrees before it hit the bridge. Four persons in a car on the bridge within several hundred feet from the point of impact claimed that large sheets of ice fell on their car.

A driver whose car was on the bridge at about the wingtip of the aircraft stated, "I heard screaming jet engines... The nose was up and the tail was down. It was like the pilot was still trying to climb but the plane was sinking fast. I was in the center left lane...about 5 or 6 cars lengths from where (the red car) was. I saw the tail of the plane tear across the top of the cars,, smashing some tops and ripping off others...I saw it spin...(the red car)...around and then hit the guardrail. All the time it was going across the bridge it was sinking but the nose was pretty well up...I got the impression that the plane was swinging around a little and going in a straight direction into the river. The plane ...seemed to go across the bridge at a slight angle and the dragging tail seemed to straighten out. It leveled out a little. Once the tail was across the bridge the plane seemed to continue sinking very fast but I don't re- call the nose pointing down. If it was, it wasn't pointing down much. The plane seemed to hit the water intact in a combination sinking/plowing action. I saw the cockpit go under the ice. I got the impression it was skimming under the ice and water I did not see the airplane break apart. It seemed to plow under the ice. I did not see any ice on the aircraft or any ice falloff the aircraft. I do not remember any wing dip as the plane came across the bridge. I saw nothing fall from the airplane as it crossed the bridge."

Between 1519 and 1524, a passenger on an arriving flight holding for gate space near Flight 90 saw some snow accumulated on the top and right side of the fuselage and photographed Flight 90.

No witnesses saw the flight crew leave the aircraft to inspect for snow/ice accumulations while at the gate. Departing and arriving flight crews and others who saw Flight 90 before and during takeoff stated that the aircraft had an unusually heavy accumulation of snow or ice on it. An airline crew taxiing parallel to, but in the opposite direction of, Flight 90's takeoff, saw a portion of Flight 90's takeoff roll and discussed the extensive amount of snow on the fuselage. The captain's statement to the Board included the following: "I commented to my crew, look at the junk on that airplane, ..Almost the entire length of the fuselage had a mottled area of snow and what appeared to be ice...along the top and upper side of the fuselage above the passenger cabin windows...".

None of the witnesses at the airport could positively identify the rotation of liftoff point of Flight 90; however, they testified that it was beyond the intersection of Runways 15 and 36, and that the aircraft's rate of climb was slow as it left the runway. Flight crews awaiting departure were able to observe only about the first 2,000 feet of the aircraft's takeoff roll because of the heavy snowfall and restricted visibility.

At 1600:03, as Flight 90 was on the takeoff roll, the local controller had transmitted to an approaching Eastern 727, Flight 1451, " the wind is zero one zero at one one, you're cleared to land runway three six; the runway visual range touchdown two thousand eight hundred rollout one thousand six hundred." At 1600:11, Eastern Flight 1451 acknowledged, "... cleared to land, over the lights." At 1600:56, the local controller transmitted, "Eastern fourteen fifty-one, turn left at the next taxiway, advise when you clear the runway, no delay clearing."

During witness interviews, one witness at the airport stated, "Immediately after I noticed the Air Florida 737, an Eastern 727 landed unbelievably close after (Air Florida) 737. I felt it was too close for normal conditions- let alone very hard snow."

Flight 90 crashed during daylight hours at 1601:01 at 38 degrees 51' N longitude and 77 degrees 02' W latitude. Elevation was 37 feet mean sea level.

INJURIES TO PERSONS

	Crew	Passengers	Other*	Total
Fatal	4	70**	4	78
Serious	1	4	1	6
Minor	0	0	3	3
None	0	0	0	0
Total	5	74	8	87

*Persons in vehicles on the bridge.
** Including three infants

DAMAGE TO AIRCRAFT

The aircraft was destroyed by impact with the bridge, ice, and water.

OTHER DAMAGE

Seven vehicles in the northbound span of the 14th Street Bridge were destroyed. A section of the bridge sidewall barrier structure and bridge railing were torn away.

PERSONNEL INFORMATION

Both pilots were trained and certificated in accordance with current regulations.

The captain was described by pilots who knew him or flew with him as a quiet person. According to available information, he did not have any sleep or eating pattern changes recently; the 24 to 72 hours before January 13 also were unremarkable. Pilots indicated that the captain had good operational skills and knowledge and had operated well in high workload flying situations. His leadership style was described as not different from other captains. On May 8, 1980, during a line check in B-737, the captain was found to be unsatisfactory in the following areas: adherence to regulations, checklist usage, flight procedures such as departures and cruise control, approaches and landings. As a result of this line check, the captain's initial line check qualification as a B-737 captain was suspended. On August 27, 1980, he received a satisfactory grade on a line check and was granted the authority to act as pilot-in-command. On April 24, 1981, the captain received an unsatisfactory grade on a recurrent proficiency check when he showed deficiencies in memory items, knowledge of aircraft systems, and aircraft limitations.

Three days later, the captain took a proficiency recheck and received a satisfactory grade. On October 21, 1981, the captain satisfactorily completed a B-737 simulator course in lieu of a proficiency check. His last line check was satisfactorily completed on April 29, 1981.

The first officer was described by personal friends and pilots as a witty, bright, outgoing individual. According to available information, he had no recent sleep or eating pattern changes. The 24 to 72 hours before January 13 were spent with his family and were unremarkable. On the morning of January 13, the first officer was described as well rested and in a good mood. Acquaintances indicated that he had an excellent command of the physical and mental skill in aircraft piloting. Those who had flown with him during stressful flight operations said that during those times he remained the same witty, sharp individual "who knew his limitations." Several persons said that he was the type of pilot who would not hesitate to speak up if he knew something specific was wrong with flight operations. He had completed all required checks satisfactorily.

Neither pilot had any record of FAA violations.

The Safety Board reviewed the winter operations conducted by the captain and first officer and found that the captain, after upgrading to captain in B-737 aircraft, had flown eight takeoffs or landings in which precipitation and freezing or near-freezing conditions occurred, and that the first officer had flown two takeoffs or landings in such conditions during his employment with Air Florida, Inc. The captain and first officer had flown together as a crew only 17 1/2 hours.

FLIGHT 90

Air Florida Flight 90 crashes into 14th Street Bridge over Potomac River

NTSB Blamed the Accident of Flight 90 on the Pilots' Lack of <u>Experience</u>

In the aftermath, the NTSB blamed the accident on the pilots' failure to abort the takeoff, even though they knew the jetliner wasn't performing up to par. The pilots also were blamed for failure to have the wings properly de-iced. There were other, less obvious factors.

At the time, Air Florida was a fast-growing start-up carrier, putting young pilots into the cockpit and allowing first officers to move quickly into the captain's seat.

The result: Pilots were not as experienced as they should have been, particularly for tricky operations in snowy weather, experts said. The Captain was 34 years old and had made only eight takeoffs and landings in snow in a Boeing 737. The co-pilot was 31 and had flown twice in snow. The two were working under an old-fashioned airline protocol: The captain is not to be questioned, even if he appears to be taking a flight into danger. As a result of the Air Florida crash, the airline industry formalized a concept known as "crew resource management," which in practical terms means: if either pilot, but notably the co-pilot, spots trouble, he should voice it loudly. Had the co-pilot been more aggressive, he would have aborted the takeoff, with or without the captain's permission, said Burnett, the former Safety Board Chairman.

"Once the plane was committed to the air, either pilot still could have prevented disaster if he had added power," Burnett said. "The pilots never gave an order to give full throttle, which, in opinion of the safety board, would have saved the plane, at least until it hit the bridge," he said.

The crash prompted airlines to adopt strict policies ensuring inexperienced captains are paired with experienced co-pilots. It also spurred airlines to be more cognizant to de-ice wings shortly before takeoff.

Clear For the Approach

It doesn't give you permission to leave your assigned altitude unless........!

Let's say that you are at 8000 feet and about 40 to 45 miles from the airport. MSA is 2500 feet and the initial approach altitude is 2000 feet and ATC cleared you for the approach. When will you leave the 8000 feet and descend to what altitude? The pilot may receive this clearance while the aircraft is still a considerable distance from the airport, in either a radar or non-radar environment. In these cases, the pilot may descend, at his/her convenience, to whichever is the lowest of the following IFR altitudes applicable to the position of the aircraft:

(A) Minimum end route altitude (MEA);

(B) Published transition or feeder route altitude

Some pilots think that they can descend to MSA (2,500 feet) which is completely wrong and dangerous.

MSA is for emergency and loss of communications reference only. Nothing to do with any instrument approaches.

In terms of terrain it may be safe to descend to 2500 ft with MSA radius, but this action will cause the aircraft to leave a controlled airspace, and might enter a restricted area or might have a conflict with other traffic which will completely compromise safety.

Read about the following accident regarding the misinterpretation of clear for an approach on the following pages.

NATIONAL TRANSPORTATION SAFETY BOARD
AIRCRAFT ACCIDENT REPORT
TRANS WORLD AIRLINES, INC.
FLIGHT 514
BERRYVILLE, VIRGINIA

SYNOPSIS

At 1110 E.S.T., December 1, 1974, Trans World Airlines, Inc., Flight 514, a Boeing 727-231, N54328 crashed about 25 nautical miles northwest of Dulles International Airport, Washington, D.C. The accident occurred while the flight was descending for a VOR/DME approach to runway 12 at Dulles in instrument meteorological conditions. The 92 occupants - 85 passengers and 7 crewmembers were killed, and the aircraft was destroyed.

The NTSB determines that the probable cause of the accident was the crew's decision to descend to 1,800 feet before the aircraft had reached the approach segment where that minimum altitude applied. The crew's decision to descend was a result of inadequacies and lack of clarity in the air traffic control procedures which led to a misunderstanding on the part of the pilots and of the controllers regarding each other's responsibilities during the operations in terminal areas under instrument meteorological conditions. Nevertheless, the examination of the plan view of the approach chart should have disclosed to the captain that a minimum altitude of 1,800 feet was not a safe altitude.

Contributing factors were:

1. The failure of the FAA to take timely action to resolve the confusion and misinterpretation of air traffic terminology although the Agency had been aware of the problem for several years;

2. The issuance of the approach clearance when the flight was 44 miles from the airport on an unpublished route without clearly defined minimum altitudes; and

3. Inadequate depiction of altitude restrictions on the profile view of the approach chart for the VOR/DME approach to runway 12 at Dulles International Airport.

As a result of the accident, the Safety Board submitted 14 recommendations to the Federal Aviation Administration.

HISTORY OF THE FLIGHT

TWA, Flight 514 was a regularly scheduled flight from Indianapolis, Indiana, to Washington, D.C., with an intermediate stop at Columbus, Ohio. There were 85 passengers and 7 crewmembers aboard the aircraft when it departed Columbus.

The flight was dispatched by TWA's dispatch office in New York through the operations office in Indianapolis. The captain received a dispatch package which included enroute and destination weather information. The flight operated under a computer-stored instrument flight rules (IFR) flight plan.

Flight 514 departed Indianapolis at 0853 e.s.t. and arrived in Columbus at 0932. The crew obtained weather and aircraft load information. The flight departed Columbus at 1024, 11 minutes late.

At 1036, the Cleveland Air Route Traffic Control Center (ARTCC) informed the crew of Flight 514 that no landings were being made at Washington National Airport because of high crosswinds and that flights destined for that airport were either being held or being diverted to Dulles International Airport.

At 1038, the captain of Flight 514 communicated with the dispatcher in New York and advised him of the information he had received. The dispatcher, with the captain's concurrence, subsequently amended Flight 514's release to allow the flight to proceed to Dulles.

At 1042, Cleveland ARTCC cleared Flight 514 to Dulles Airport via the Front Royal VOR, and to maintain flight level (FL) 290. At 1043, the controller cleared the flight to FL230 and to cross a point 40 miles west of Front Royal at that altitude. Control of the flight was then transferred to the Washington ARTCC and communications were established with that facility at 1048.

During the period between receipt of the amended flight release and the transfer to control to Washington ARTCC, the flight crew discussed the instrument approach to runway 12, the navigational aids, and the runway at Dulles, and the captain turned the flight controls over to the first officer. When radio communications were established with Washington ARTCC, the controller affirmed that he knew the flight was proceeding to Dulles. Following this contact, the cockpit voice recorder (CVR) indicated that the crew discussed the various routing they might receive to conduct a VOR/DME approach to runway 12 at Dulles.

They considered the possibilities of proceeding via Front Royal VOR, via Martinsburg VOR, or proceeding on a "straight-in" clearance.

At 1051, the Washington ARTCC controller requested the flight's heading. After being told that the flight was on a heading of 100, the controller cleared the crew to change to a heading of 090 degrees to intercept the 300 radial of the Armel VOR, to cross a point 25 miles northwest of Armel to maintain 8,000 feet, and "... the 300 degree radial will be for a VOR approach to runway 12 at Dulles." He gave the crew an altimeter setting of 29.74 for Dulles. The crew acknowledged this clearance. The CVR recording indicated that the Armel VOR was then tuned on a navigational receiver. The pilots again discussed the VOR/DME approach to runway 12 at Dulles.

At 1055, the landing preliminary checklist was read by the flight engineer and the other crewmembers responded to the calls. A reference speed of 127 kts. was calculated and set on the airspeed indicator reference pointers. The altimeters were set as 29.74 inches.

At 1057, the crew again discussed items on the instrument approach chart including the Round Hill intersection, the final approach fix, the visual approach slope indicator and runway lights, and the airport diagram.

At 1059, the captain commented that the flight was descending from 11,000 feet to 8,000 feet. He then asked the controller if there were any weather obstructions between the flight and the airport. The controller replied that he did not see any significant weather along the route. The captain replied that the crew also did not see any weather on the aircraft weather radar. The CVR recording indicated that the captain then turned on the anti-icing system.

At 1101, the controller cleared the flight to descend to and maintain 7,000 feet and to contact Dulles Approach Control. Twenty-six seconds later, the captain initiated a conversation with Dulles Approach Control and reported that the aircraft was descending from 10,000 feet to maintain 7,000 feet. He also reported having received the information "Charlie" transmitted on the ATIS broadcast.

The controller replied with a clearance to proceed inbound to Armel and to expect a VOR/DME approach to runway 12. The controller then informed the crew that ATIS information Delta was current and read the data to them. The crew determined that the difference between information Charlie and Delta was the altimeter setting which was given in Delta as 29.70. There was no information on the CVR to indicate that the pilots reset their altimeters from 29.74.

At 1104, the flight reported it was level at 7,000 feet. Five seconds after receiving that report, the controller said, "TWA 514, you're cleared for a VOR/DME approach to runway 12." This clearance was acknowledged by the captain. The CVR recorded the sound of the landing gear warning horn followed by a comment from the captain that "Eighteen hundred is the bottom" The first officer then said, "Start down" The flight engineer said, "We're out here quite a ways. I better turn the heat down."

At 1105:06, the captain reviewed the field elevations, the minimum descent altitude, and the final approach fix and discussed the reason that time to the missed approach point was published. At 1106:15, the first officer commented that, "I hate the altitude jumping around." Then he commented that the instrument panel was bouncing around. At 1106:25 the captain said, "We have a discrepancy in our VOR's, a little but not much." He continued, "Fly yours, not mine." At 1106:27, the captain discussed the last reported ceiling and minimum descent altitude. He concluded,"...should break out."

At 1106:42, the first officer said, "Gives you a headache after a while, watching this jumping around like that" At 1107:27, he said,"...you can feel that wind down here now." A few seconds later, the captain said, "You know, according to this dumb sheet it says thirty-four hundred to Round Hill - is our minimum altitude." The flight engineer then asked where the captain saw that and the captain replied, "Well, here Round Hill is eleven and a half DME." The first officer said, "Well, but -" and the captain replied, "When he clears, that means you can go to your " An unidentified voice said, "Initial approach," and another unidentified voice said, "Yeah" Then the captain said, "Initial approach altitude." The flight engineer then said, "We're out a - twenty-eight for eighteen." An unidentified voice said, "Right," and someone said "One to go."

At 1108:14, the flight engineer said, "Dark in here," and the first officer stated, "And bumpy too." At 1108:25, the sound of an altitude alert horn was, recorded. The captain said "I had ground contact a minute ago." and the first officer replied, "Yeah, I did too." At 1108:29, the first- officer said, "power on this #." The captain said "Yeah - you got a high sink rate." The first officer replied, "Yeah." An unidentified voice said, "We're going uphill," and the flight engineer replied, "We're right there, we're on course." Two voices responded, "Yeah!" The captain then said, "You ought to see ground outside in just a minute - Hang in there, boy." The flight engineer said, "We're getting seasick." At 1108:57, the altitude alert sounded. Then the first officer said, "Boy, it was - wanted to go right down through there, man," to which an unidentified voice replied, "Yeah!" Then the first officer said, "Must have had a # of a downdraft."

At 1109:14, the radio altimeter warning horn sounded and stopped. The first officer said, "Boy!" At 1109:20, the captain said, "Get some power on." The radio altimeter warning horn sounded again and stopped. At 1109:22, the sound of impact was recorded.

At 1109: 54, the approach controller called Flight 514 and said, "TWA 514, say your altitude." There was no response to this or subsequent calls.

CONCLUSIONS

1. The flight operated without reported difficulty and in a routine manner until the diversion to Dulles Airport from Washington National Airport was approved.

2. The crew of flight 514 reviewed the approach chart for the VOR/DME approach to runway 12 at Dulles several times before beginning the approach.

3. The Washington Air Route Traffic control Center controller vectored the flight to intercept the 300 degrees radial of the Armel VOR at a point about 80 miles from the VOR. This portion of the radial was not part of the published instrument approach.

4. The crew of Flight 514 intercepted the radial and tracked inbound on it, and control of the flight was passed to the Dulles approach controller.

5. The Dulles approach controller cleared the flight for a VOR/DME approach to runway 12 when the aircraft was about 44 miles from the airport. The clearance contained no altitude restrictions.

6. The captain assumed that the flight could descend to 1,800 feet immediately. The first officer, who was flying the aircraft, initiated an immediate descent to 1,800 feet.

7. The flight encountered icing and turbulence during the descent. Neither of these conditions should have appreciably endangered or restricted the control of the aircraft, but contributed in the apparent inability of the crew to arrest the descent at 1,800 ft.

8. The first officer allowed the aircraft to descend below the target altitude of 1,800 feet and did not take sufficient corrective actions to regain and maintain that altitude.

9. The first officer's altimeter was set properly.

10. It is possible that wind velocity over the hilly terrain may have induced an altimeter error which could have caused

the instrument to indicate that the aircraft was higher than its actual altitude. However, the crew's last comments regarding altitude indicated that they knew they were below 1,800 feet.

11. The altitude alerting system and the radio altimeter aural warnings sounded at appropriate altitudes to indicate to the pilots that the aircraft was below 1,800 feet and that the aircraft was within 500 feet and 100 feet of the ground. These latter warnings occurred 7 seconds and 1 second, respectively, before impact.

12. The flight crew apparently did not have sufficient time to avoid the accident after these warnings.

13. The approach clearance was given to the flight without altitude restrictions because the flight was not being handled as a radar arrival and because the controller expected the crew to conduct the approach as it was depicted on the approach chart.

14. Procedures contained in FAA'S Terminal Air Traffic Control Handbook were not clear and resulted in the classification and handling of TWA 514 as a "nonradar"

arrival. The terms "radar arrival" and "none radar arrival" were not defined.

15. In view of the available ATC facilities and services and since the flight was receiving radar service in the form of radar monitoring while under the jurisdiction of a radar approach control facility, the procedure should have provided for giving altitude restrictions in an approach clearance for an aircraft operating on an unpublished route prior to its entering a segment of the published approach procedure.

16. The ATC system was deficient in that the procedures were not clear as to the services the controllers were to provide under circumstances of this flight.

17. The flight crew believed that the controller would not clear them for an approach until they were clear of all obstructions.

18. The depiction of the profile view of the approach charts neither indicated the position of Round Hill intersection nor did it contain all minimum altitudes associated with

the approach procedure. This information was available on the plan view of the approach chart.

19. The captain noticed the minimum altitude associated with the approach segment from Front Royal to Round Hill but he decided that the flight could descend to 1,800 feet without regard for the 3,400-foot minimum altitude depicted on the chart because he was not on that segment.

20. The captain of Flight 514 did not question the controller after receiving the approach clearance, regarding the action the flight crew was expected to take. Another crew that questioned a similar clearance received further instructions and information which resulted in their accepting a radar surveillance approach to Dulles.

21. Both military and civil aviation officials for several years had indicated concern regarding a lack of understanding on their part of what the Air Traffic Control procedures and terminology were intended to convey to the pilots. They were also concerned about the possibility of misunderstandings which could result in pilots descending prematurely.

22. The FAA was not responsive to the long standing, expressed needs and concerns of the users of the Air Traffic Control System with regard to pilot/controller responsibilities pursuant to the issuance of an approach clearance for a nonprecision approach. Furthermore, the FAA did not provide users of the Air Traffic Control System with sufficient information regarding the services provided by the system under specific conditions.

23. The FAA did not utilize the capability of the ARTS III system to insure terrain clearance for descending aircraft conducting none precision instrument approaches in instrument meteorological conditions.

24. The flight crew of Flight 514 was not familiar with the terrain west and northwest of Dulles. However, they did have information regarding the elevation of obstacles west of Round Hill intersection depicted on the plan view of the approach procedure.

PROBABLE CAUSE

The National Transportation Safety Board determines that the probable cause of the accident was the crew's decision to descend to 1,800 feet before the aircraft had reached the approach segment where that minimum altitude applied. The crew's decision to descend was a result of inadequacies and lack of clarity in the air traffic control procedures which led to a misunderstanding on the part of the pilots and of the controllers regarding each other's responsibilities during the operations in terminal areas under instrument meteorological conditions. Nevertheless, the examination of the plan view of the approach chart should have disclosed to the captain that a minimum altitude of 1,800 feet was not a safe altitude.

CONTRIBUTING FACTORS

1. The failure of the FAA to take timely action to resolve the confusion and misinterpretation of air traffic terminology although the Agency had been aware of the problem for several years.

2. The issuance of the approach clearance when the flight was 44 miles from the airport on an unpublished route without clearly defined minimum altitudes.

3. Inadequate depiction of altitude restrictions on the profile view of the approach chart for the VOR/DME approach to runway 12 at Dulles International Airport.

RECOMMENDATIONS

As a result of the accident, the Safety Board submitted 14 recommendations to the Administrator of the Federal Aviation Administration. Subsequent to the accident, the FAA has taken several actions in an effort to prevent recurrence of this type of accident.

ACTIONS TAKEN

1. The FAA has directed that all air carrier aircraft be equipped with a ground proximity warning system by December 1975.

2. The FAA has revised the provisions of 14 CFR 91 with regard to pilot responsibilities and actions after receiving a clearance for a none precision approach.

3. The FAA has established an incident reporting system which is intended to identify unsafe operating conditions in order that they can be corrected before an accident occurs.

4. The FAA has changed its Air Traffic Control procedures to provide for the issuance of altitude restrictions during none precision instrument approaches.

5. The FAA is installing a modification to the ARTS III system that will alert air traffic controllers when aircraft deviate from predetermined altitudes while operating in the terminal area.

TWA Flight 514

CHAPTER TWENTY-ONE

RISK MANAGEMENT

RISK MANAGEMENT

Virtually, no aspect of human endeavor involving worthwhile activity can be considered absolutely risk-free. Using considerations and techniques for minimizing risks and subsequent decision-making is a process known as Risk Management. The seasoned, balanced judgment required for this decision making for pilots is an essential measure of airmanship. The state-of-the-art of risk management in aviation is the consequence of an enormous amount of information on engineering, procedures, human factors, selection and training of personnel, meteorology, communication, navigation, and some 40 other techniques. However, the basic philosophy which governs and airman's attitude towards safety furnishes the foundation on which the state-of-the-art rests and attitude cost nothing. But, the term "attitude" is general and tends to be nondescript for practical applications. Therefore, the following specific areas of attitude control (and thus- "no-cost" safety) are offered. An investigation of over 100,000 accidents involving all pilot experience levels (including highly "professional" flight crews) has identified three particularly deadly areas of attitude deterioration and vulnerability. Pilots interested in longevity will be well advised to consider these factors carefully and often.

The first killer is the insidious loss of discipline in flight operations. Commonly called complacency, this trait is evident in all areas of human endeavor from snake handling to the practice of medicine. Seldom, however, is it as deadly as in flight operations. It is manifested by departure from standard operating practices, shortcuts in procedures, acceptance of distractions, disregard for regulations, and general apathy. It is controlled by disciplined thought, precise planning and intensive self-examination. These are not "easy" fixes. Subsequently, pilots with truly professional attitudes may be the exception.

The second accident-enabling factor is psychological pressure. All pilots deal with pressures of aviation decision-making. Some, however, do not consciously realize the impact of social and/or managerial environment in which aviation decisions are made. The most successful way to deal with these pressures is to impose a standard of limitations or minimums decided upon at a time when the pressure is not "on" Thereafter, the essential ingredient in managing pressure (real or imagined) is strength of character known as "back-bone" to stand for your convictions, limitations and minimums.

The final accident-enabling factor is emotional instability. This means the usually short-term effects of certain major life events or a combination of small events, which can produce an unstable mental condition in an otherwise "solid" individual.

All persons face these factors on various occasions, and the wise pilot realizes that during such times he is prone to accepting high risks. He will then limit or curtail his flying activities accordingly. The achievement of safety is much more dependent on no-cost attitudes, on a no-cost cooperative sense of care, accountability and responsiveness than on expensive equipment. A continuous sense of awareness, beginning with a thorough knowledge of the limitations of men and equipment, is essential to avoid undesirable events. This must be nurtured by all levels of management. The Captain is management's most important representative.

CHAPTER TWENTY-TWO

PILOT INCAPACITATION

"PILOT INCAPACITATION"

Despite long hours of training on how to recognize and resolve emergencies dealing with the loss of some mechanical component, very little attention has been given to recognizing and coping with the loss of the human component. Yet pilot incapacitation has happened more frequently, and presents a greater hazard, than many of the mechanical failures emergencies for which pilots are constantly trained emergencies such as decompression, engine failure or loss of hydraulic systems.

Pilot incapacitation is a serious aviation hazard. Accidents have occurred; lives have been lost. Incapacitation can happen to any pilot at any age, and at any phase of flight. A recent study revealed that during a seven-year period there were 17 instances of pilot deaths in the cockpit. Of these 17 deaths, five led to fatal accidents causing 158 fatalities. Of these five, four deaths occurred during the approach phase of the flight. It was also found that 2/3 of the 17 pilots who died were under the age of 50.

Definitions

Incapacitation in the above context is defined as any physiological or psychological condition which adversely affects flight crew performance in flight. Incapacitation is classified into two categories:

Obvious (usually maximal loss of function)

Subtle (usually partial loss of function).

Obvious Incapacitation

Obvious incapacitation is frequently sudden, usually prolonged and usually results in a complete loss of operating function. By definition, it is immediately apparent to the remaining flight crew members.

Included in this category is the case where flight crew members are aware of their own significant discomfort or pain. In such an event they should immediately advise the other flight crew members of their condition.

Subtle Incapacitation

Subtle incapacitation is frequently partial in nature and often transient (for periods of seconds or minutes). It presents a significant operational hazard because it is difficult for other crew members to detect. The affected flight crew members may look well and be conscious, but with their brain only functioning partially. They may be unaware of, or incapable of assessing the consequence of their condition.

Action

In the case of flight crew incapacitation, the fit crew member should apply the following actions:

1. Take over the control of the aircraft. If the incapacitated flight crew member causes interference with handling the aircraft, press the sidestick pushbutton for 40 seconds.
2. Engage autopilot.
3. Inform ATC.
4. PA announcement if there is a medical doctor on board.

5. Advise cabin crew to remove incapacitated flight crew member.
6. To reduce cockpit workload ask the cabin crew if there is another company pilot on board.
7. Early approach preparation.
8. Perform an auto land.
9. Arrange medical assistance after landing.

The following examples of incapacitation include some fatal accidents:

EXAMPLE #1 -At the time the first officer got the approach lights in sight; he informed the captain and also mentioned that the aircraft was a little bit left of the centerline. The deviation was so slight that he was not surprised that the captain did not immediately take corrective action. With the runway less than one mile distant, the aircraft was still to the left of centerline, so the first officer again mentioned the fact to the captain. Still no correction followed but after some seconds the aircraft turned slightly to the right. The crew assumed that this was the expected correction, however, the turn continued, crossing the centerline, at which time the first officer took over the aircraft. The first officer looked at the captain and saw him slumped forward in his shoulder harness and his right hand was slowly slipping off the power levers. At 150 feet, the first officer executed a missed approach. He informed ATC and requested medical assistance to standby after landing.

EXAMPLE #2 -The captain, age 44, died or collapsed due to heart failure associated with myocarditis on a night final approach. He attempted to leave his seat and fell across the throttle quadrant, pushing all throttles back to the idle position. The accident was fatal to both the captain and copilot.

EXAMPLE #3 -The copilot made a particularly good landing - so smooth that the other crewmembers commented on it. However, when he put the engines into reverse the aircraft started to drift toward the edge of the runway. The captain then noticed that reverse thrust had not been applied symmetrically and that the copilot had slumped over as if he was still reaching for the throttles. The captain had no problem taking over control of the aircraft. The copilot did not regain consciousness.

In these examples of total incapacitation, the pilot flying the aircraft simply ceased to function. Total incapacitation ranged from consciousness to death. The second form of pilot incapacitation is subtle or partial incapacitation, in which the pilot remains conscious, but for some mental or emotional reason is partially incapacitated. This form is perhaps the most dangerous because it occurs with greater frequency and is even more difficult to detect. Look at these examples of partial incapacitation:

EXAMPLE #4 -A three man crew on final approach was proceeding to the VOR. Approach control cleared the aircraft directly to the outer marker. The captain continued to fly to the VOR. The second officer noticed the captain was still flying to the VOR and warned him about it. The captain told him to "shut up". Eventually, approach control vectored them out of the conflicting traffic area for a missed approach. The captain recovered and made a normal approach and landing, but could not figure out what had happened. The cause of the subtle loss of the ability to function was preoccupation with personal problems.

EXAMPLE #5 -A captain with a particularly good record made a very erratic instrument approach. The aircraft broke out at 300 feet in heavy rain. Just before reaching the threshold, the captain felt he was too high and pushed the nose over, resulting in a very high rate of sink. A crash landing resulted with major damage to the aircraft. The cause of the poor performance and judgment was attributed to hypoglycemia.

EXAMPLE #6 -A two-man crew reached minimums on approach and then executed a missed approach. The captain, on initial climb out, put the aircraft into a very steep climbing turn approaching a stall. The co-pilot forcibly took the aircraft away from the captain. The cause of this abnormal action was increased sensitivity to vertigo secondary to brain disease.

EXAMPLE #7 -The aircraft was on final approach with the captain at the controls. Just prior to the outer marker, the rate of sink was noted to be slightly high and the altitude substantially below the outer marker level. The captain did not respond to the altitude warning. The co-pilot took over the aircraft and executed a missed approach. After the co-pilot landed the aircraft, the captain reversed the engines properly. He was totally unaware of the missed approach. The cause of this loss of function was petit mal or silent epilepsy.

As seen from these examples, partial or subtle incapacitation may or may not be for an extended period of time. Despite the time involved or the reason for the incapacitation, it is critical that the problem be recognized and resolved. The purpose of this section is to reemphasize the volatile potential for human failure in the cockpit, how to recognize it, and how to deal with it.

As with any emergency in an aircraft, coping with human incapacitation involves three phases: (1) recognition, (2) regaining and/or maintaining control of the aircraft, and (3) solution. Of these three, the most critical and most difficult is recognition. It has been ingrained into every pilot that the captain is the sole authority in the cockpit and that every flight crewmember knows his duties and is totally competent in performing them. These are valid assumptions designed to allow a smoothly operating team effort coordinated by a single team leader. It is, therefore, extremely difficult for any member of the flight crew to challenge the actions of another crewmember, particularly if the person challenged is the captain. However, just as there are warning signals built into the mechanical systems of the aircraft, there are warning signals built into the operational system of the cockpit. Based on these warning signals augmented by sound judgment, any flight crewmember should feel not only authorized but obligated to challenge another pilot. These warning systems are based on a "crew concept" operation, in which each crewmember performs his own assigned tasks while monitoring the overall operation of the aircraft. Crewmembers must maintain regular use of standard operational procedures, and be alert to any other crewmember who appears to be deviating from those procedures without a clear, concise reason for doing so.

The major key to the operations' warning system is the "two communication rule". Under this rule, crewmembers should instantly be alerted to possible incapacitation of any pilot if the pilot does not respond appropriately to two verbal communications, or the pilot does not respond to any verbal communication associated with a significant deviation from a standard profile.

Once a crewmember's suspicions are aroused, he should waste no time in ascertaining whether or not the other pilot is incapacitated. Once incapacitation is recognized, the other pilot should immediately take full command of the aircraft despite the rank or seniority of the incapacitated pilot. When taking command, the crewmember must respond instantly and decisively, since it is during the most critical phases of flight, such as takeoff and landing, stress oriented failures are most likely to occur. It is during these phases that crewmembers must be most alert.

Once the aircraft is under control and the stricken pilot cared for, cockpit duties should be reorganized to ensure safe continuation of flight and landing. In many cases, an emergency should be declared and the autopilot used to reduce the workload. Care should be taken to ensure that concern for the stricken pilot does not interfere with sound judgment and rational decisions. Despite the loss of one crewmember, there is no immediate danger to the passengers and no emergency situation other than that of a stricken pilot.

Questions that should be considered when losing a cockpit crewmember in flight include:

QUESTION - What should the remaining crewmember(s) tell ATC if the incapacitation occurs in the terminal control area?

ANSWER - After declaring the emergency it would be helpful to give ATC an estimate of the duration of the hold required and the nature of the emergency. Requesting a holding vector rather than a holding pattern can reduce the cockpit workload. Do not shortcut the procedure. It is very important not to let understandable concern for the incapacitated pilot rush orderly handling of the operational problems to the point that safety of the aircraft is jeopardized.

QUESTION - If the captain becomes incapacitated, should the co-pilot change seats? If so, when in the air or after landing?

ANSWER - is NO. At this stage the prime task for the co-pilot is to make a safe landing. It is probably not desirable to do it under conditions not completely familiar. Most aircraft have sufficient directional control from either seat to bring the aircraft to a complete stop after landing. After the landing roll has been completed, there may be a case for changing seats, especially if the only full nose wheel steering is on the left side. Ground personnel normally signal to the pilot on the left side, and self-parking systems are also predicated upon the aircraft being controlled from the captain's seat.

QUESTION - How should cockpit duties be revised and the aircraft be set up to land?

ANSWER - This will vary from aircraft to aircraft. It will include such items as putting the aircraft in a landing configuration earlier than normal. It may be easier for the pilot in control to handle all operational communications. These should be minimal because of the declared emergency.

QUESTION - What about removing the incapacitated pilot from his seat?

ANSWER - It takes two people to remove the dead weight of an unconscious body from an aircraft seat without endangering any controls or switches. Incidentally, if the incapacitated pilot is given oxygen, it should be at 100% and maximum flow.

QUESTION -What sort of medical assistance should be requested?

ANSWER - Simply asking for a doctor to meet the aircraft after landing is not enough, even if one were available. The absolute essential request is for an ambulance. It is always helpful to give as much factual information regarding the problem as is possible, as long as it does not interfere with or delay the landing procedure.

QUESTION - Should the aircraft be taxied to a regular loading gate or stopped just off the runway?

ANSWER - Once the aircraft is safely landed, the prime consideration should be for the incapacitated crewmember. In most cases, this means getting him off to a hospital as soon as possible. The fastest way is to taxi the aircraft to where he can be expeditiously removed. Having an ambulance by the nose wheel of most aircraft will not expedite removal unless passenger loading facilities are also available.

QUESTION - How can the individual pilot ensure that he does not become "A Pilot Lost in Flight"?

ANSWER - If you don't feel well, say so! If on the ground, take yourself off the flight. If in the air, let the other guy fly.

While frequently there is considerable warning before an incapacitating incident, pilots have not always recognized it. In one of the cited examples, the captain was not feeling well and even took oxygen on the ground at an enroute stop. Despite almost clear skies, he flew the final leg himself and became unconscious after going into reverse at about 100 knots. **Cause of death**: "A sudden heart attack".

Routine adherence to "Standard Operating Procedures" and standard flight profiles, particularly during takeoff and landing, is stressed because frequently a procedural deviation provides the first indication of a problem. In these cases, the procedural deviation is the first communication and any inappropriate verbal response associated with it should be enough to trigger the "index of suspicion".

Once the incapacitation is known to exist, follow the steps suggested in your company's procedures and guidelines.

For your information, let me bring to your attention an accident prevention bulletin suggested by the Flight Safety Foundation cautioning pilots of the possible hazards of accepting "goodies" offered by their grateful passengers.

Two male passengers offered a flight attendant some cookies. At the time the aircraft was enroute from Philadelphia to Chicago. The flight attendant ate three of the cookies and, during descent into Chicago, she began feeling light headed and the feeling progressed to one of extreme intoxication. Laboratory analysis of the remaining cookies showed they were laced with cocaine. Interestingly enough, here is where the caution extends to the flight crews. The same two male passengers asked the flight attendant to offer the cookies to the cockpit crew. The moral of this story is: Don't accept any goodies from seemingly "grateful" passengers, and if you do accept the goodies, "don't eat them". It may be better to appear rude than to actually become incapacitated.

Here is an interesting twist to this subject. A captain becomes incapacitated on a DC-10 flight from Bombay to Zurich. During the flight, the captain very frequently visited the rear lav for personal relief with some sense of urgency. Approximately one hour before landing the captain asked the flight attendant if he had any pills that might control his problem. The flight attendant talked to a male passenger… a doctor, who offered the captain some pills "great for the stomach - take three!" The captain replied he was a very healthy person, seldom took medicine and would take one.

The doctor reassured him that three were okay. Back in the cockpit the captain compromised, took two pills then began to prepare for descent. In less than five minutes, the captain was sound asleep and the crew, hard as they tried, could not wake him. The reason for this reaction was the doctor mistakenly gave the captain prescription sleeping pills. The captain woke up five hours later, surprised to find himself in the airport clinic. "One of the best rests I ever had", he said, but quickly added he would not take medicine in flight in the future.

CHAPTER TWENTY-THREE

TAKEOFF DEFINITIONS

TAKEOFF DEFINITIONS

Accelerate-Stop Distance-The horizontal distance to accelerate from a standing start to the V 1 speed and thereafter, assuming an engine failure at this speed, to bring the airplane to a full stop. The accelerate-stop distance, used in entering the chart, must not exceed the length of the runway plus the length of any stop way.

Balanced Field length -The condition where the takeoff distance is equal to the accelerate-stop distance. This distance must not exceed the length of the runway.

Takeoff Distance-(Turbine)-The horizontal distance from the start of the takeoff to the point at which the airplane is 35 feet AGL. (Assuming engine failure at V1 or 115% of above value if no engine failure, whichever is greater.)

The takeoff distance available, used when entering the performance charts, is the sum of the runway length plus the actual or maximum allowable clearway length. The length of

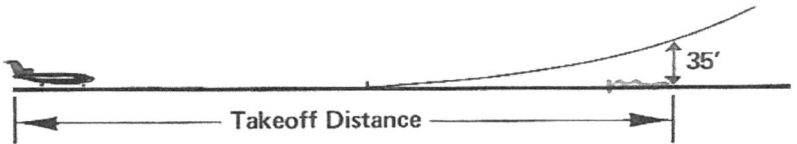

the clearway used must not be greater than one-half the length of the runway.

Takeoff Path – The horizontal path from the takeoff point to a point at which the aircraft is 1,500 feet above the takeoff surface.

Takeoff Run (Turbine) – If the takeoff distance includes a clearway, the takeoff run is the horizontal distance from the start of the takeoff to a point equidistant between the location of Vlof and the point at which the airplane is 35 feet AGL. (Assuming engine failure at V1 or 115% of above value if no engine failure, whichever is greater).

The takeoff run used when entering the performance charts must not exceed the length of the runway.

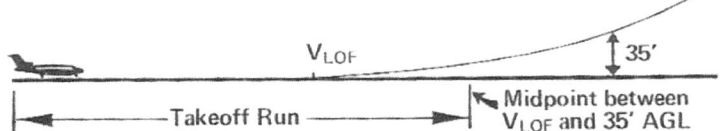

Unbalanced Field Length – The condition where the takeoff distance and accelerate-stop distance are not equal.

V1 – **Critical Engine Failure Speed**. The speed below which the takeoff must be aborted and the aircraft brought to a stop in the event of an engine failure and the speed above which a takeoff is continued.

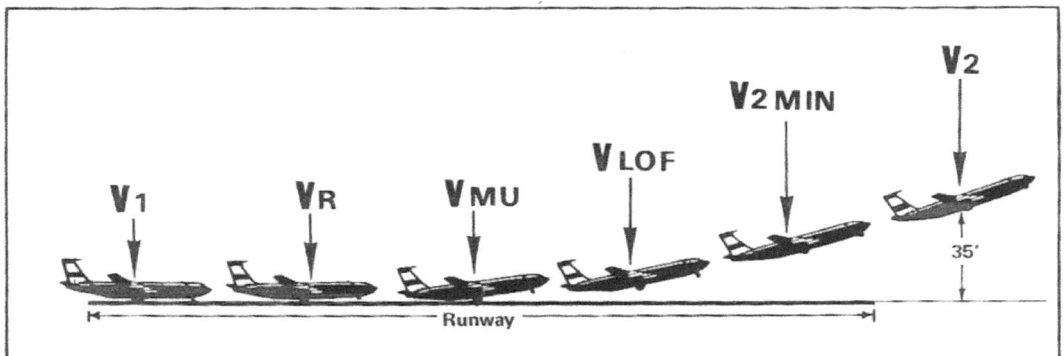

Vr – **Rotation Speed**. The speed at which the airplane is rotated to the takeoff attitude. Vr may not be less than V1 nor less than 105 percent of Vmc. This speed also allows reaching V2 (see V2 definition) before reaching a height of 35 feet above the takeoff surface.

Vmu – **Minimum Unstick Speed**. The minimum speed at and above which the airplane can safely lift off the ground and continue the takeoff.

Vlof – **Liftoff Speed**. The speed at which the aircraft first becomes airborne. If the airplane is rotated at its maximum practical rate, Vlof must not be less than 110 percent of Vmu with all engines operating, nor less than 105 percent of Vmu with one engine inoperative.

V2min – **Minimum Takeoff Safety Speed**. This speed may not be less than 120 percent of Vs, or less than 110 percent of Vmc.

V2 – **Takeoff Safety Speed**. The speed that meets the required climb gradient with one engine inoperative. It cannot be less than V2min and must be attained before reaching a height of 35 feet.

TAKEOFF PERFORMANCE

In essence, there are two main factors which must be considered in determining the takeoff performance of jet aircraft.

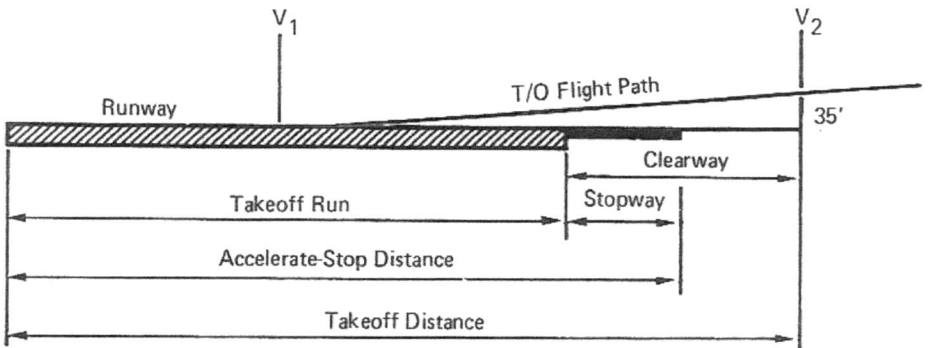

These are:

1. The runway requirement of the aircraft if one engine fails at V1. The airplane should be able to accelerate to V1 and then stop, or assuming engine failure at V1, the takeoff can be continued to a height of 35 feet. From this point, the airplane must now meet certain takeoff climb requirements. The above illustration shows the runway requirements when both a stopway or clearway are used.

2. The takeoff climb requirements insure that the aircraft will be able to maintain climbout gradient with one engine out.

The climbout is normally divided into three separate segments. These segments are:

First – actual lift-off to landing gear retraction;
Second – landing gear retraction to 400 feet above runway surface;
Third – 400 feet to 1,500 feet above the runway.

Occasionally, the takeoff weight of the jet aircraft is limited by the climb compliance in the second segment. This segment is based upon using the takeoff safety speed (V2) and that speed must be attained at or prior to reaching a height of 35 feet. In general, the takeoff weight restrictions are usually associated with low altitude airports because of runway length limitations. The climb compliance limitations are more common at high altitude airports.

TAKEOFF CLIMB SEGMENTS – FAR PART 25 AIRPLANE
APPROACH CLIMB – FAR PART 25 AIRPLANE

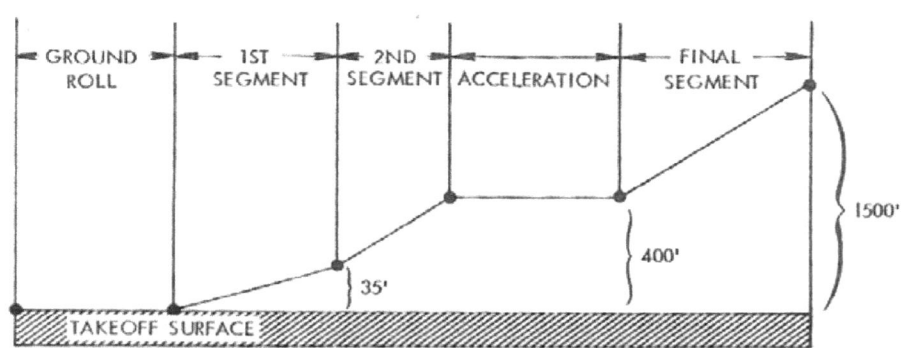

		1ST SEGMENT	2ND SEGMENT	ACCELERATION	FINAL SEGMENT
CLIMB GRADIENT	2 ENG.	POSITIVE	2.4%	POSITIVE	1.2%
	3 ENG.	0.3%	2.7%	POSITIVE	1.5%
	4 ENG.	0.5%	3.0%	POSITIVE	1.7%
FLAPS		←——— TAKEOFF ———→			UP
GEAR		DOWN	←——— UP ———————→		
CRITICAL ENG.		←——————— INOPERATIVE ———————→			
POWER		←——— TAKEOFF ———→			MAX. CONT.
AIRSPEED		V$_{LOF}$ → V$_2$	V$_2$	V$_2$ → 1.25V$_s$	1.25V$_s$

	2 ENG	3 ENG	4 ENG
CLIMB GRADIENT	2.1%	2.4%	2.7%
CONFIGURATION	←——————— APPROACH ———————→		
CRITICAL ENG.	←——————— INOPERATIVE ———————→		
WEIGHT	←——————— MAXIMUM LANDING ———————→		
AIRSPEED	←——————— NOT TO EXCEED 1.5V$_s$ ———————→		

DESTINATION AND ALTERNATE AIRPORT REQUIREMENTS
(FAR PART 121, 185, 187, 195, and 197)

To use an airport as a destination or alternate, the airplane must be able to stop within:

	% OF EFFECTIVE RUNWAY LENGTH	
	DESTINATION	ALTERNATE
Reciprocating	60%	70%
Turbojet	60%*	60%
Turboprop	60%	70%

The percentage figures represent the percent of the effective runway length required assuming the airplane flew 50 feet above point "b".

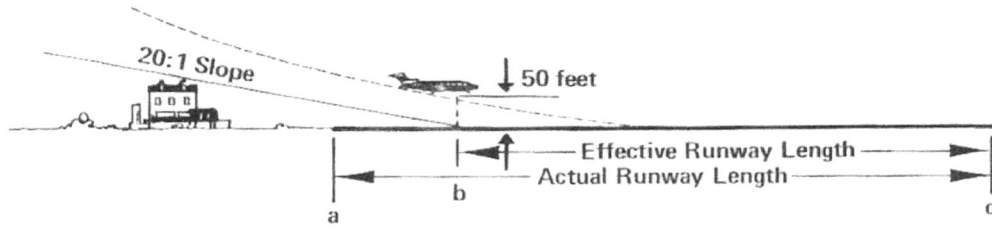

*For wet runway, use 115% of requirement for a dry runway.

For computations, most favorable runway in still air is used if no wind is forecast. If wind is forecast, most suitable runway is used.

For aircraft using most suitable runway when wind is forecast, not more than 50% of headwind nor less than 150% of tailwind can be used. (Certification of transport category aircraft is included in FAR Part 25).

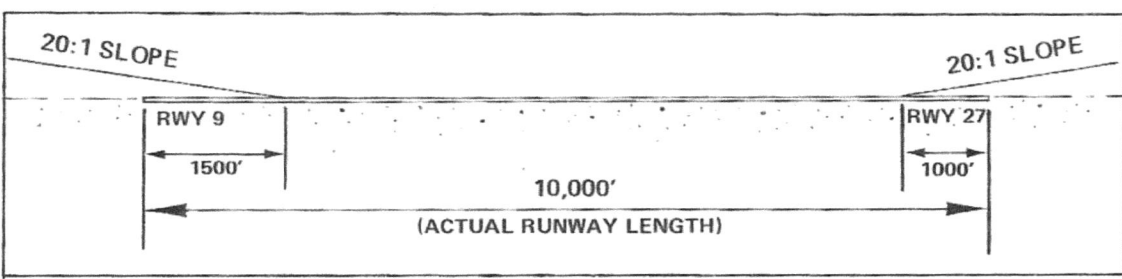

LANDING PERFORMANCE

There are also two main factors which must be considered in the discussion of landing performance. These are:

1. The distance required to land and come to a full stop. This is based on the effective runway length which states the aircraft must be able to stop within 60 percent of available runway after crossing the threshold at a height of 50 feet and at a speed of at least 1.3 times Vso.

The ability of the aircraft to climb out with the critical engine inoperative in the event of a go-around or missed approach. This is an approach climb compliance criteria whereby the landing weight of the aircraft is such that it can make a safe climb out with the critical engine inoperative.

Generally speaking, the maximum allowable landing weight is restricted by the landing field length available. However, at high altitude airports, the approach climb criteria may be more restrictive, but is seldom encountered by jet aircraft.

Airbus 330 The Ultimate Guide for Pilots

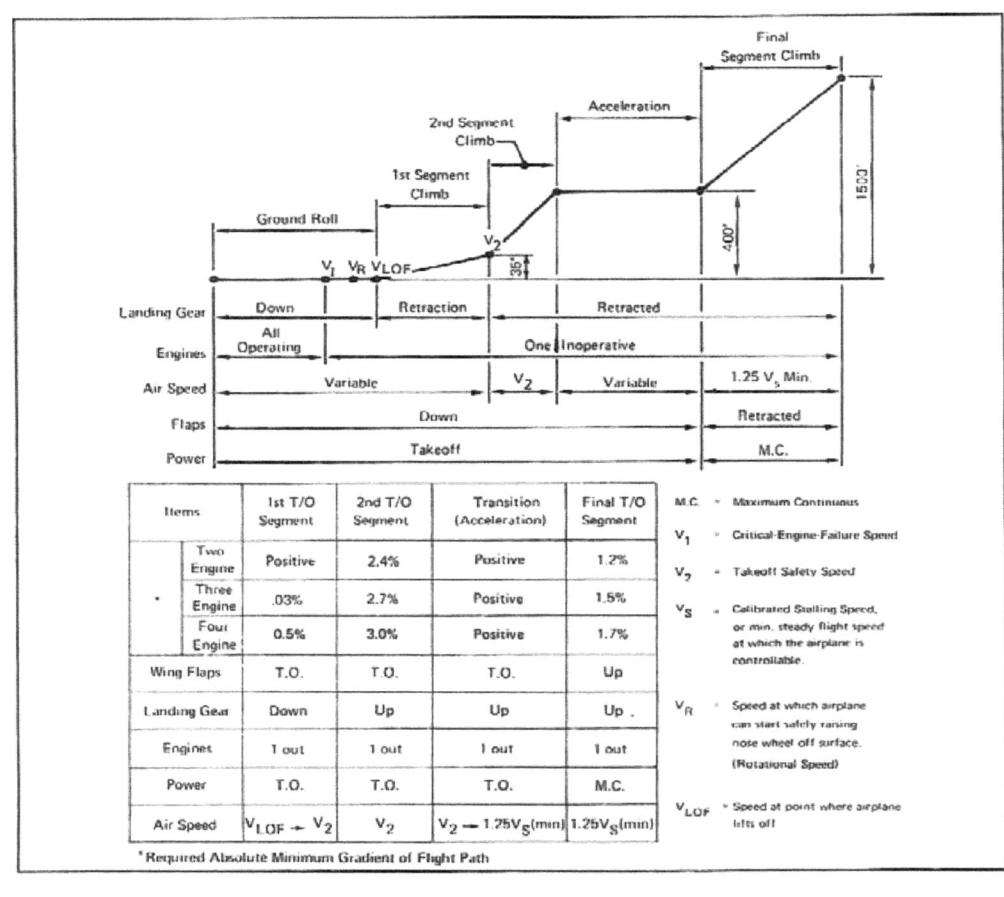

NORMAL DESCENT CALCULATIONS

In the absence of the headwind/tailwind chart or when you are comfortable with the formula, you can also use the following rule-of-thumb to calculate normal descent from altitude or flight level. Descent from cruise altitude may be performed in several configurations. The clean descent is preferred, and should be used whenever operating conditions permit, as it saves time and fuel. The following rule-of-thumb has been found workable in determining the DME distance at which to begin a normal descent.

Altitude (in 1000s of feet) X 4 = DME distance to start descent

EXAMPLE (1)
-Cruise Flight Altitude 31,000 feet
-DME Transmitter on Field
Cruise Altitude. …31(000)
X 4
Start Descent at 124 miles DME

EXAMPLE (2)

-Same Cruise Altitude as Example (1)

-Airport 10 miles beyond DME transmitter

From Example (1)………….. 124 miles DME

Airport beyond Transmitter…-10 miles

Start Descent at…………….. 114 miles DME

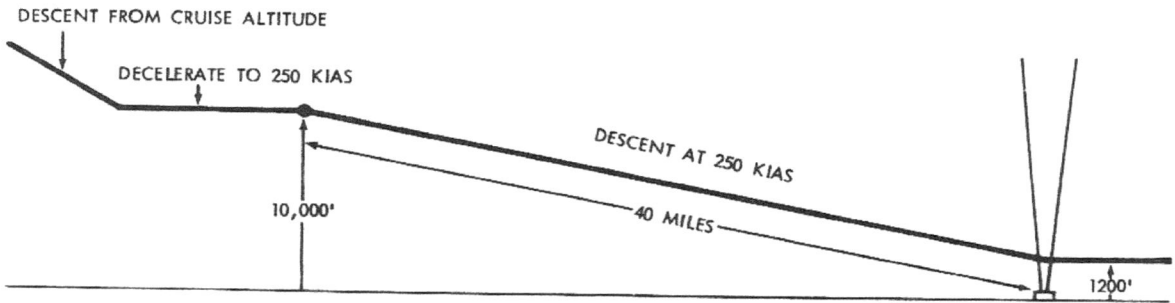

In order to develop an efficient rate-of-descent and speed profile, the following should be considered:

Whenever practical, descend at flight idle thrust. From cruise altitude to crossover altitude, descend at Cruise Mach. From crossover altitude to 10,000 feet, descend at 280 knots.

At 10,000 feet:

-If 250 knot speed restriction applies, decelerate and descend at 250 knots.

-If 250 knot speed restriction does not apply, continue descent at 280 knots.

CHAPTER TWENTY-FOUR

NOISE ABATEMENT

Difference Between NADP 1 and NADP 2

Noise abatement departure procedure one (NADP 1), is designed to meet close-in noise abatement objective. At minimum 800' AAE reduce to climb thrust, continue with V2 +10 to maximum 3000' AAE. Maintain positive climb, accelerate and retract flaps and slats on schedule.

Noise abatement departure procedure two (NADP 2), is designed to meet distant noise abatement objective. At minimum 800' AAE maintain positive climb, accelerate and retract flaps and slats on schedule and set climb thrust (if not already done together with initial flap/slat retraction) and climb with Vzf +10 until reaching 3000' AAE.

Let me put it in very simple terms - NADP 1 is to climb as fast as you can from your departure airport and NADP 2 is to get as far as you can from your departure airport.

NOTE:

NADP2 saves fuel over NADP1 simply because high lift devices create drag. The engines deliver the same amount of power so more of that power is used to compensate for drag (less excess power to climb). You climb slower (vertical speed) with flaps and slats vs a clean aircraft (same aircraft same speed). Of course this is difficult to demonstrate, but it is also applied to F1 departure vs F2 or F3 departure (more flaps reduces runway length needed but it worsens your climb performance).

So since NADP2 cleans up the aircraft about 2000 ft. earlier then NADP1 (most accelerate at 1000' nowadays I believe) it is more efficient fuel burn wise. On top of that you will reach your most efficient climb speed earlier. Of course this assumes same routing, no climb restrictions, no shortcuts etc.

However in the short-term, accelerating will reduce the climb rate and climb angle over the ground. So when there is a buildup area close to the airport, you can achieve a better initial climb gradient over the ground putting 2000 ft extra air between the aircraft and the people on the ground before accelerating. The total noise that the aircraft makes is the same; the total noise that reaches the ground is less.

In the example shown below, on reaching an altitude of 800 ft. above aerodrome elevation, engine power or thrust is adjusted in accordance with the noise abatement power thrust schedule provided in the aircraft operating manual. A climb speed of V2 plus 10 to 20 kt is maintained with flaps and slats in the take-off configuration.

On reaching an altitude of 3000 ft. above aerodrome elevation, the aircraft is accelerated and the flaps/slats are retracted on schedule while maintaining a positive rate of climb to complete the transition to normal enroute climb speed.

NADP1

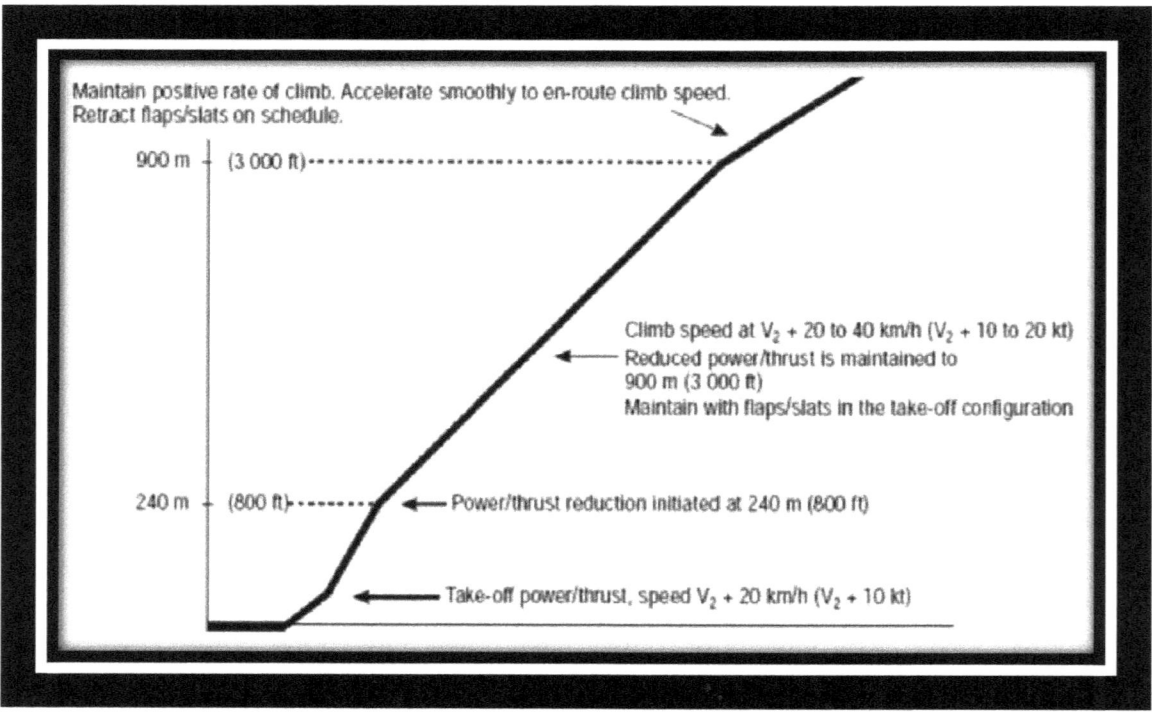

In the example shown below, on reaching 800 ft. above aerodrome elevation, the aircraft body angle/angle of pitch is decreased, the airplane is accelerated towards Vzf, and the flaps/slats are retracted on schedule. Power or thrust reduction is initiated at a point along the acceleration segment that ensures satisfactory acceleration performance. A positive rate of climb is maintained to 3000 ft. above aerodrome elevation. On reaching this altitude, a transition is made to normal enroute climb speed.

NADP2

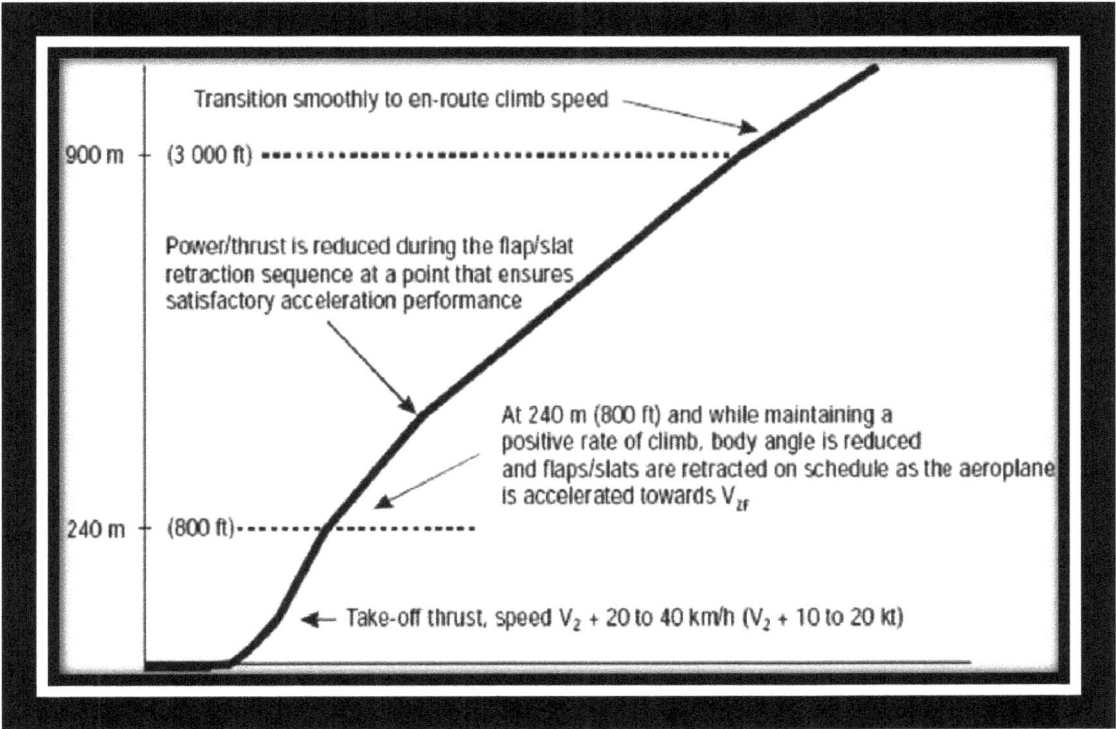

CHAPTER TWENTY-FIVE

REJECTED TAKEOFF

REJECTED TAKEOFF

DEFINITION: A take-off that is discontinued after take-off thrust is set and initiation of the take-off roll has begun. The Rejected Take-Off (RTO) is a maneuver performed during the take-off roll if the flight crew determines that the take-off should not be continued. Most RTOs (approximately 95%) are initiated at speeds below 100 knots and are executed without incidents. However, the potential for an accident or incident following a high speed RTO remains high. A review of the available data over the history of western built transport jet operations shows that approximately one in 3,000 take-offs has been rejected. Of these RTOs about one in 1,000 was unsuccessful, resulting in an overrun accident or incident.

That is an accident/incident rate of one per 3,000,000 take-off attempts.

From the above statistics one can conclude that:
-An RTO is not a very common event.
-The probability of an RTO incident/accident is remote.
-The infrequency of RTO events may lead to an ease off with regard to maintaining sharp decision-making skills.

In spite of these statistics pilots should be prepared to make the correct go/no go decision on every take-off.

Note: V1 is the maximum speed at which the RTO maneuver can be initiated and the aircraft stopped within the remaining field length under the conditions and procedures defined in the FARs / JARs. It is the latest point in the take-off roll where a stop can be initiated. If an engine failure is recognized before V1, an abort can be made within the remaining runway. If an engine failure is recognized at or after V1, the take-off can be continued within the remaining take-off distance.

REMEMBER: V1 is the end of the go/no go decision process, not the beginning!!

Since an actual RTO situation is rare, the need to emphasize the potential adverse consequences of an improperly performed RTO (miscalculation of actual runway versus speed, complacency, etc.), realistic situations should be presented to all crewmembers during simulator training and checks. The RTO maneuver should be initiated in the simulator with a critical length runway (i.e., at a maximum gross takeoff weight for that runway considering ambient temperature), and at speeds just before V1. **A REJECTED TAKEOFF SHOULD NOT BE ATTEMPTED AFTER V1.** Pilots should be aware that there will always be exceptions to the general philosophy regarding the decision to abort. There is not one procedure or set of procedures which could possibly cover all situations. This training should enable all crews to gain adequate and realistic experience to perform a maximum effort RTO if the necessity should arise in actual line operation.

NOTE: On a balanced field length runway, a main gear tire blowing, or the separation of a recap at or slightly before V1, will decrease the braking capability of the aircraft and preclude stopping on the remaining runway.

Not enough emphasis can be placed on the two words: **EARLY ABORT**. If we must reject a takeoff (abort), the earlier the decision is made, the better the chance of a no-damage no-injury completion. Aviation literature is fraught with examples of abort decisions made too late, and of abort decisions made early enough but not carried out properly, all resulting in unnecessary loss of life and/or property damage. This section is not intended to help you decide whether to reject a takeoff, but rather to give you more information on which to base your decision, and to help you build a set of habits, which will ensure a successful abort when it does occur.

Pilots are, by nature, GO-oriented. We do all our planning with the thought that we are going from point A to point B. Our employer assumes that we will indeed make that trip, and our pay scale is based on that assumption. As a result of this 360-degree GO orientation, we are often surprised on that rare occasion when we must make, in a split second, a GO-NO-GO decision. Yet it is at this time that we face one of the most difficult situations in all of flying...the high-speed abort.

Let's look briefly at some of the criteria used to arrive at allowable gross weights and V speeds: From the aircraft Gross Weights Manual we get two basic kinds of gross weight capabilities information...that which is RUNWAY LIMITED and that which is CLIMB LIMITED.

Runway Limited takeoff weights are normally referred to as WIND/TEMP gross weights, and, for any given wind and temperature condition, satisfy the following criteria:

1. **Field length limits.**
2. **Obstacle clearance limits.**

3. **Tire speed limits.**
4. **Brake energy limits**.

CLIMB LIMITED takeoff weights reflect climb performance, which varies only with airfield elevation and temperature...wind, runway length, and obstacle clearance has no effect.

(One other caution need be made: CDL items may or may not impact climb limit weights.) A particular CLIMB LIMIT gross weight is the maximum gross weight, which satisfies all the following engine-out criteria:

1. **First, Second, Third, and Final Segment Climb requirements.**
2. **Five minute limit from brake release to flaps up with flap retraction initiated at a specified altitude.**

Because a Gross Weights Manual or Runway Analysis takes all the preceding into consideration, we are assured that we can (or cannot) operate safely from a particular runway at a particular gross weight. Once so assured, we can go to the Performance Charts to get data such as EPR or N1 settings and V-speeds.

Even though a rejected takeoff, or RTO, is by definition a before-getting-airborne procedure, we are concerned here not only with WIND/TEMP, or Runway Limited, gross weights and speeds, but with CLIMB LIMITED weights and speeds as well. After all, we find our weights and V-speeds on the basis of the most limiting of wind/temp or climb limit.

As we all know, V1 (commonly called Decision Speed) is that speed at which we can reject the takeoff - for whatever reason - and safely stop in the remaining runway without using reverse thrust. The distance (runway length) required to do this is called the accelerate-stop distance. If we select a V1 such that we can lose the most critical engine and still be at V2 and 35 feet AGL at the accelerate-stop distance, we have defined what is known as a balanced field length. A number of our takeoffs are balanced-field takeoffs.

At first blush a V1 abort looks like the safest of procedures since, almost without exception, reverse thrust on one or more engines will be available to help us stop. And, after all, the test pilots who performed the aborts from which much of the V1-VR-V2 information is derived didn't use reverse thrust in their tests. **Piece of cake, right? WRONG!! !**

Wrong? Why?

The basic reason is the manner in which rejected takeoffs differ in real life from the rejected takeoffs performed by the test pilots, and those differences are substantial. Consider the following and see how many you can lay claim to each time you start your takeoff roll.

1. **Complete review of RTO procedures before starting takeoff.**

2. **New brakes and tires.**

3. **Clean, dry runway.**

4. **Takeoff started from the end of the runway.**

5. **Takeoff thrust before brake release.**

6. **Knowing that the takeoff will be aborted.**

7. **Knowing that max braking means maximum pressure on the brake pedals.**

8. Knowing that, having practiced RTOs over and over, you will do everything right.

9. Knowing that everything done in preparation for this takeoff was done absolutely right.

10. No worry about traffic congestion.

11. No worry about passenger comfort.

12. No worry about scheduled departure time.

13. Knowing that your airplane will come to a stop at the same airport your car's parked at.

The test pilot has all the above working for him; if you have three out of that baker's dozen in your corner, it's an exception to the norm.

Let's take a for instance out of Miami International Airport and consider the options.

It's warm...in fact, it's hot; winds are calm; you're at max taxi weight as you're pushed back; and you're cleared for runway

8R. This time you're just under the climb limit weight (it crosses your mind that since you're not wind/temp limited, you have at least some extra runway to play with if you need it); you also note that use of alternate (or reduced, or flex) power is out of the question. Traffic is heavy, and you anticipate possible clearance for Runway 12, so you sneak a peek at the performance calculation for 12. Ah, still good; still climb limited (and that comforting thought about some extra runway again crosses your mind). And it happens just as you had expected; tower clears you for immediate, with emphasis on the word immediate, takeoff on 12. To keep from obstructing traffic flow, you advance the throttles as you roll onto the runway, make your power check as the engines are spooling up and you're on your way. Now stop for a moment and consider how many of the thirteen items listed above are working for you. Depending on each individual's approach to his/her job, some will have more working for them than others, but nobody, and I mean nobody, will have them all.

For example, captains religiously discuss item 1 (RTO procedures) immediately prior to every takeoff; others do so, at best, infrequently. As a result, if the takeoff must be rejected, you must flawlessly perform a most difficult procedure that you might not have really thought about for days or even weeks.

If you have item 2...well, Congratulations!

I know you don't have item 3.

Items 4, 5, and 6? No way! But does this prevent the possibility of a successful RTO? By no means, but it does complicate the RTO considerably. You know you had some extra runway since you were not wind/temp limited, but you don't know how much, and you ate up a lot of runway with the rolling takeoff, making the validity of your V1 speed questionable. It is therefore essential that you make your RTO decision early, and that, once made, you consummate it immaculately...the so-called immaculate rejection.

Item 7? Well, possibly so, but probably not. Max braking is available only via an operational anti-skid system, and then only when you're literally standing on the brakes. You cannot soft-pedal this procedure, or, to make another pun, you can't pussyfoot around. The brake energy required (i.e., kinetic energy absorption) to stop a fast- moving, heavily-loaded airplane is enormous (from Physics 101 we recall that kinetic energy is directly proportional to the square of the velocity). **Remember**, the output pressure from the anti-skid control valves to the brakes can never be greater than the supply pressure metered by the pilot's feet; if you haven't fowled the brake pedals; you're getting less than maximum braking from the anti-skid system. Don't worry about overbaking when the anti-skid system is operational...it can't be done. And I'm sure your passengers would rather spill their martinis than end up on the other side of the Dolphin Expressway, so get on the binders!

Item 8? Do we ever practice RTOs except in the simulator?

Item 9? No comment.

Item 10? That's how you got into this mess.

Item 11? See the last sentence in Item 7.

Item 12? No comment.

Item 13? Don't laugh; more accidents result from get-home-itis than we'd like to believe. But always remember, it's much better to be on the ground wishing you were in the air than to be in the air wishing you were on the ground. So, how much do you have going for you? Not much, and that brings us to the basic point of this whole discussion: **PLAN AHEAD!!!**

If you get everything possible on your side, and if you start your takeoff roll with a review of takeoff emergency procedures, and if you consummate immaculately, an RTO can become the most satisfying procedure imaginable rather than the disaster it too often is.

The takeoff data available to you is valid, but it has to be used properly. Emergency procedures developed for your aircraft are valid, but they must be reviewed regularly, and you must be prepared to use them when needed. The airplanes provided for you are the best in the world, but they do occasionally break; you must plan in advance so that a "what was that?" on takeoff roll doesn't lead you down the primrose path to disaster. Next time when deciding to take off from an intersection and your calculation shows 10 Meter Stopping Margin think twice and **BE PREPARED!!!**

ABOVE 100 kts and BELOW V1 referred to ("High speed regime")
Captain should be go-minded. Reject only for: ENG FIRE
 APU FIRE
 Severe damage
 ENG FAIL or sudden loss of engine thrust
 CONFIG warning
 Red/Warning (- ENG OIL LO PR)

ENG REV UNLOCKED
Red/Warning
SIDESTICK FAULT
(NEW)
L+R ELV FAULT (- pitch control only by trim wheel)
Red/Warning
Tire failure when speed is less than V1-20 kts.

Above this speed it's better to get airborne, dump fuel and land with a long runway, unless the tire debris has caused major engine anomalies.

Nose gear vibration should or a window coming open should not lead to an RTO above 100kts.

Until takeoff power set (all of these should give a caution):

F/CTL   PRIM 1 FAULT

F/CTL   PRIM 1 PITCH FAULT

F/CTL   ELEV SERVO FAULT on 1 green servo control

HYD G SYS LO PR

A further hidden failure may result in loss of one elevator control in flight.

A return to the gate for maintenance is required in each case above.

Above V1 pilot must reject only if the aircraft will not fly able.

PERFORMANCE/SYSTEMS IMPACTS
Factors Which May Affect RTO Stopping Performance and/or Stopping Distance

PILOT FACTORS

Delay in recognition of problem requiring RTO

Delay in initiating RTO

Improper techniques. Eg. Late or no use of reverse thrust, not maximum braking when braking manually.

Instinctively taking over from autobrakes and not using maximum manual braking.

Error in performance calculations (improper speeds)

Runway line-up uses more distance than allowed in calculations (Distance to V1 more than calculated in the performance figures)

Improper (low) thrust setting (longer, slower acceleration)

Slow to set takeoff thrust whilst rolling (longer, slower acceleration)

SYSTEM FACTORS

Damaged tires

Deflated tires

Brakes deactivated (MEL). A V1 reduction usually applies to accommodate for this. A brake failure during the RTO will not be accounted for.

Anti-skid faulty or unserviceable (MEL). A large V1 reduction usually applies. (Unplanned) failure of the antiskid will be much more of an issue with a contaminated runway.

A/C weight greater than predicted by load sheet

Residual brake temperature (with brake temps past a certain point the braking efficiency reduces and the brakes may fail altogether). The A330 does not have Min Turnaround tables.

The basic 150 and 300 degree limitations make brake energy matters an easy assessment for departure.

Speed brake (no speed brake in RTO affects drag – some 30%) and more so weight on the wheels to aid proper braking (30% increase in braking efficiency).

ENVIRONMENTAL FACTORS

Less headwind or more tailwind than used for calculations

Hot temperature (performance figures account for)

High pressure altitude (QNH adjustment accounts for).

Engine performance

Higher density altitude so acceleration to V1 takes longer and more runway.

CHAPTER TWENTY-SIX

FLYING IN AND OUT OF HIGH ALTITUDE AIRPORTS

FLYING IN AND OUT OF HIGH ALTITUDE AIRPORTS

Due to the peculiarities of maneuvering for an approach and landing into (and takeoff from) such airports as Bogota, Guatemala City, La Paz, Mexico City, etc. it is recommended that the initial entry into such airports be accompanied by a check airman. This will familiarize yourself with the airport, approach procedures and the surrounding area prior to flying into the airport on your own. Extra care should be exercised on foreign operations. Even though all controllers are supposed to be able to speak English, difficulty may be encountered in understanding them.

In addition, foreign traffic control procedures often are not as sophisticated. The two items just mentioned should be ample justification for careful monitoring of all clearances by all cockpit crewmembers entering and leaving any foreign airport. Listed below are basic guidelines to follow, which will help insure safe operation into any high altitude airport.

Carefully view the PART films for the airport (s) you intend to qualify into. There is plenty of useful information available if you view the presentation properly. Where there are high mountains or other obstacles around an airport, it pays to be most attentive to the PART films (i.e. Kabul, Afghanistan (Hamid Karzai International), Guatemala City (La Aurora International), La Paz, Bolivia (El Alto International Airport) and Mexico City (Benito Juarez International).

Study your enroute chart. Know what the MEA is at all times, especially in preparation for your descent. Do not start a descent until you know your exact position. This cardinal rule can be assured by identifying all radio facilities that are to be used.

Study your approach chart carefully. Look for notes that might be inadvertently overlooked. Some foreign high altitude airports list speed restrictions. Observe them, or your flight path can very well take you close to some terrain you really don't want to be near. For operation into and out of foreign stations, as mentioned before, listen to all transmissions. Be sure you understand each and every clearance prior to accepting it. Do not expect traffic control and separation like you receive in the continental United States and its possessions. Make all turns with a 25-30 degree bank. Shallow banks result in large radius turns, and in combination with a high TAS, may result in marginal obstacle clearance altitude above the surrounding terrain.

Plan and discuss the approach well in advance during the approach briefing. Last minute briefings, and delayed speed reductions can result in a poorly executed approach. When approaching the FAF, just prior to initiating the approach, have the aircraft slowed up to the proper speed and flap configuration for starting the descent. This will result in a well-controlled flight path. If enroute cabin altitude is lower than field elevation of landing airport, confirm cabin altitude has been properly set prior to landing.

Do not rely on VASI indications for obstacle clearance on approaches over hilly and mountainous terrain. There is a natural tendency to rely on them at distances far out from the runway. This is especially tempting on a clear night, in the absence of an ILS. DON'T DO IT. Fly the approach as depicted on the approach chart. Review the "Additional Runway Information" section on the airport drawing side of the chart for any specific restrictions on the use of a particular VASI.

Stay on speed and in slot on final approach. Ground speed will be much higher due to higher TAS. Make normal landing in target touchdown area. Make sure spoilers are deployed and utilize reverse thrust as soon as practical after touchdown. Due to the higher actual touchdown speed, it is easy to overheat the brakes.

If runway is wet, as on any wet runway, use extreme caution. A slippery runway at high airport elevation makes decelerating and stopping a maneuver requiring TLC (tender loving care).

Takeoffs at high altitude airports are also different from a sea level operation. Due to the less dense air, aircraft acceleration is slower, and time to obtain rotation speed takes longer especially during high outside temperatures. Use all available runway for every takeoff. If the Gross Weights for Takeoff specifies a non-standard level-off height or specific departure procedures, review procedures on pre-takeoff briefing (example: BOG), maintain green dot speed till you are about MSA altitude. In the event of an aborted takeoff, use maximum braking, assure that ground spoilers are deployed and use max reverse.

Ariana Afghan Airline Boeing 727 Landing on Runway 29 in Kabul, Afghanistan one of the toughest and most challenging airports in the world

KABUL APPROACH PLATES

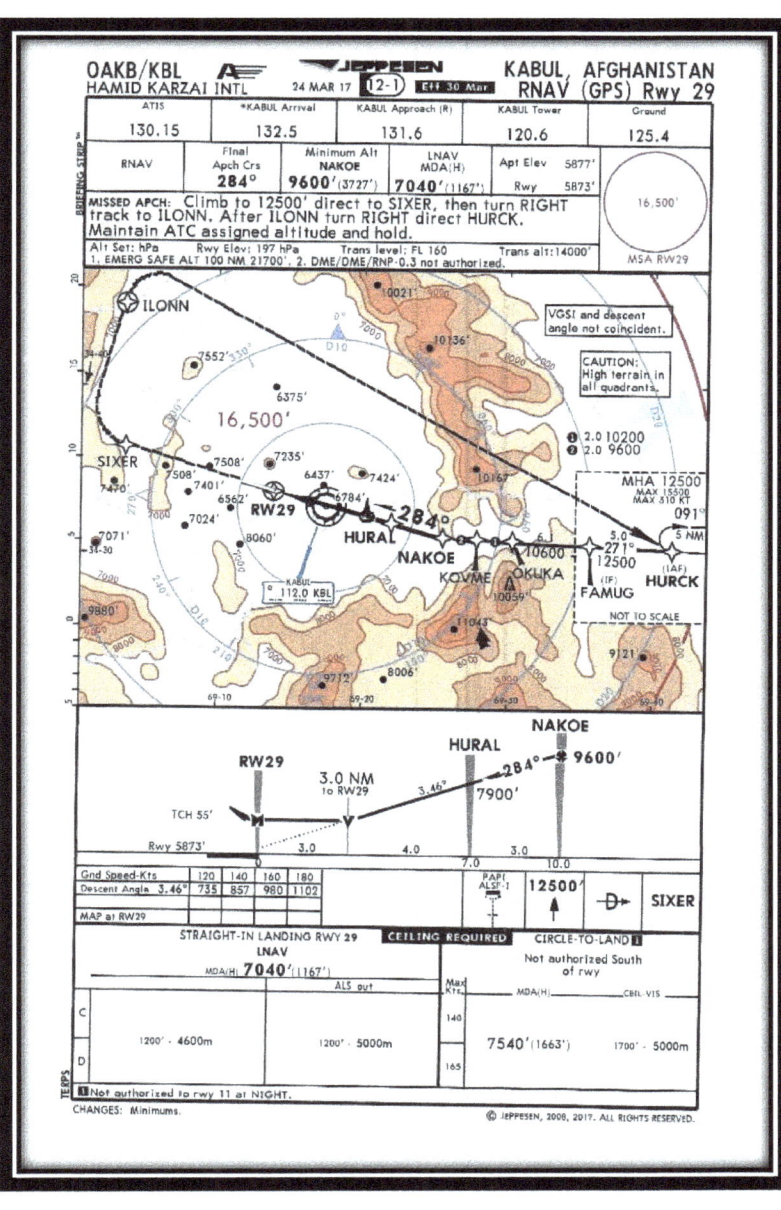

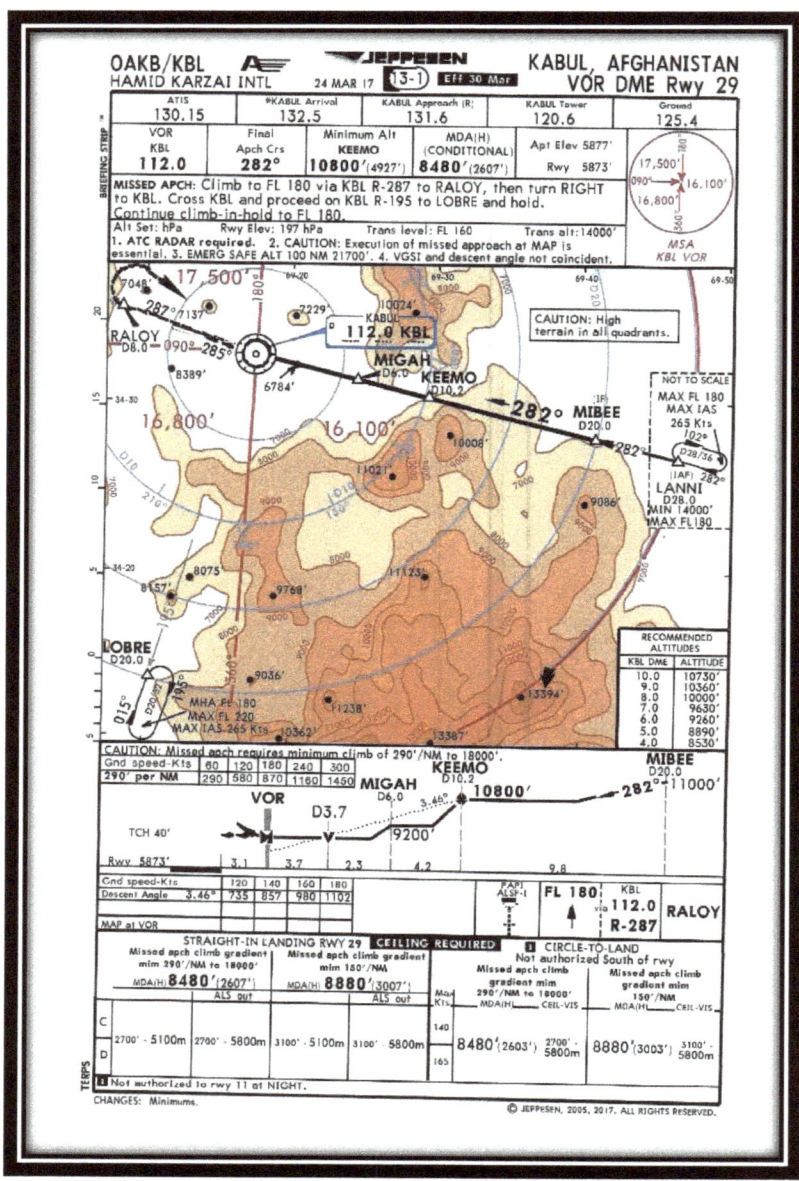

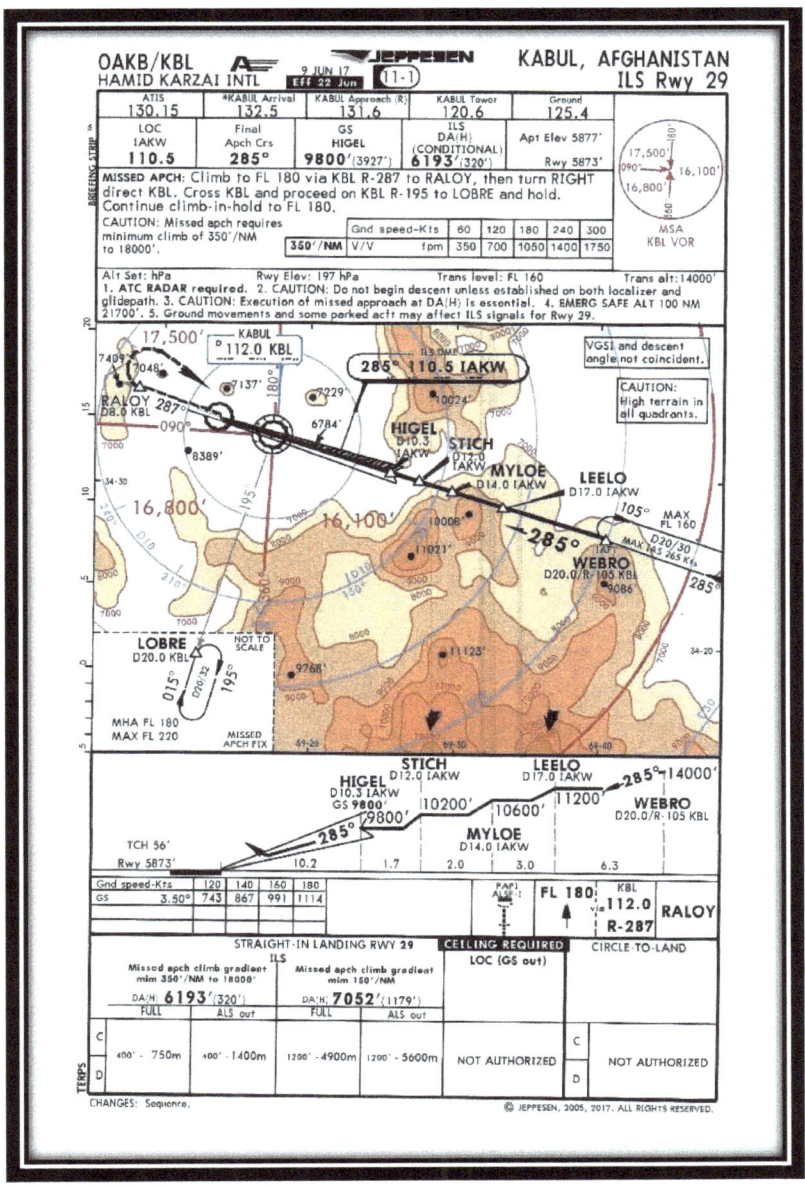

CHAPTER TWENTY-SEVEN

HOW TO MAKE AN A330 GO DOWN AND SLOW DOWN

How to Manage a "Go Down and Slow Down" in the A330

Managing the Princess on approach continues to be a challenge for those new to the airplane.

We're often vectored in fast, and slowing down early is not an option. There are too many planes in the sky competing to land at the same airports. Besides with the price of fuel, flying fast and getting on the ground is the most efficient. The problem is, the A330 doesn't like to go down and slow down. And she sure doesn't like to descend on the glideslope at 180 knots. She will accelerate unless you do something.

I've noticed we're required to keep our speed up to 180 knots more times than not. And we're often vectored in high. How do we manage the approach in this case?

Don't activate the approach speed until you're on the glideslope and ready to slow. If you attempt to slow this plane then think you're going to capture the glideslope, it won't happen. Fly the plane to the glideslope first, and then slow down. That's the only way you'll get on profile and make a stabilized approach.

Once capturing the glideslope extend flaps, gear, and/or speed brakes to allow her follow the glideslope while maintaining the requested speed. The speed, and distance you capture the glideslope, will determine your configuration.

There are also some tricks of the trade the long-term bus pilot's use that we can stick in our toolkits too.

A great gouge:
"170 knots with Flaps 3 gives you the best rate of descent." Or Flaps 2, Gear Down and fly at 170 knots is the other option. Depends on how far out you're intercepting the glideslope and your speed. If you're way out you may want to delay putting down the gear. One benefit the Airbus has over the Boeing is the ability to use speed brakes, with gear and flaps extended, to slow. So with the Airbus you can fly down with faster speeds and have greater ability to slow up while on the glideslope.

A dot above the glideslope... Flaps 3, intercept the glideslope, gear down. When it's time to slow... 1800 feet... Activate managed speed, and flaps full. If you're going too fast, you may need speed brakes to help slow her down.

One very important thing A330 pilots must remember is, if you go high on the glideslope during the approach, and push the nose over and attempt to fly back to capture the glideslope by pushing the nose over - your speed will increase. To compensate for this, she will reduce the thrust to idle. If you're low to the ground, she will not have enough altitude and time for the engines to spool up when power is needed, and you'll hit hard.

For example:

This kind of situation caused an accident with fatalities when a Turkish B737 was above the glideslope on approach. The crew pushed the nose over to capture glideslope, then thrust went to idle. Crew continued descending on to the GS at idle thrust, the flight crew forgot to increase to approach thrust when established, stalled and went down in a field.

A preliminary investigation found that the crash was caused primarily by the engine's automated reaction which was triggered by a faulty radio altimeter, which had failed twice in the previous 25 hours. This caused the auto throttle to decrease the engine power to idle during approach and the crew noticed this too late to take appropriate action to increase the throttle and recover the aircraft before it stalled and crashed. Boeing has since issued a bulletin to remind pilots of all 737 series and BBJ aircraft of the importance of monitoring airspeed and altitude, advising against the use of autopilot or auto throttle while landing in cases of radio altimeter discrepancies. Because of their lack of experience the crew didn't realize the thrust was in "idle" for "90" seconds? They had more than enough time...ample time... to save the plane. We will always have faulty equipment, things breaking. I've seen faulty flags many times. The key is to pay attention and know what your plane is doing. So many pilots flying automated aircraft become complacent. Unfortunately this time many died.

Moral of that story... Don't follow your plane. The automation is on you to babysit it and make sure it's doing what it's supposed to do.

Remember these jets are not designed to approach with power off. They're not gliders.

In the Airbus, Open descent mode gives you idle thrust. You don't want the aircraft to go to idle thrust during approach too close to the ground to capture the glideslope from above.

Vertical speed mode gives you control of how quickly you will capture it plus prevent thrust from going in to the idle position.

ALWAYS REMEMBER - THE KEY TO A SAFE APPROACH IS A STABILIZED APPROACH.

CHAPTER TWENTY-EIGHT

HOW TO PREVENT A HARD LANDING

How to Prevent a Hard Landing (and a Trip to the Fleet Manager's Office)

Always remember there are two key elements that will prevent you from making a hard landing. **Stabilized Approach and Flare are keys to avoiding hard landings**. The captain of a Malaysia Airlines Airbus A330-300 aircraft should have initiated a go-around to avoid the hard landing it made at Melbourne Tullamarine airport on 15 March 2015.

The final report on the incident by the Australian Transport Safety Bureau found that the A330, registered 9M-MTA, experienced a downward acceleration of 2.6g at touchdown, requiring the landing gear to be changed before it returned to service.

As the captain was flying the approach, he disconnected the autopilot when the A330 was around 700ft above ground level. This was accompanied by frequent and heavy inputs to the sidestick controls as the precision approach path indicator lights showed that the jet was coming in under the required glidescope for the runway.

The captain attempted to recapture the glideslope when the aircraft was around 60 ft above ground level by moving the throttles to the take-off/go-around detent, which caused the flight mode annunciator on the primary flight display to change modes. The first officer, as the pilot monitoring, noticed the change in modes and assumed that a go-around was taking place and awaited further announcement from the captain. Instead, the captain reduced the thrust levels, at which point the first officer noticed that the aircraft was not flaring, and both pilots applied nose-up inputs to their sidestick controls, just as the aircraft touched down. The aircraft experienced a vertical acceleration of around 700ft/min on at touchdown, and came down around 170 m from the runway's landing threshold.

There were no injuries as a result of the incident, however a number of landing gear components had been stressed beyond their design limits and required replacing and supplemental inspections.

Company procedures called for the crew to initiate a go-around if the approach becomes unstable at any point below 500 ft above ground level, with the pilot monitoring the approach to communicate with the pilot flying, or even take over the approach if necessary.

The captain and first officer advised at interview that, in retrospect, they should have conducted a go-around in accordance with the operator's training procedures. It also noted that communication between the two pilots was inadequate, which led to a "lack of recognition of the undesirable flight state and the continuation of an unstable approach." This incident clearly highlights the importance of a stable approach, flare and called on pilots to maintain a philosophy of "if in doubt, GO AROUND".

The handling differences in a Fly-By-Wire aircraft are significantly different in some maneuvers--- especially landing. The A330 shifts modes during the landing, slipping the aircraft becomes a bit of a challenge, therefore Airbus recommends landing in a crab because wings level approach provides a better chance of not catching an engine upon landing.

If a slip is to be flown just before landing, lateral stick input is used to establish the amount of bank and must be returned to a neutral position to hold the amount of bank requested, while opposite rudder is established. Not a big deal. Now we're flying neutral stick with a bank established and cross rudder, creating a slip. But there is a little more to landing A330 due to the modes of operation in Normal Law.

Normal Law--- the flight control law used for normal operations when everything is working.

Flight Mode
Landing Mode
Ground Mode

Flight Mode becomes operational 5 seconds after takeoff. We climb, cruise, and approach with full Fly-By-Wire technology.

Landing Mode is when the logic begins to change. Airbus decided that when descending below 100 feet RA, they wanted to give us a "conventional feel" for the flare and touchdown. This feel only affects the pitch handling characteristics. Then at 50 feet RA a slight pitch down elevator input is applied requiring the pilot to give a bit of aft stick movement to maintain the same pitch. At 30 feet— flare. The pilot brings the nose up just enough to arrest the descent rate. Not the traditional flare that you'd expect in a Cessna or a Boeing 727. Then bring the power to idle when commanded. The aft main wheels touchdown first. Front main wheels land second. Then

fly the nose to the runway. Do not hold the nose off. If you hold it off too long, she'll run out of airspeed and drop hard.
During the flare, rudder should be applied to align the aircraft with the runway heading.

Ground Mode is where the fun begins in crosswind conditions. Sidestick control of elevators, ailerons, and spoilers, is now directly proportional to the deflection of the sidestick. Therefore, if we had a bank established, but our stick was neutral--- once on the ground we'd be required to input the same amount of bank as necessary to counteract the wind, and hold the stick in that direction.

If you had no bank established, once on the ground, you may need to add some, remembering the direct stick to controls logic--- just like Direct Law. The flying does not stop when this plane is on the ground. It may just begin.

CHAPTER TWENTY-NINE

NIGHT LANDING

LANDING VISUAL ILLUSIONS

Landing is without a doubt one of the hardest things to do well in aviation. Landing at night is even harder. With significantly fewer visual cues, you need to rely on your instruments and airport lighting much more to make it down in one piece. There are a lot of different ways to screw up your night landing (more than we can possibly list here), but these are 5 of the main reasons things don't go well on night landings.

1) Black Hole Effect

When you're flying into an airport that has very few ground features around it, it gives you the illusion that you're higher than you actually are. That's because the airport looks like an island of bright lights, with nothing but darkness around it.

Pilots tend to fly lower approaches into these kinds of airports, hence the name "black hole effect". The darkness sucks you in, and if you aren't careful, can cause you to crash short of the runway.

2) High Intensity Light.

When you're trying to locate the airport, it's usually best to bring the lights up to high. But once you've spotted it, the high intensity lights can cause problems. That's because when the lights are bright, you feel like you're closer to the runway than you actually are, causing you to fly a higher-than-normal approach. Why? Because when the lights are bright, you have the illusion that you're lower and closer to the runway, causing you to fly a higher glide path than you normally would.

But that's not the only problem with high intensity lights. As you approach your round out and flare, the lights can be blinding, making is very hard to see the runway itself. And when you can't see the runway, it's hard to make a good landing.

3) Rain/Night time

Landing in rain at night is a lot like the black hole effect. If you're landing in rain, you get the illusion that you're higher than you actually are. And that means you're going to fly a lower than normal approach.

4) Runway Width Illusions

We've all been there in the daytime, trying to land on an unusually wide or narrow runway, and being way off on glide.

The same problems happen at night too. If you're landing on a wide runway, you have the illusion that you're too low, and you fly a higher than normal glide path.

And if you're landing on a narrow runway, you have the illusion that you're too high, which can fool you into flying a lower than normal glide path.

5) Locating the Airport, And NOT the Highway
Aside from all these problems we've already listed, just finding the airport can be a challenge.

Some airports, like Cortez, CO, have brightly lit highways near them. And believe it or not, the highway can be pretty easily mistaken for a runway or approach lighting system.

If you find yourself lining up for a highway instead of the runway, you're going to find yourself with all sorts of problems, from being too high or too low, or getting dangerously close to terrain and unlit obstacles.

Using VASI/PAPI and the ILS

So what's the solution to all of these problems? Navigate, navigate, and navigate.

Almost all lighted runways have a glideslope system, whether it's visual, electronic, or both.

When it comes to visual glideslopes, PAPI and VASI systems are the most popular ones out there. For PAPIs, you want to see two red, and two white. (Remember the saying "two red, two white, just right"?) And for VASIs, you want to see red over white ("red over white, just right") If the runway has an ILS, that's even better. When you combine it with a PAPI or VASI, you'll have a combination of the best guidance for a perfect night landing.

CHAPTER THIRTY

JET PERFORMANCE TERMS

JET PERFORMANCE TERMS AND DEFINTIONS

Accelerate-Stop Distance -The distance to accelerate from a standing start to the critical engine failure speed (V1) and thereafter, assuming an engine failure at this speed, to bring the airplane to a full stop. The accelerate-stop distance must not exceed the length of the runway plus the length of the stop way.

Approach Climb -The landing weight of the aircraft must be such that it can climb out after a go-around with the most critical engine put at a maximum climb gradient of 2.1 percent for two-engine airplanes, 2.4 percent for three-engine airplanes, and 2.7 percent for four-engine airplanes.

Balanced Field Length -The condition where the takeoff distance is equal to the accelerate-stop distance. This distance must not exceed the length of the runway. The aircraft can either accelerate to V1 and then stop, or accelerate to V1 and continue to a height of 35 feet, with one engine cut at V1.

Calibrated Airspeed (CAS) -CAS is IAS corrected for instrument and static system or position errors.

Clearway -Expressed in terms of a clearway plane, extending above the end of the runway with an upward slope not exceeding 1.25 percent, above which no object nor any terrain protrudes.

Compressibility -The compressing together of the molecules of air by an object moving faster than the molecules can move out of the way; the result of compressibility is to increase the density of the air in the immediate vicinity of the object.

Compressibility Drag -Compressibility drag is caused by turbulence and an airflow separation associated with shock wave formation when airflow exceeds the speed of sound locally over the wing. This increase in drag is often referred to as the "drag rise."

Compressor Speed (rpm or percent)
N - for a single compressor engine
N1 - speed for the low-pressure compressor of a dual-compressor engine, or the compressor speed (rpm or percent) of a single-compressor engine equipped with a free turbine.
N2 - speed of the high-pressure compressor of a dual-compressor engine, or the free-turbine speed (rpm or percent) of a single-compressor engine equipped with a free turbine.

Critical Engine Failure Speed (V1) -This is the speed at which the engine is assumed to fail. It is usually selected to make the accelerate-stop distance equal to the distance to 35 feet for the continued takeoff.

Critical Mach Number (MCRIT) -A Mach number representing the speed of a given aircraft at which a Mach number of one is attained at any local point on the aircraft. Generally, the shape of the airfoil determines the critical Mach number. Planform, angle of attack, and sweepback also have an appreciable effect.

Density Altitude -Density altitude is pressure altitude corrected for temperature. It is the altitude in standard atmosphere corresponding to a particular value of air density.

Drag Rise -The rapid increase in drag encountered by an airplane as it approaches the speed of sound.

Engine Pressure Ratio (EPR) -The ratio of tailpipe total pressure divided by engine inlet total pressure.

Equivalent Airspeed (EAS) -The calibrated airspeed of an aircraft corrected for adiabatic compressible flow for the particular altitude. Equivalent airspeed is equal to calibrated airspeed in standard atmosphere at sea level.

Exhaust Gas Temperature (EGT) - The gas temperature downstream of the last turbine.

Feel Simulation -A means of providing the pilot with a sense of proper feel of control surfaces.

Free-Turbine Speed (N3) -The rpm or percent of a dual-compressor engine equipped with a free turbine.

Indicated Airspeed (IAS) -IAS is the reading obtained directly from the airspeed instrument. This reading includes no correction for static system, instrument position, or compressibility errors.

Indicated Air Temperature (IOAT) -This is the temperature indicated on the ram temperature gauge. This instrument reading is higher than the ambient outside air temperature due to adiabatic compressibility temperature rise felt on the temperature gauge pickup.

Landing Field Length -At a destination airfield, the aircraft must be able to stop within 60 percent of the available runway after crossing the threshold at a height of 50 feet and a speed of at least 1.3 Vso.

Leading Edge Flaps -Small flaps on portions of the wings' leading edges. They are flush with the underside of the wing during cruise and are extended during takeoff and landing to maintain excellent lift characteristics of the wing even at low flying speeds.

Local Velocity -The velocity of air at some specific point on a moving body as distinguished from the velocity of the moving body.

Mach number (M) -A number expressing the ratio of the speed of a moving body to the speed of sound in air.

Mach 1.00 - speed of sound

Maximum Operating (Mach) (MMO) - This is the certified maximum Mach number permissible in flight operations which is limited by high speed buffet characteristics of the airplane. VMO is a "buffet" limit.

Maximum Operating (Velocity) (VMO) -This limit is the FAR certified speed establishing the limiting normal operating air load (impact or dynamic pressure) permissible on the aircraft structure during "smooth" flight conditions.

Mean Aerodynamic Chord (MAC) -The chord of an assumed rectangular airfoil, representing the mean chord of an actual airfoil.

Minimum Control Air (VMCA) -Minimum speed at which control can be recovered and straight flight maintained if the most critical engine suddenly fails with the air- plane airborne and out of ground effect.

Minimum Control Ground (VMCG) -Minimum speed during the takeoff run while in ground effect at which controllability by primary aerodynamic controls alone permits a safe continued takeoff if any engine suddenly fails. This permits forward pressure on the yoke to use the nose gear reaction to aid control, but not nose wheel steering.

Minimum Liftoff Speed (VLOF) -The minimum speed at which the aircraft will lift off the ground if the airplane is rotated at its maximum practical rate.

Minimum Takeoff Safety Speed (V2MIN)- May not be less than 110 percent of VMCA or 120 percent of VS at takeoff flap setting.

Minimum Unstick Speed (VMU) -The minimum speed at which the aircraft can be made to lift off the ground (unstick) and to continue the takeoff without displaying any hazardous characteristics. VMU may be low enough so that the airplane would have to be rotated beyond the point where the tail would hit the ground before a high enough altitude could be reached to give an unsafe takeoff.

Ram Pressure -Ram pressure is the aerodynamic pressure rise resulting from high velocities. It is also called dynamic pressure and is usually expressed in pounds per square foot. It is expressed, in the cockpit, as indicated airspeed (IAS).

Rotation Speed (VR) -The speed at which the pilot should initiate raising the nose gear off the ground.

Shock Waves -Waves formed by the pileup of air at the point where the air reaches the speed of sound. These waves first form when the airplane itself is still traveling considerably below the speed of sound, but the air moving over curved portions attains the speed of sound.

Speed of Sound -The speed at which sound waves travel through a medium is primarily a function of temperature. At standard sea level conditions, the speed of sound in air is 661 knots, or 761 miles per hour.

Speed Ranges

Subsonic -Mach numbers below 0.75

Transonic -Mach numbers from 0.75 to 1.20

Supersonic -Mach numbers from 1.20 to 5.00

Hypersonic -Mach numbers above 5.00

<u>Note</u>: With the possibility of having both subsonic and supersonic flow on the same aircraft, it is convenient to establish approximate speed ranges, as shown above.

Spoilers -Panels located on the upper chamber of the wing which aid in lateral control and act as speed brakes to slow aircraft on landing roll.

Stalling Speeds

VS -zero thrust stalling speed or minimum steady flight speed at which the airplane is controllable

VS1 -stalling speed in the particular configuration under consideration

VSO -stalling speed in the landing configuration

Static Pressure -The pressure exerted on an object not taking into consideration any movement of the air on the object.

Stop way -An area beyond the runway not less in width than the runway for use in decelerating the airplane during an aborted takeoff. A stop way can be used for increasing the accelerate-stop distance.

Swept Wing- A wing that slants backward from wing root to wingtip. The sweep of the wing has the aerodynamic effect of permitting higher speeds before encountering shock wave formation.

Takeoff Distance -The greater of:

(1) the horizontal distance from the point of brake release to a point where the airplane attains a height of 35 feet above the takeoff surface, assuming an engine failure at the VI speed; or

(2) 1.15 times the horizontal distance from the point of brake release to the point where the airplane attains a height of 35 feet above the takeoff surface with all engines operating.

The takeoff distance available is the sum of the runway length plus the actual or maximum allowable clearway length. The length of the clearway used must not be greater than one-half the length of the runway.

Takeoff Run -The greater of:
(1) the horizontal distance from the point of brake release to a point equidistant between the lift-off point and the point where the airplane attains a height of 35 feet above the takeoff surface, assuming an engine failure a V1 speed; or

(2) 1.15 times the horizontal distance from the point of brake release to point equidistant between the lift-off point and the point where the airplane attains a height of 35 feet above the takeoff surface with all engines operating.

Takeoff Safety Speed (V2) -The speed at which the airplane should be flown after lift-off (for the case when an engine fails during the takeoff run).

Thrust -Thrust is the forward pull expressed in pounds. In uncelebrated, level flight conditions, thrust is equal to the total drag of the airplane. Basically, a jet engine is considered to have a somewhat constant thrust with increase in TAS as compared to piston-engine aircraft which have a sharp drop in thrust with increasing TAS.

Total Pressure -The pressure actually felt by an object moving through the air. Total pressure would be slightly greater than static conditions would be.

Transonic Speed -A speed at which an aircraft will have both subsonic and supersonic air-flows around the wings or fuselage.

True Airspeed -True airspeed is the true speed of the airplane relative to the air.

Tuck Under -Tuck under is the tendency of the airplane to pitch down during acceleration as shock waves form on the wing causing flow separation. The resultant loss of lift locally over the wing changes the location of the center of pressure (center of lift) which, in turn, affects the trim required when accelerating at high Mach numbers.

Unbalance Field Length -The condition where the takeoff distance and accelerate-stop distance are not equal.

Vortex Generators - Airfoil-like small surfaces protruding into the airstream which reduce buffeting at high flight speeds.

Yaw Damper -A system that automatically counteracts yaw.

CHAPTER THIRTY-ONE

SUMMER AND WINTER OPERATIONS

SUMMER OPERATIONS

Summertime and the living is HOT! The sun, heat, humidity and thunderstorms create an environment which can be very difficult for airline crews. Nature's forces combine to cause failures in both men and machinery.

Thunderstorms, hail, turbulence, tornadoes, and other meteorological offspring of summer weather will provide a challenge to us during the summer months. Summer is also the time for us to be concerned with high temperatures and the problems of overheated brakes and tires as well as the degradation of aircraft performance during all phases of flight. Let's look at some procedures and techniques that are particularly important during summer operations.

PREFLIGHT

Summertime preparation for flight, although more pleasant than a winter walk around, is as necessary, and just as time-consuming as it is in the winter months. The items that must receive extra attention change somewhat with the season.

Pitot heats and static ports, brake and tire condition and inflation, as well as aircraft skin and control surfaces, require renewed attention during the summer months. Wasps and even birds have been known to quickly build nests in parked aircraft, clogging static ports and intakes. Tire and brake condition becomes more critical during the hot summer months. Heat is still THE most significant detriment to tire life.

REPORTS AND LOG ENTRIES

While checking the condition of lightning diverters on the radome, wings, and tail, look for other evidence of lightning strikes and hail damage. Dents and other evidence of loss of "aerodynamic cleanliness" are of special interest for the purposes of fuel conservation. Much needed are your reports and log entries of pressurized compartment leakage, as well as dents and other discrepancies.

RAMP AND RUNWAY HIGH TEMPERATURES

Actual temperatures out on the ramp and runway are often in excess of those reported for a particular airport. Strict adherence to weight and runway limitations is mandatory. Runway limitations become more critical during the summer months.

The ramp and runway surface becomes soft; more employees, passengers and terminal spectators appear in the open; more carts, equipment and light aircraft seem to be around; and more windows are open. All this means that there is a greater exposure to jet engine blast and noise, especially at the smaller airports. So, please review and adhere to published procedures in the appropriate flight manuals regarding thrust limitations and noise abatement procedures. Extra care in these areas, especially in the summer months, will save dollars and enhance our reputation as a good neighbor.

Under the summer sun, taxiways and runways reach egg-frying temperatures during the day, followed by nighttime cooling which leads to accelerated surface breakdown. This means loose asphalt chunks to be reported; airport repair crews and vehicles to be avoided; and heat-softened tar to be written up and cleaned from landing gear and wheel well components. And there is the ever-present yellow tractor/mower cutting grass right alongside runways and taxi strips.

HOT BRAKES AND TIRES

Brakes and tires that appreciate kind treatment during the cooler months demand it when the mercury climbs up toward the triple digits. Increased heat accumulation calls for longer cooling periods. Good pilot technique can reduce total brake/landing costs by over a million dollars a year, cut delays due to brake and tire changes, and add a measure of safety to the operation. Flight crews can help a great deal by remembering that spoilers and reverse thrust are most effective at high speed, brakes are most effective at low speed, and those first taxiway turnoffs are expensive.

Passengers too, appreciate kind treatment in the form of a crisp, pre-cooled passenger cabin - not to mention the comfort of a ride that is relaxing: and free from turbulence.

PASSENGER COMFORT

Passengers too, appreciate kind treatment in the form of a crisp, pre-cooled passenger cabin – not to mention the comfort of a ride that is relaxing and free from turbulence.

THUNDERSTORMS

Thunderstorms present the most obvious summer weather hazards. The thunderstorm season in the latitudes that bracket the United States, arrives in late spring, when the temperatures rise, and continues until early fall.

THUNDERSTORMS AND SQUALL LINES

There is no reliable method by which a pilot can foretell whether a given thunderstorm is truly hazardous to flight. There are certain signals that indicate an individual storm is especially dangerous, of course. We know to avoid storms with continuous lightning; hooked scalloped or pointed echoes; and those with unusually great vertical development or rainfall. But we also know that these signals can appear and disappear in time intervals of only a few minutes, and this is indicative of the rapid changes of severity possible in these storms. We need to be reminded of the violent winds and wind shears generated beneath a potent thunderstorm. In short, our respect for the truly awesome forces generated by these storms has been renewed.

Meteorologists can forecast thunderstorm areas along with an overall assessment of severity prior to actual storm development. They cannot forecast an individual storm or cell until after it has appeared, and it is largely a matter of radar tracking and measurement.

Squall lines are a different breed of cat. Thunderstorms that are a part of a squall line tend to be more violent than "area" or air-mass thunderstorms. Line storms can form almost anywhere, but they are commonly found in the warm sector of a wave cyclone about 50 to 300 miles in advance of a cold front. Commonly called pre-frontal squall lines, they are usually oriented parallel to the cold front and move in about the same manner as the cold front. It is the pre-frontal squall line that most often gives rise to tornadoes and damaging surface winds in the spring and fall seasons. Reaching their most violent stages in late afternoon and evening, pre-frontal squall lines often dissipate at night and reform the next day. They can be forecast more accurately than the air-mass variety of storm.

THE AVERAGE STORM CELL

It has been estimated that an average storm cell may contain some five hundred thousand tons of condensed water in the form of liquid droplets and ice crystals. In terms of energy, it has been calculated that a typical squall line thunderstorm dissipates several times the energy released by the Hiroshima or Nagasaki bombs.

HAIL

Large hail is most often found in association with thunderstorms containing strong updrafts, lots of moisture, and clouds of great vertical height. It is during the mature stage of the thunderstorm cycle when hail is most frequently encountered - usually between the 10,000 and 30,000-foot levels.

Hail of damaging size has been known to fall well outside of the storm cloud. It is especially hazardous to fly downwind of the storm cloud beneath the anvil overhang. When possible, divert around the storm on the upwind side. When one must fly to the lee of a thunderstorm, give it a wide berth, allowing at least 20 miles separation and be prepared for turbulence.

SUMMER TAKEOFF RISK

When analyzing the weather situation, don't overlook the departure phase of flight. Several aircraft have been thrust violently into the ground by unpredictable cells poised just off the departure end of the runway. The competent pilot knows that any penetration of a thunderstorm situation presents a calculated risk to be avoided if at all possible. Taking off into severe weather is definitely not recommended.

WEATHER AVOIDANCE

Familiarity with weather patterns before flight should enable a crew to achieve optimum weather avoidance profile during climb out and cruise. But don't allow complacency to enter the picture and have an effect on crew coordination and weather vigilance. Remember that even the best of weather forecasters have been humbled from time to time by freakish weather happenings.

DETERIORATION OF PERFORMANCE IN THE SUMMER

Here are some examples of ways in which high temperatures can affect performance:

1. An increased demand for cooling may cause an overworked APU to overheat or shutdown.
2. Fuel tanks will not find room for the maximum placarded quantity.
3. More thrust will be required to "break away" on soft parking ramps.
4. Tires and brakes become hot from rolling friction alone - not to mention from needed braking.
5. Heated air is thin. Takeoff performance is reduced as a result.
6. True airspeeds on takeoffs are higher. A rejected takeoff could require more stopping distance with increased exposure to overheated brakes, melted fuse plugs, and resultant flat tires.

RESTRICTIONS TO VISIBILITY

In the summer, rain, smoke, haze, and fog are all common over our system routes. When confronted with one of these obscurations, we must concern ourselves with distinction between horizontal, vertical and slant- range visibility. When the weather observer finds the sky totally obscured, he reports the vertical visibility into the obscuring phenomena as the ceiling. The RVR is, of course, the horizontal visibility. Neither of these reported visibilities tells the pilot on the glide slope at what altitude or distance out that the runway will become visible (the slant-range visibility). In rain, smoke, haze or fog, the pilot must be aware that his/her ceiling and visibility in the approach zone may well be less than reported. The transition from instrument to visual flight will normally occur at an altitude lower than the reported ceiling whenever the sky is reported as obscured. The slant-range visibility to the runway is often less than reported RVR in the presence of a visibility restriction.

VISUAL ILLUSIONS

An awareness of those conditions which produce illusory phenomena during the approach phase of flight is of particular importance in the summer with more frequent VFR approaches. Obstructions to vision - haze, smoke, even glare and darkness - cause the illusion that the aircraft is higher than it actually is.

The same illusion is caused by dimmer-than-normal runway lights, approach zone terrain sloping upward toward the threshold, and an upsloping or shorter-than-normal runway. Exceptionally clear air, bright runway lighting, and downward sloping terrain to the runway threshold, cause the opposite visual illusion. In addition, rain on the windshield causes objects to appear lower (aircraft to appear higher) by as much as 200 feet at one mile. A complacent pilot may be prone to overlook or disregard altimeter cross checks, altitude callouts, and instrument indications during VFR flight under these illusionary conditions. Flight crews should minimize illusions and their effects by flying precision approaches whenever possible.

LOW LEVEL WIND SHEAR

There is nothing new about the phenomenon we call wind shear. It has been with us for years, we have all felt its effect, and its recognition has always been of vital importance.

Research and published materials have greatly increased our knowledge and understanding of wind shear and how to cope with it, so for a change, let's discuss a few points regarding the anticipation and detection of this hazardous condition.

1. Anticipate and be alert for wind shear condition in departure or arrival areas if thunderstorms are in the vicinity. Under these conditions, large changes in direction and velocity can occur.
2. Check the latest available surface weather charts for frontal activity.

a) Determine the temperature difference across the front using surface reports within approximately 50 miles of the frontal zone. The greater this temperature difference, the stronger the front and the greater the probability of encountering a significant wind shear.

b) Look closely at the weather (if any) associated with the frontal zone. Thunderstorms, rain showers and other evidence of turbulent activity may serve to mask or impair recognition of the shear zone from the cockpit. Vertical currents, when encountered at the same time as horizontal wind shear, can be particularly disconcerting.

3. When a descent or climb is anticipated through a frontal zone at low levels, make the following checks:

a) Compare the reported wind direction and speed on both sides of the front to determine the probable pattern and intensity of the shear you may encounter.

b) Query the tower or approach control for any reports or other indications of unusually strong low level winds or turbulence not evident at ground level.

THUNDERSTORMS

During the thunderstorm season, it's time to review the conditions required for a thunderstorm to develop, the types of weather conditions associated with thunderstorms and some techniques to use for avoidance.

For a thunderstorm to develop the following conditions must be present: (1) sufficient water vapor; (2) unstable air; and (3) a lifting force.

First, let's consider how air obtains water vapor. As the air mass is transported from one area to another, moisture is absorbed due to evaporation. The amount of moisture a mass of air can absorb prior to the saturation point is dependent upon its temperature. The warmer the air, the more moisture it can hold. You can expect the greatest frequency of low ceilings, fog and precipitation in areas where prevailing winds have an over-water trajectory. If cool air is moving over a warm body of water you can expect showers to appear on the leeward side of the water. Also, if warm air is moving over a cold body of water you can expect fog to develop on the leeside.

For this scenario we want to consider the situation of cool air blowing over a warm area. It should be remembered that whenever cool/cold is stated in relation to warm/hot the temperatures are considered as relative to each other. Warm over cold or cold over warm is another way of saying stability. Stability can be further defined as how something (airplane, person or air) will react when its present condition is disturbed. Stable air, like a stable airplane, when disturbed will return to its original condition/course. This would be the condition of the atmosphere when we have warm air over cold. Unstable air, like an unstable airplane, when disturbed will go out of control and either never return to its original condition or return at such a rate that it will overshoot. Unstable air exists when we have cold air over warm. This unstable condition exists because the warm air wants to rise and the cold air wants to descend.

Now we have warm, moist, unstable air over land. The only condition we lack for a thunderstorm to develop is a lifting force. This is the disturbing force necessary to start the action. Lifting of this air can be caused by surface heating, converging winds, sloping terrain, a frontal surface, or any combination of these conditions. What needs to happen is for the warm air to move up to replace the cool air above and the cool air to start down.

This forced upward motion creates an initial updraft. As the air in this updraft cools, the moisture will condense and a cumulus cloud will begin to form. As the water vapor condenses, latent heat is released, partially offsetting the cooling. This allows the updraft to continue until it reaches a point where the air in the updraft is at the same temperature as the surrounding air. Once the temperatures are the same, the updraft ceases to exist and the droplets of water increase in size to the point where they start to fall. These descending water droplets drag air down with them causing a down draft co-existing with the updraft.

As rain starts to fall, the cell has entered into the mature stage. During the mature stage, the thunderstorm packs just about every known aviation weather hazard into one vicious bundle. These hazards are tornados, turbulence, icing, hail, low ceilings and visibilities, lightning and wind shear. Although all of these hazards do not exist in each thunderstorm, the crew can expect to encounter turbulence, icing, lightning and wind shear, to some degree, in all thunderstorms.

What are the vital statistics of a thunderstorm? First, the storm can measure from less than five miles to more than thirty miles in diameter with cloud bases ranging from a few hundred feet in moist climates to 10,000 feet or higher in drier climates. The tops can range from a nominal of 25,000 to 45,000 feet to altitudes exceeding 65,000 feet. The duration of the storm depends on its severity with a life cycle from as low as twenty minutes to as long as 1.5 hours with lines of storms lasting for several hours. The up and down draft's vertical speed may exceed 6,000 feet per minute and, when in the close proximity of each other, will create strong vertical shear. Combined with these statistics are possible roll clouds on the leading edge, the wind shear turbulence area and the ground based gust front. All of which create a formidable threat to aviation.

So far, we have reviewed the ingredients necessary for a thunderstorm to develop and the hazards associated with these storms. Next, we will consider some techniques to use when confronted with the requirement to operate in or through thunderstorm areas.

Airborne Weather Avoidance Radar is, as its name implies, for avoiding severe weather - NOT for penetrating it. The decision whether to fly into an area of radar echoes depends on echo intensity, spacing between echoes and the capabilities of you and your aircraft.

Remember that the weather radar detects only precipitation drops; it does not detect minute cloud droplets. Therefore, you may be in instrument conditions with no radar return indicated on the radarscope. Because radar detects precipitation drops, the size of the return will depend on the amount of rainfall. Meteorologists have determined that the greatest rainfall rates are in thunderstorms. This means that the significant return you note on the radar (red area on color radars) is the center of the thunderstorm and should be avoided.

There are some limitations on the use of the radar, which, depending on the situation may be severe. First of all, the radar is limited in its ability to "see through" a thunderstorm. Therefore, an aircrew never really knows what lies behind the closest cell or cells depicted on the radarscope. Because of this, a crew could unknowingly, fly into a blind canyon with no way out. This is especially true when penetrating a line of thunderstorms. This limitation emphasizes the need for avoidance as compared to "threading the needle" when flying in thunderstorm areas.

Next is the short-range resolution of the present radars. At short ranges, it is difficult to accurately determine the storm's intensity and exact position. Due to this limitation, the crew should use a higher range scale, have the correct ground track established and concentrate on the conditions further down track.

The last limitation to be covered is tilt management. Effective tilt management is the single, most important key to more informative weather radar displays. Poor tilt management can have the radar scanning the wrong area at the wrong time causing the crew to fly into a thunderstorm.

Here is a list of some DOs and DON'Ts of thunderstorms flying as provided by the FAA Aviation Weather Manual:

1. Don't land or takeoff in the face of an approaching thunderstorm. The visible thunderstorm cloud is only a portion of a turbulent system whose updrafts and downdrafts often extend far beyond the visible cloud. Severe turbulence can be expected up to twenty miles from severe thunderstorms decreasing to about ten miles in less severe storms. Therefore, "approaching" is loosely defined as being within twenty miles of a storm.
2. Don't attempt to fly under a thunderstorm; even if you can see through to the other side.

3. Don't try to navigate, either visually or by airborne radar, through thunderstorms covering .6 or more of an area.
4. Don't fly without airborne radar into a cloud mass containing scattered, embedded thunderstorms.
5. Do avoid, by at least twenty miles, any thunderstorm identified as severe or giving an intense radar echo.
6. Do clear the top of a known or suspected severe thunderstorm by at least 1,000 feet altitude for each 10 knots of wind at the cloud top.
7. Do remember that bright and frequent lightning indicates a severe thunderstorm.
8. Do regard as severe any thunderstorm with tops 35,000 feet or higher whether the top is visually sighted or determined by radar.

Finally, never regard any thunderstorm as "light". Avoidance is the best policy.

We have reviewed how to build a thunderstorm, the hazards associated with a thunderstorm and some additional techniques to consider when confronted by a thunderstorm. Experience and knowledge should convince even the bravest pilot that a thunderstorm should be regarded as a threat, regardless of its "intensity". You should think about that!

SAFETY CONCERNS DURING WINTER OPERATIONS

It has been years since the Air Florida tragedy at Washington National Airport. Many of the environmental hazards and operational circumstances that existed at that time continue to be unwelcome aspects of our winter operations today. Contributory factors concluded by the National Transportation Safety Board include the following:

- The flight crew had limited experience in jet transport winter operations.
- The aircraft was improperly deiced by another carrier's personnel who did not follow their own company's procedures.
- Neither the Air Florida maintenance representative who was responsible for the proper accomplishment of deicing/anti-icing nor the Captain, who was responsible for assuring that the aircraft was free from ice or snow, verified that the aircraft was clean before pushback.
- The flight was delayed, awaiting clearance, for 49 minutes after deicing before initiation of takeoff.
- The flight crew did not use anti-ice during ground operations or takeoff.
- The EPR gauge readings were erroneous due to ice blocked PT2 probes.

- The F/O expressed concern that something was "not right" four (4) times during the takeoff roll, but the Captain took no action to abort the takeoff.
- Although the flight crew initiated pitch control, they did not add <u>thrust in time</u> to prevent impact.

FAR 121.629, Operation in Icing Conditions requires that:

a) No person may dispatch or release an aircraft, continue to operate an aircraft enroute, or land an aircraft when in the opinion of the pilot in command or aircraft dispatcher (domestic and flag carriers only), icing conditions are expected or met that might adversely affect the safety of the flight.

b) No person may take off an aircraft when frost, snow, or ice is adhering to the wings, control surfaces, or propellers of the aircraft.

It is clear that the ultimate responsibility for this determination rests with the pilot in command of the aircraft. Just how the Captain is to go about making this determination is the subject of considerable discussion. Reference material on the subject of aircraft icing and winter operations procedures and cautions are endless, but few venture into the discretionary arena as to how a crewmember in the cockpit can ascertain that he/she does, indeed, have a clean airplane. There is no one answer due to the variety of environmental factors that allows one method to be valid in one case and unsatisfactory in another.

FAA Advisory Circular (AC 20-117) states:

"The consensus of the aviation community and the conclusion reached by the FAA is that the only method of assuring flight safety following ground operations in conditions conducive to aircraft icing, is by either close inspection prior to takeoff to ascertain that critical aircraft components are clean (free of ice, frost, or snow formations) or a determination that any formations are not adhering to critical surfaces and will blow off in the early stages of takeoff roll."

This is qualified somewhat, further on in the Advisory Circular:

"The fact that it is impractical for an aircraft crewmember to disembark at the end of a runway and perform pre-takeoff inspections, means that the crewmember should perform that inspection from the best vantage point available from within the aircraft. The crewmember may elect to open windows, doors, or hatches to improve the view, but in many aircraft even this is impractical. In the darkness of night the crewmember must rely upon wing and other aircraft illumination lights that may not provide sufficient reflection to make appropriate visual observations. The crewmember may, where practical, call upon the assistance of qualified ground personnel. If under any circumstance, the pilot in command cannot ascertain that the aircraft is clean, takeoff should not be attempted."

In practice, a clean aircraft determination is a judgmental assessment based on the flight crews' seasoned visual observations, professional experience, knowledge of the elements, reliance on trained ground personnel and procedures, and heavily influenced by an understanding of aerodynamic lift and flight control dynamics.

Visual observations required recognition of the various ice forms and their characteristics. These states are generally classified as clear, rime or frost.

Clear ice is generally smooth and glassy in appearance. It sometimes has a rough appearance when mixed with solid precipitation and it adheres very firmly to surfaces and is difficult to remove.

Rime ice is ordinarily relatively rough in appearance and milky white in color. It is less compact than clear ice and does not adhere to surfaces as strongly.

Frost has a light, whitish, crystalline structure and frequently forms on parked aircraft when the temperature falls below 0 degrees C. Frost usually forms in a thin coating.

Although extra care and attention may be required to deice/anti-ice an aircraft with clear ice, all ice forms constitute hazards which affect the aircraft's performance characteristics and must be removed before takeoff. Even a thin coating of frost can cause a 5 to 10 percent increase in stall speed.

Contamination at the wing leading edge or along the upper profile surface results in a sharp reduction in the maximum lift capabilities of an efficient profile. A rough surface can reduce lift by 50%. This increases stalling speed by 30%.

What about past experience? Should we not be able to use years of experience for guidance? We can to a certain degree. Experience can tell us when the contamination is sufficient to cause an accident or serious incident.

But, when a successful takeoff is made with no apparent effect of contamination, we have no experience to tell us how much the margin before stall or loss of control has deteriorated. It is easy in such instances to conclude that the contamination effect was zero and gain the false impression that deicing would have been a waste of time. The truth is that <u>there is always some effect of wing contamination.</u> The question is only whether it is sufficient to cause an accident.

It is not advisable to use the false "no-effect" experience as an excuse for neglecting deicing. If you do, you may one day experience the real danger of contamination. Many general aviation and air transport pilots who have fallen for this temptation have later shared their experience with accident investigators. Others have not been so fortunate. The following examples of accidents and incidents illustrate what can happen:

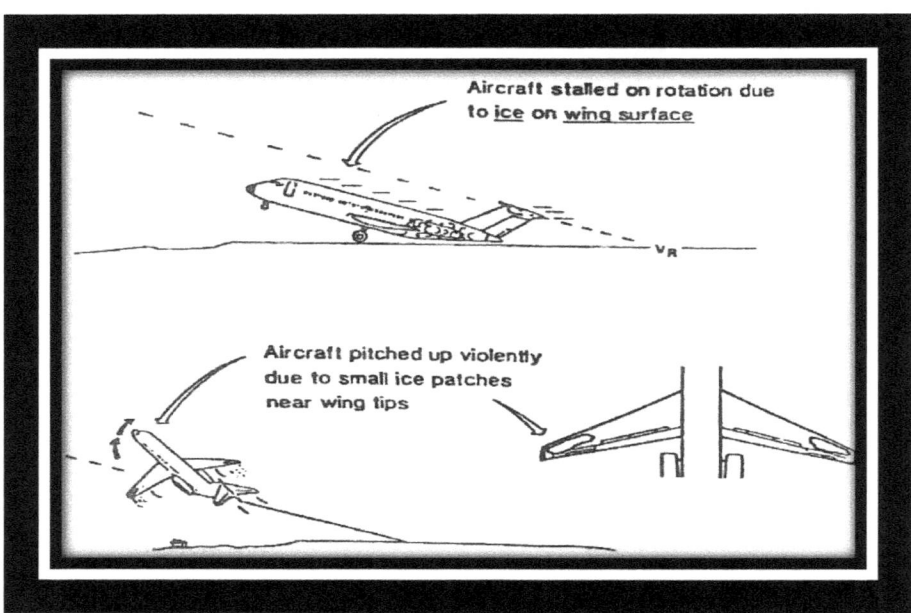

Aircraft rolled 45° after lift off due to ice on one flap (picked up while reversing in dry snow)

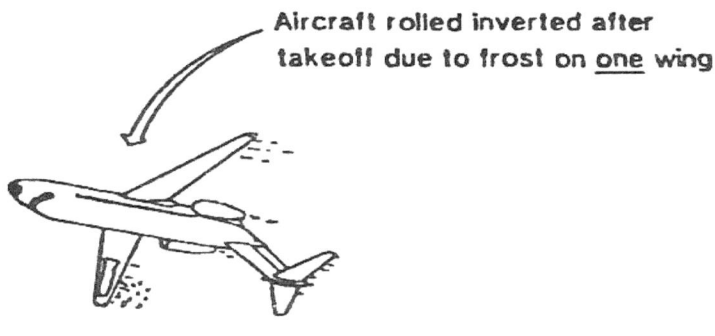

Aircraft rolled inverted after takeoff due to frost on <u>one</u> wing

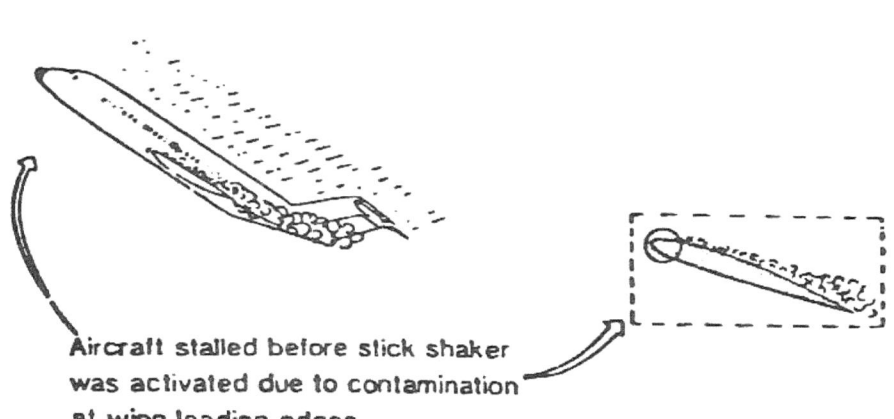

Aircraft stalled before stick shaker was activated due to contamination at wing leading edges

WINTER OPERATING REMINDERS

During preflight, check to see that the airplane is free of snow, ice or frost. When in doubt, follow recommended snow, ice, or frost removal procedures...KEEP IT CLEAN!

DO NOT assume snow will blow off the wings; a layer of ice could be under the snow.

Anti-icing/deicing procedures should be followed whenever they are needed... THERE IS NO SET RULE REGARDING FREQUENCY OF ANTI-ICING/DEICING.

TAXI

Maintain distance GREATER THAN NORMAL between airplanes while taxiing on ice or snow covered taxi and runway surfaces...blown snow and slush CAN ADHERE to YOUR AIRPLANE.

DO NOT use reverse thrust on snow or slush covered ramps, taxiways or runways unless ABSOLUTELY NECESSARY. If reverse thrust is used during taxi, the airplane (especially the leading edges) must be carefully re-inspected for accumulation of snow, slush, ice and frost.

Taxi with FLAPS UP if taxi route is through slush or standing water in low temperatures. Do not accomplish takeoff checklist until flaps are extended.

During icing conditions, periodically run up the engines to as HIGH a thrust setting as practicable (see AFM for appropriate procedures for your particular aircraft) ...this is necessary to provide sufficient energy for icing protection thereby REDUCING the possibility of ICE ACCUMULATION on ENGINE PROBES.

During icing conditions, turn ENGINE ANTI-ICE ON IMMEDIATELY after engine start.

As necessary, verify that the airplane is FREE of snow or ice before moving into position for takeoff.

TAKEOFF PROCEDURES

DO NOT use reduced thrust for takeoff during icing conditions or when runway is contaminated with snow, ice, slush, or standing water.

DO accomplish an engine run-up to as high a thrust as possible and check for STABLE engine operation BEFORE brake release.

After takeoff EPR has been set, DO check to see that it is in agreement with N1 and other cockpit indications are normal.

DO rotate smoothly and normally (not to exceed 3 degrees per second) at VR...NOT BEFORE

DESCENT AND LANDING

ANTICIPATE the need for engine/nacelle and/or wing anti-ice at all times, especially DURING descent.

CLOUDS ARE considered visible moisture when visibility is less than one mile.

OBSERVE Aircraft Operations Manual minimum Nl limits during DESCENT when anti-icing systems are used.

If available, arm the AUTOBRAKE and AUTOSPOILER systems before landing.

DEPLOY speed brakes IMMEDIATELY after main gear contact runway.

Lower nose wheel to the runway IMMEDIATELY as the speed brakes and thrust reversers are being actuated.

DO NOT hold nose gear off runway.

Apply brakes smoothly and symmetrically with moderate-to-firm pressure UNTIL a safe stop is ASSURED.

LET THE ANTI-SKID SYSTEM DO ITS WORK.

BE PREPARED for possible downwind drift on slippery runways with a crosswind when using reverse thrust.

DO NOT ATTEMPT to turn off the runway until speed is reduced to a PRUDENT level.

NO ONE GETS READY FOR AN EMERGENCY IN A MOMENT. WHAT A PERSON DOES IN AN EMERGENCY IS DETERMINED BY WHAT HE/SHE HAD BEEN DOING REGULARLY FOR A LONG TIME.

A REVIEW OF FAA AC20-117

Over a twenty year span, icing accidents accounted for 1.1% of total takeoff accidents. This may not sound significant, but consider this: these accidents account for 4.4% of fatal takeoff accidents or 2.3% of all fatalities from accidents.

Wind tunnel and flight tests have been conducted on leading edge and upper wing surfaces and the results have been dramatic. Ice, frost, and/or snow accumulations on these surfaces that may amount to no more than the thickness and roughness of course sandpaper can reduce wing lift by as much as 30% and increase drag by 40%, according to AC 20-117. Naturally, this would reduce controllability and will increase the stall speed significantly.

So what constitutes ice contamination or, better yet, is there an acceptable amount of ice or frost contamination where I may still be safe and legal to fly? What does the flight manual say? What does the company say? Finally, what does the FAA say?

It is safe to say that FARs 121.629, 135.227, and 91.209 define what is legal and what the FAA says is acceptable when it comes to taking off with an accumulation of ice, snow or frost. The "clean wing concept" (even "clean aircraft concept") makes it a requirement that takeoff not be attempted should there be ANY adhering of snow, ice and/or frost to the critical components of an aircraft. Safe to say, this is company policy, too.

Many factors influence the formation and accumulation (with resulting surface roughness) of ice, snow and/or frost. Some environmental factors include:

- Precipitation Type and Rate
- Ambient Temperature
- Relative Humidity
- Wind Velocity and Direction
- Solar Radiation

Some man-made factors include:

- Aircraft Surface Temperature
- Aircraft Component Inclination Angle, Contour, and Surface Roughness
- Operation of Aircraft or Surrounding Equipment on Snow, Slush or Wet Surfaces
- Deicing Fluid Presence, Type, and Mixture Ratio

From the list of variable factors mentioned above you should be able see that it is impossible to guarantee that just because you've deiced your aircraft, that icing-type contamination won't occur before you takeoff or that you can be assured of any predetermined period of time you will be free of ice. The only method of making certain that your aircraft is free of contaminates prior to takeoff is by visually inspecting your flight control and lift surfaces immediately before takeoff to the maximum extent possible. Conducting pre-takeoff inspection as it should be done requires the pilot in command to be knowledgeable of ground deicing procedures, that the ground deicing process was conducted in a thorough and uniform manner, and that critical surfaces or components not in view during pre-takeoff inspection will also be clean.

Some suggested practices for pilots to assure they are complying with the clean aircraft concept are:

- Be knowledgeable of the adverse effects of surface roughness on aircraft performance and flight characteristics.
- Be knowledgeable of ground deicing and anti-icing practice and procedures being used on your aircraft whether this service is being performed by your own company, a service contractor, or a fixed-base operator.

- Do not allow deicing or anti-icing until you are familiar with the ground deicing practices and quality control procedures of the service organization.
- Be knowledgeable of critical areas of your aircraft and assure these areas are properly deiced and anti-iced, proper precautions are being taken during the deicing process to avoid damage to aircraft components, and proper preflight inspections are performed even though this is also the responsibility of other organizations or personnel.
- Be knowledgeable of ice protection system function, capabilities, limitations, and operation.
- Perform additional preflight inspections related to deicing or anti-icing as necessary or required.
- Be aware that no one can accurately determine the time of effectiveness of a freezing point depressant deicing or anti-icing treatment because of the many variables that influence this time.
- Be knowledgeable of the variables that can reduce time of effectiveness and their general effects.
- Assure that deicing or the anti-icing treatment is performed at the last possible time prior to taxi to takeoff position.
- Do not start engines until it has been ascertained that ice deposits are removed. Ice particles shed from rotating components under centrifugal and aerodynamic forces can be lethal.
- Be aware that certain operations may produce recirculation of ice crystals, snow or moisture.
- Be aware that operations in close proximity to other aircraft can induce snow, other ice particles, or moisture to be blown onto critical aircraft

- components, or allow dry snow to melt and refreeze.
- Do not take off if snow or slush is observed splashing onto critical areas of the aircraft, such as wing leading edges, during taxi.
- Always perform pre-takeoff inspections just prior to takeoff.
- Do not take off if positive evidence of a clean aircraft cannot be ascertained.

With all of this in mind, the decision to takeoff remains the responsibility of the pilot in command.

Airbus 330 The Ultimate Guide for Pilots

UNDERWING FROST

While you are aware of the impact made by upper wing and/or leading edge surface ice, snow and/or frost accumulation, let's check into something somewhat less understood. This type of ice contamination can occur in above freezing weather situations which could cause problems if your particular airport usually has no need for deicing equipment or the equipment has been deactivated for the summer. While we're sure that there isn't a spec of upper wing surface that was missed in your preflight, let's look a bit closer into underwing frost contamination.

Where would you expect to find underwing icing? Well, just like upper wing icing, critical surface temperatures are usually found in the area of integral wing fuel tanks due to the materials and fluids involved. This type of contamination usually is a factor after a long cruise (where the fuel in the wing tanks becomes cold soaked to below freezing temperatures) and a normal descent into a region of high humidity. Frost will probably form during the ground turn-around time and tends to quickly re-form even after being removed. This does NOT rule out ice/frost forming elsewhere/anywhere, however.

An excerpt from AC 20-117 bears repeating here. It states: "Many aircraft in service today (generally large aircraft) are permitted by maintenance manuals to be dispatched for flight with slight amounts of frost adhering to fuel tank areas of wing undersurfaces. Maintenance manuals of such aircraft specify limits of frost thickness (generally between 1/8" and 3/8") depending upon the aircraft characteristics." Keep in mind that there is no FAA certification for this practice and this is not an approved practice found in a <u>flight</u> manual. For this reason, underwing frost should be removed. If practical, the surface should be anti-iced.

Just what will be the impact of a rough surface on the underwing portion of our wing? Frost initially forms as individual grains about 0.004 of an inch in diameter, but once it has started to form, it grows quickly and is usually larger, about 0.010 of an inch. Even a slight surface roughness can have significant effects on stall speed and power required to achieve or to sustain flight. Available test data on underwing icing/frost build-up does not indicate significant effect on lift, but it will increase drag and thereby <u>decrease</u> climb gradient capability. See Figure 1 for the impact of frost and/or ice on the second segment climb limits for three different aircraft types.

Obviously, some wing designs are more sensitive to underwing frost than others.

In summary, just as there are two sides to every coin, remember to keep in mind that there are two sides to every wing and conduct a thorough preflight for ice build-up this winter.

HYDROPLANING

When icing and rain conditions are present, hydroplaning is a common phenomenon. During these conditions, the pilot should remain vigilant during takeoffs, aborted takeoffs and landings. I will briefly explain the three different types of hydroplaning (dynamic, viscous and rubber reversion) below.

Dynamic Hydroplaning

Dynamic hydroplaning occurs when the standing water on a runway is not displaced from under the tire at a rate fast enough to allow the tire to make contact over its complete footprint area. This type of hydroplaning can be either partial (Figure 1) with a portion of the tire still in contact with the runway surface, or total (Figure 2) with the tire fully detached from the ground surface.

During total dynamic hydroplaning, wheel spin-down occurs and wheel rotation can stop completely. Minimum total hydroplaning speed in knots has been found to be nine times the square root of tire inflation pressure in pounds per square inch or V= square root of 9 x p (p=pressure). Partial dynamic hydroplaning can occur at considerably lower speeds.

Figure 1

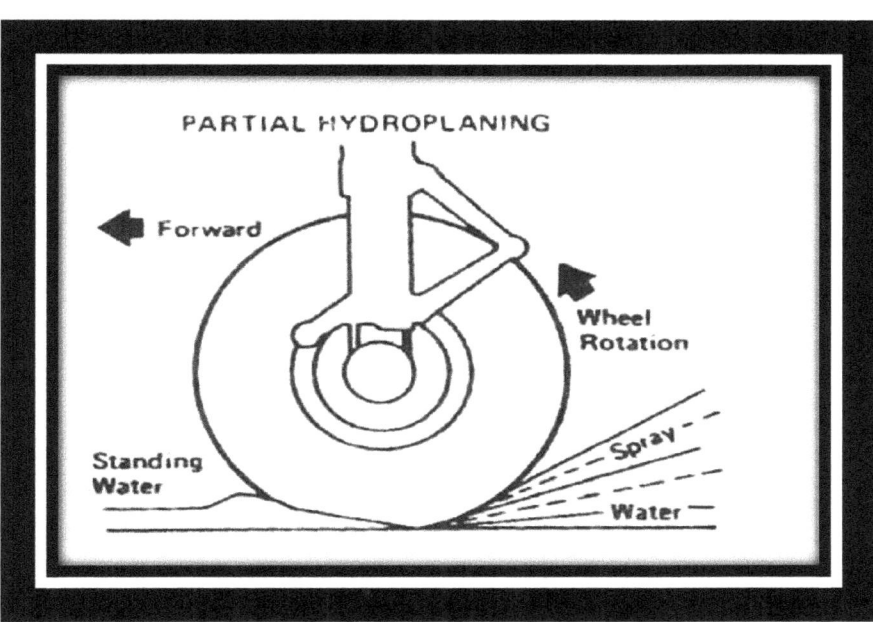

Figure 2

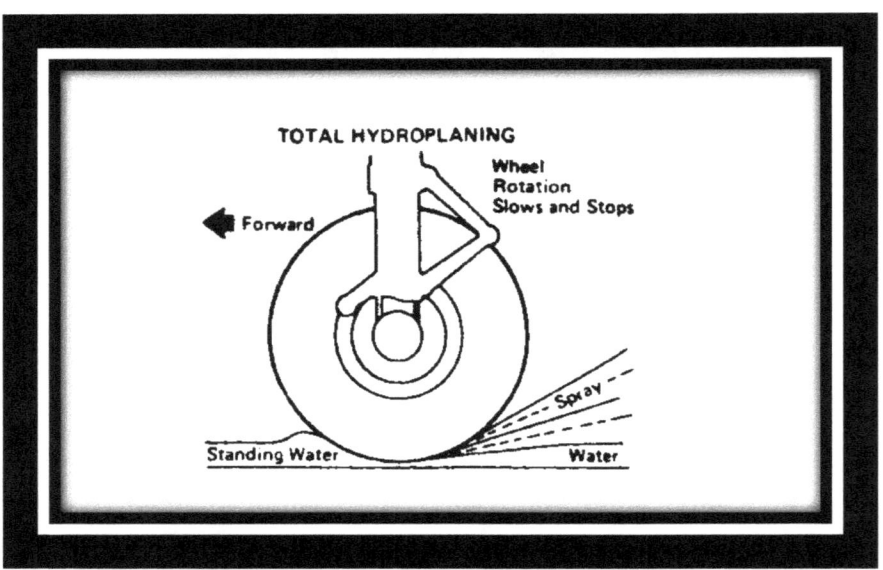

Viscous Hydroplaning

Viscous hydroplaning is defined as due to fluid of a viscosity higher than that of plain water. Thick fluids such as slush or water mixed with dust, rubber particles, oil, etc., are not as readily displaced by the tires. For this reason, viscous hydroplaning can occur at very low speeds and is probably the most hazardous of all types.

There are several techniques that can be used to lessen the possibility of entering a hydroplaning skid. Slower touchdown speeds and a firm landing minimize exposure time to hydroplaning. Earliest possible spoiler deployment assists wheel spin-up by increasing the weight on the wheels. Brakes should not be applied prior to wheel spin-up, and the anti-skid systems should be used. Once the airplane is on the runway and hydroplaning, maximum reverse thrust provides the most effective means of deceleration. Caution must be exercised during a crosswind rollout due to the tendency to weathercock.

RUBBER REVERSION

Rubber reversion hydroplaning is believed to be quite rare. It is due to friction-generated steam beneath the tire which causes the rubber to revert to its uncured state. It can occur on damp runways or when touchdown is made on a wet spot on a dry runway such that no wheel spin-up occurs.

MINIMIZING HYDROPLANING EFFECTS

Strict adherence to established operating procedures relative to approach and landing, followed by a "firm" touchdown rather than a "grease job" are important courses of action to follow.

Spoiler deployment, to get the aircraft weight on the wheels right away, is important. This action helps to prevent delayed wheel spin up. Monitor spoiler operation if spoilers are deployed automatically. See that they are extended immediately after the nose wheel touches the pavement.

Don't hold the nose wheel off. Land it without delay.

Apply reverse smoothly and evenly to all engines. Use the maximum recommended if conditions indicate the need. If the aircraft begins to weathervane into a crosswind, ease off on the reverse until the rudder becomes effective.

After nose wheel has contacted the runway and aircraft is tracking, increase reverse thrust. Apply brakes smoothly and symmetrically with moderate to firm steady pedal pressure. If hydroplaning conditions develop, the use of reverse thrust may be the most effective deceleration means available to the pilot. However, improper use of reverse thrust on wet slippery runways can be critical to directional control, especially during crosswind conditions. Avoid the use of nose wheel steering as long as possible. It is virtually useless on a wet runway until the speed is quite low. Often its use can create more problems than it corrects. Nose wheel tire pressures are lower than main gear tire pressures on most airplanes, and this allows the nose wheel to hydroplane long after the main gear wheels have stopped.

SUMMARY

In summary, the key factor in hydroplaning is <u>SPEED</u>. The water skier serves as good example of total hydroplaning. It can be easily seen that with no tire to runway contact, braking is reduced to practically zero levels. The loss in directional control may also be appreciated if it is realized that when the wheels are not in contact with the runway, any unbalanced forces on the aircraft-such as crosswinds-may induce an out-of-control situation.

CHAPTER THIRTY-TWO

OPTIMUM USE OF WEATHER RADAR

Best Possible Use of Weather Radar

In recent years, there have been a number of flights where passengers or crew suffered injuries due to severe turbulence. In some other instances, the aircraft structure was substantially damaged following a hailstorm encounter. Clearly adverse weather can pose a threat to the safe and comfortable completion of a flight, thus it needs to be detected and avoided in a timely manner.

WEATHER RADAR LIMITATIONS

Weather Radar Detection Capability

One of the weather radar limitations is that it indicates only the presence of liquid water. The consequence is that a thunderstorm does not have the same reflectivity over its altitude range because the quantity of liquid water in the atmosphere decreases with the altitude.

Yet, the convective cloud and associated threats may extend significantly above the upper detection limit of the weather radar (called "radar top"). This means that reflectivity is not directly proportional to level of risk that may be encountered. A convective cloud may be dangerous, even if the radar echo is weak. This is particularly true for equatorial overland regions where converging winds produce large scale uplifts of dry air. The resulting weather cells have much less reflectivity than mid-latitude convective cells. However, turbulence in or above such clouds may have a higher intensity than indicated by the image on the weather radar display. On the other hand, air close to the sea can be very humid. In this case, thermal convection will produce clouds that are full of water. These clouds will have a high reflectivity, but may not necessarily be a high threat.

Consequently, limitations of weather radars must be well understood and complemented by basic meteorological knowledge of the crew and, where possible, visual observation.

How To Make the Best Possible Use Of The Airborne Weather Radar

The weather radar is a tool for detecting, analyzing and avoiding adverse weather and turbulence. As with any other tool, adequate skills and the crew's involvement are needed in order to use it efficiently. In fact, the management of adverse weather still relies primarily on the crew to actively monitor the meteorological situation throughout the flight, and make a full use of the available technology:

1. Awareness of weather radar capabilities and limitations, according to the specificities outlined in the FCOM and the manufacturer's user guide.

2. Preflight briefing (knowledge of the route climatology and weather forecast – charts and online simulation) and during flight (update on weather information)

3. Adapted use of the weather radar, with the crew regularly assessing the range, gain and tilt, and making use of weather threat assessment functions when available in order to display an optimum weather radar picture on the ND.

4. Regular manual vertical and horizontal scanning by the crew to increase situation awareness.

5. Correct understanding of the radar image displayed.

6. Adequate strategic (mid-term) and tactical (short term) decision making for trajectory planning.

How to optimally tune the weather radar and manage flights in convective weather?

Flight Planning: The Importance of Weather Briefing and Weather Reports

Weather avoidance already starts in the briefing room before commencing the flight, with a thorough assessment of enroute weather and decisions on possible mitigation means. Before boarding, a weather briefing should reveal areas of predicted significant weather activity. Equally, this briefing should include the assessment of typical weather patterns in the area. For example: in the tropics, cumulonimbus intensity and development is greater at certain times of the day. The crew has the opportunity at this stage to plan a route to avoid active weather based on both the weather briefing and their knowledge of local climatology. Changing the flight route could be an option as well as taking additional fuel for enhanced strategic and tactical options in flight. Once airborne, the weather radar should be used and tuned regularly in combination with all available information, e.g. pre-flight briefing, pilot's knowledge and experience of the area's typicality, reported turbulence, updated weather reports... If possible, the weather information should be updated in flight regularly. Information sought by ATC of turbulence encounters are an additional means.

Weather Radar Antenna Tilt

Effective management of the antenna tilt along with an appropriate ND range selection, are key tools to obtaining an informative weather radar display on the ND. The ND might not display cells at aircraft flight level, only cells that are cut by the radar beam are shown. For this reason, the antenna tilt needs to be adjusted up and down regularly to scan weather ahead, and it needs to be adjusted to the ND range selection (except with the most recent radar models where this adjustment is made automatically).The flight crew needs to periodically scan:

Vertically, using the antenna tilt function

Horizontally, using the range change.

If available, the automatic mode should be used as the default mode (unless mentioned differently in the FCOM), for detection and initial evaluation of displayed weather. Then, if adverse weather is suspected (e.g. according to information gathered during the pre-flight briefing), manual control should be used regularly and actively to analyze the weather ahead.

Note: The automatic mode should be used as the default mode, for detection and initial evaluation of displayed weather. Then, manual control should be used periodically to analyze the weather.

Even when the tilt is adjusted automatically, pilots are advised to reverse to the manual mode "MAN" regularly in order to scan the immediate weather ahead. This action allows the crew to assess the vertical structure and expansion of convective clouds.

Factors that can affect the relevancy of the ND display and that should trigger a tilt adjustment is:

- A heading change

- An altitude change or even a regular flight profile change (e.g. from climb to cruise)

- The shape of thunderstorms

In the case of a change in heading or altitude, leaving the antenna tilt on Auto may induce a risk of overlooking weather or underestimating the severity of the weather. For example, at take-off or in climb, the tilt should be set up if adverse weather is expected above the aircraft.

Display Range Management

To maintain comprehensive situation awareness, the flight crew needs to monitor both the short-distance and long-distance weather. To this end, the Crew should select different ranges on the Pilot Monitoring (PM) and Pilot Flying (PF) ND.

To avoid threatening convective weather, the flight crew should make deviation decisions while still at least 40 NM away; therefore, the following ranges should be selected on the NDs:

Pilot Monitoring (PM) adjusts ranges to plan the long-term weather avoidance strategy (in cruise, typically 160 NM and below).

Pilot Flying (PF) adjusts ranges to monitor the severity of adverse weather, and decide on avoidance tactics (in cruise, typically 80 NM and below as required).

Gain Adjustment

The sensitivity of the receiver may vary from one type of radar system to another. In the CAL (AUTO) position, the gain is in the optimum position to detect standard convective clouds. Manual settings are also available and can be used to analyze weather. At low altitudes, reducing the gain might be justified for proper weather analysis. Due to increased humidity at lower levels, convective cells are usually more reflective and the weather radar display may have a tendency to show a lot of red areas. This can also be the case at higher altitude with significant positive ISA deviations in a very humid atmosphere (typically the Indian monsoon). In these cases, slowly reducing the gain allows the detection of threatening areas: most red areas slowly turn yellow; the yellow areas turn green and the green areas slowly disappear. The remaining red areas – (i.e. the red areas that are the last to turn yellow, are the most active parts of the cell and must be avoided). At high altitudes, water particles are frozen and clouds are less reflective. In this case, gain should be increased for threat evaluation purposes.

Turbulence and Weather Threats Detection

Turbulence can be difficult to predict, but signs such as frequent and strong lightning and/or the specific shape of clouds can alert the crew to the likely presence of severe turbulence. If necessary and when available (according to the standard of weather radar onboard), the TURB function can additionally be used to confirm the presence of wet turbulence up to 40 NM (or 60 NM depending on the radar standard). Remember that the TURB function needs humidity; therefore clear air turbulence will not be displayed. In addition, the flight crew may be alerted by visual cues provided by the latest generations of weather radars that offer weather threat assessment functions.

Avoidance Strategy

The flight crew needs to remain vigilant and active in using and tuning the weather radar in order to be able to initiate an avoidance maneuver as early as possible. Indeed, weather radar information becomes more intense as the aircraft gets nearer the convective weather zone, thus making avoidance decisions more difficult. For this reason, crews should consider a minimum distance of 40 NM from the convective cloud to initiate the avoidance maneuver. Once the decision to deviate course has been taken, it is preferable to avoid lateral performance instead of vertical avoidance. Indeed, vertical avoidance is not always possible (particularly at high altitude) due to the reduction of buffet and performance margins. In addition, some convective clouds may have a significant build-up speed that extends far above the radar visible top.

Lateral Avoidance

When possible, it is advisable to try to avoid a storm by flying on the upwind side of a cumulonimbus. Usually, there is less turbulence and hail upwind of a convective cloud.

The "area of threat" identified by the flight crew (e.g. a cumulonimbus cloud) should be cleared by a minimum of 20 NM laterally whenever possible. An additional margin may be applied in case the convective clouds are very dynamic or have a significant build-up speed.

If the aircraft trajectory goes between several convective clouds, if possible maintain a margin of at least 40 NM with the identified area.

Vertical Avoidance

Do not attempt to fly under a convective cloud, even when you can see through to the other side, due to possible severe turbulence, wind shear microbursts and hail. If an aircraft must fly below a convective cloud (e.g. during approach), then the flight crew should take into account all indications (visual judgement, weather radar, weather report, pilots report, etc.) before they take the final decision.

If overflying a convective cloud cannot be avoided, apply a vertical margin of 5,000 feet.

Note: If possible, it is preferable to perform lateral avoidance instead of vertical avoidance.

Regardless of how you locate a severe weather area – visual, by radar, or from a report – a key parameter to successful route planning and avoidance strategy is time. The weather radar, and enhanced models more particularly, can help you to analyze and understand distant weather accurately and evaluate weather scenarios from a distance. This system is a key tool to planning ahead to avoid last-minute decisions, and making a decision on circumnavigating a nasty convective cell with a comfortable safety margin. In addition to technology, you need to stay active in maintaining situation awareness throughout the flight. Regularly complement the radar images displayed by a manual vertical scan of surrounding cells, as well as gain and tilt adjustments as required. Last but not least, adhere to your knowledge of meteorology basics, local climatology and weather briefing to adopt the best course of actions, and navigate

Safely, effectively and comfortably to destination.

CHAPTER THIRTY-THREE

INTERCEPTION PROCEDURES

Interception Procedures

Intercepts during peacetime operations are vastly different than those conducted under increased states of readiness. The interceptors may be fighters or rotary wing aircraft. The reasons for aircraft intercept include, but are not limited to:

- o Identify an aircraft;
- o Track an aircraft;
- o Inspect an aircraft;
- o Divert an aircraft;
- o Establish communications with an aircraft
- When specific information is required (i.e., markings, serial numbers, etc.) the interceptor pilot(s) will respond only if, in their judgment, the request can be conducted in a safe manner. Intercept procedures are described in some detail in the paragraphs below. In all situations, the interceptor pilot will consider safety of flight for all concerned throughout the intercept procedure. The interceptor pilot(s) will use caution to avoid startling the intercepted crew or passengers and understand that maneuvers considered normal for interceptor aircraft may be considered hazardous to other aircraft
- All aircraft operating in US national airspace are highly encouraged to maintain a listening watch on VHF/UHF guard frequencies (121.5 or 243.0 MHz). If subjected to a military intercept, it is incumbent on civilian aviators to understand their responsibilities and to comply with ICAO standard signals relayed from the intercepting aircraft. Specifically, aviators are expected to contact air traffic control without delay (if able) on the local operating frequency or on VHF/UHF guard. Noncompliance may result in the use of force.

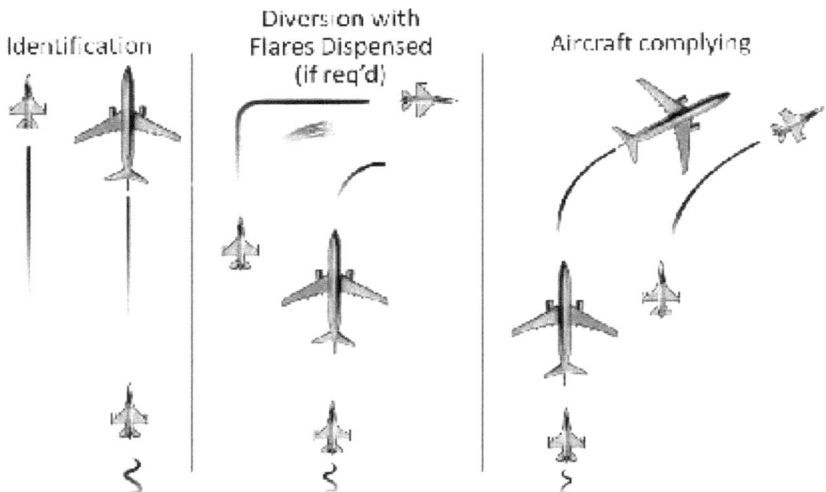

Intercept Phases

Approach Phase:

- As standard procedure, intercepted aircraft are approached from behind
- Typically, interceptor aircraft will be employed in pairs, however, it is not uncommon for a single aircraft to perform the intercept operation
- Safe separation between interceptors and intercepted aircraft is the responsibility of the intercepting aircraft and will be maintained at all times

Identification Phase:

- Interceptor aircraft will initiate a controlled closure toward the aircraft of interest, holding at a distance no closer than deemed necessary to establish positive identification and to gather the necessary information
- The interceptor may also fly past the intercepted aircraft while gathering data at a distance considered safe based on aircraft performance characteristics

Post Interception Phase:

An interceptor may attempt to establish communications via standard ICAO signals

- In time-critical situations where the interceptor is seeking an immediate response from the intercepted aircraft or if the intercepted aircraft remains non-compliant to instruction, the interceptor pilot may initiate a divert maneuver:
- The interceptor flies across the intercepted aircraft's flight path (minimum 500 feet separation and commencing from slightly below the intercepted aircraft altitude) in the general direction the intercepted aircraft is expected to turn
- The interceptor will rock its wings (daytime) or flash external lights/select afterburners (night) while crossing the intercepted aircraft's flight path
- The interceptor will roll out in the direction the intercepted aircraft is expected to turn before returning to verify the aircraft of interest is complying
- The intercepted aircraft is expected to execute an immediate turn to the direction of the intercepting aircraft
- If the aircraft of interest does not comply, the interceptor may conduct a second climbing turn across the intercepted aircraft's flight path (minimum 500 feet separation and commencing

from slightly below the intercepted aircraft altitude) while expending flares as a warning signal to the intercepted aircraft to comply immediately and to turn in the direction indicated and to leave the area
- o Note that NORAD interceptors will take every precaution to preclude the possibility of the intercepted aircraft experiencing jet wash/wake turbulence; however, there is a potential that this condition could be encountered

Law Enforcement Operations:

- Special law enforcement operations include in-flight identification, surveillance, interdiction, and pursuit activities performed in accordance with official civil and/or military mission responsibilities
- To facilitate accomplishment of these special missions, exemptions from specified sections of the CFRs have been granted to designated departments and agencies. However, it is each organization's responsibility to apprise ATC of their intent to operate under an authorized exemption before initiating actual operations
- Additionally, some departments and agencies that perform special missions have been assigned coded identifiers to permit them to apprise ATC of ongoing mission activities and solicit special air traffic assistance

Intercept and Escort:

- Based on SAR aircraft establishing visual and/or electronic contact with aircraft in difficulty
- If a bailout or crash occurs SAR can be conducted without delay
- Must be requested by a pilot in difficulty or a distress condition is declared

Intercept Signals

Series	Intercepting aircraft signals	Meaning	Intercepted Aircraft Responds	Meaning
1	**Day:** Rocking wings from a position slightly above and head of, and normally to the left of, the intercepted aircraft and, after acknowledgment, a slow level turn, normally to the left, on to the desired heading **Night:** Same and, in addition, flashing navigational lights at irregular intervals **NOTE:** Meteorological conditions or terrain may require the intercepting aircraft to take up a position slightly	You have been intercepted, follow me	**Aeroplanes:** **Day:** Rocking wings and following **Night:** Same and, in addition, flashing navigation lights at irregular intervals **Helicopters:** **Day or Night:** Rocking aircraft, flashing navigational lights at irregular intervals and following	Understood, will comply

	above and ahead of, and to the right of, the intercepted aircraft and to make the subsequent turn to the right **NOTE:** If the intercepted aircraft is not able to keep pace with the intercepting aircraft, the latter is expected to fly a series of race-track patterns and to rock its wings each time it passes to the intercepted aircraft			
2	**Day or Night:** An abrupt break-away maneuver from the intercepted aircraft consisting of a climbing turn of 90 degrees or more without crossing the line of flight of the	You may proceed	**Aeroplanes:** **Day or Night:** Rocking wings **Helicopters:** **Day or Night:** Rocking aircraft	Understood, will comply

	intercepted aircraft			
3	**Day:** Circling aerodrome, lowering landing gear and overflying runway in direction of landing or, if the intercepted aircraft is a helicopter, overflying the helicopter landing area **Night:** Same and, in addition, showing steady landing lights	Land at this aerodrome	**Aeroplanes:** **Day:** Lowering landing gear, following the intercepting aircraft and, if after overflying the runway landing is considered safe, proceed to land **Night:** Same and, in addition, showing steady landing lights (if carried) **Helicopters:** **Day or Night:** Following the intercepting aircraft and proceeding to land, showing a steady landing light (if carried)	Understood, will comply
4	**Day or Night:** Raising landing gear (if fitted) and flashing landing lights while passing over	Aerodrome you have designated is inadequate	**Day or Night:** If it is desired that the intercepted aircraft follow the intercepting aircraft to an alternate	Understood, follow me Understood, you may proceed

	runway in use or helicopter landing area at a height exceeding 300m (1000') but not exceeding 600m (2000') (in the case of a helicopter, at a height exceeding 50m (170') but not exceeding 100m (330') above the aerodrome level, and continuing to circle runway in use or helicopter landing area. If unable to flash landing lights, flash any other lights available		aerodrome, the intercepting aircraft raises its landing gear (if fitted) and uses the Series 1 signals prescribed for intercepting aircraft. If it is decided to release the intercepted aircraft, the intercepting aircraft uses the Series 2 signals prescribed for intercepting aircraft	
5	**Day or Night:** Regular switching on and off of all available lights but in such a manner as to be distinct from flashing lights	Cannot comply	**Day or Night:** Use series 2 signals prescribed for intercepting aircraft	Understood
6	**Day or Night:** Irregular flashing of all available lights	In distress	**Day or Night:** Use 2 signals prescribed for intercepting aircraft aircraft	Understood

Special Emergency (Air Piracy):

- A special emergency is a condition of air piracy, or other hostile act by a person(s) aboard an aircraft, which threatens the safety of the aircraft or its passengers
- The pilot of an aircraft reporting a special emergency condition should:
  - If circumstances permit, apply distress or urgency radio-telephony procedures including the details of the special emergency
  - If circumstances do not permit the use of prescribed distress or urgency procedures, transmit on the air/ground frequency in use at the time, as many as possible of the following elements spoken distinctly and in the following order:
    - Name of the station addressed (time and circumstances permitting)
    - The identification of the aircraft and present position
    - The nature of the special emergency condition and pilot intentions (circumstances permitting)
    - If unable to provide this information, use code words and/or transponder as follows:

Spoken Words: **TRANSPONDER SEVEN FIVE ZERO ZERO"** which means I am being hijacked/forced to a new destination

Transponder Setting: Mode 3/A, Code 7500

Code 7500 will never be assigned by ATC without prior notification from the pilot that the aircraft is being subjected to unlawful interference

The pilot should refuse the assignment of Code 7500 in any other situation and inform the controller accordingly

- Code 7500 will trigger the special emergency indicator in all radar ATC facilities

ATC will acknowledge and ask to confirm correct setting of 7500

If affirmative, or no reply is heard then ATC will not ask further questions but will flight follow, respond to pilot requests and notify appropriate authorities

If it is possible to do so without jeopardizing the safety of the flight, the pilot of a hijacked passenger aircraft, after departing from the cleared routing over which the aircraft was operating, will attempt to do one or more of the following things, insofar as circumstances may permit:

- Maintain a true airspeed of no more than 400 knots, and preferably an altitude of between 10,000 and 25,000'
- Fly a course toward the destination which the hijacker has announced

If these procedures result in either radio contact or air intercept, the pilot will attempt to comply with any instructions received which may direct the aircraft to an appropriate landing field or alter the aircraft's flight path off its current course, away from protected airspace

Visual Warning System (VWS)

The VWS signal consists of highly-focused red and green colored laser lights designed to illuminate in an alternating red and green signal pattern

These lasers may be directed at specific aircraft suspected of making unauthorized entry into the Washington, DC Special Flight Rules Area (DC SFRA) proceeding on a heading or flight path that may be interpreted as a threat or that operate contrary to the operating rules for the DC SFRA

The beam is neither hazardous to the eyes of pilots/aircrew or passengers, regardless of altitude or distance from the source nor will the beam affect aircraft systems

- If you are communicating with ATC, and this signal is directed at your aircraft, you are required to contact ATC and advise that you are being illuminated by a visual warning system
- If this signal is directed at you, and you are not communicating with ATC, you are advised to turn to the

- most direct heading away from the center of the DC SFRA as soon as possible
- Immediately contact ATC on an appropriate frequency, VHF Guard 121.5 or UHF Guard 243.0, and provide your aircraft identification, position, and nature of the flight
- Failure to follow these procedures may result in interception by military aircraft
- Further noncompliance with interceptor aircraft or ATC may result in the use of force

Pilots planning to operate aircraft in or near the DC SFRA are to familiarize themselves with aircraft intercept procedures

- This information applies to all aircraft operating within the DC SFRA including DOD, Law Enforcement, and aircraft engaged in aeromedical operations and does not change procedures established for reporting unauthorized laser illumination as published in FAA Advisory Circulars and Notices

Emergency Airborne Inspection of Other Aircraft:

Providing airborne assistance to another aircraft may involve flying in very close proximity to that aircraft

- Most pilots receive little, if any, formal training or instruction in this type of flying activity
- Close proximity flying without sufficient time to plan (i.e., in an emergency situation), coupled with the stress involved in a perceived emergency can be hazardous

The pilot in the best position to assess the situation should take the responsibility of coordinating the airborne intercept and inspection, and take into account the unique flight characteristics and differences of the category(s) of aircraft involved

Some of the safety considerations are:

- Area, direction and speed of the intercept;
- Aerodynamic effects (i.e., rotorcraft down-wash);
- Minimum safe separation distances;
- Communications requirements, lost communications procedures, coordination with ATC;
- Suitability of diverting the distressed aircraft to the nearest safe airport; and
- Emergency actions to terminate the intercept

Close proximity, inflight inspection of another aircraft is uniquely hazardous

- The pilot-in- command of the aircraft experiencing the problem/emergency must not relinquish control of the situation and/or jeopardize the safety of their aircraft
- The maneuver must be accomplished with minimum risk to both aircraft

Conclusion

If you are intercepted by a U.S. Military or law enforcement aircraft, immediately:

- Adhere to instructions relayed through the use of visual devices, visual signals, and radio communications from the intercepting aircraft
- Attempt to communicate with the intercepting aircraft and/or ATC on the emergency frequency 121.5/243.0 MHz, giving the identity and position of your aircraft and the nature of the flight
- If equipped with a transponder, squawk Mode 3/A code 7700, unless otherwise instructed by ATC
- If any instructions received by radio from any sources conflict with those given by the intercepting aircraft by visual or radio signals, request clarification while continuing to comply with the instructions given by the intercepting aircraft until positively released.

CHAPTER THIRTY-FOUR

TIPS AND PROCEDURES FOR PILOTS

TIPS AND PROCEDURES FOR PILOTS

Visibility must be reported at or above the published minimum

Regulations prohibit a pilot from beginning the final segment of an instrument approach procedure unless the latest weather report indicates that flight visibility is equal to, or more than, the visibility minimum published for that procedure.

Conversely, if you have already initiated the final approach segment, based on legal weather minimums and you receive a subsequent weather report of below minimums, you can consider the report as advisory, and continue the approach.

These rules are simple enough, but in practice, the determination of what part of the approach constitutes the "final segment" is sometimes confusing.

NON-PRECISION APPROACHES
(LOC, VOR, VORTAC, NDB, ETC)

The final approach segment is defined as a non-precision approach as beginning at the FINAL APPROACH FIX (FAF). This is usually identified by a Maltese cross on Jeppesen charts.

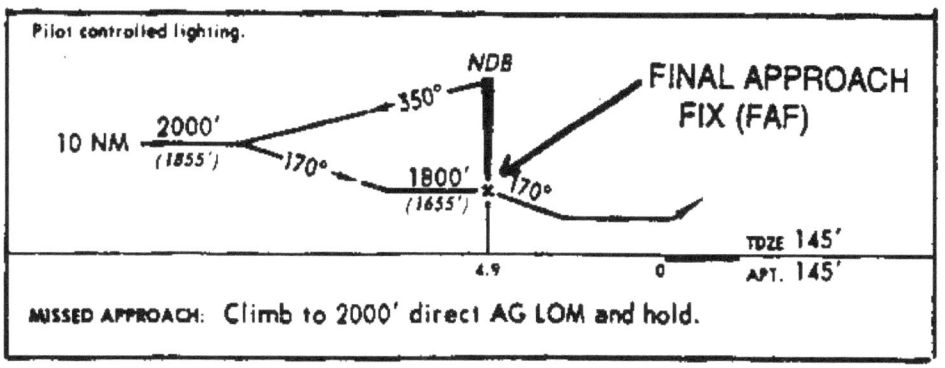

If no FAF depicted, the final approach segment begins at the final approach point (FAP). The Airman's Information Manual defines this as "the point, applicable only to a non-precision approach with no depicted FAF (such as an on-airport VOR), where the aircraft is established inbound on the final approach course from the procedure turn and where the final approach descent may be commenced. The FAP serves as the FAF and identifies the beginning of the final approach segment."

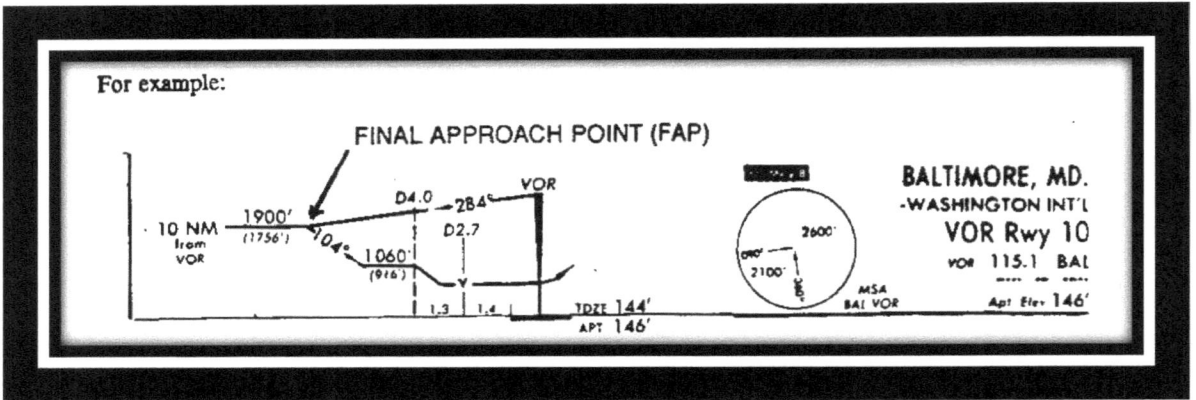

PRECISION APPROACHES

The final approach segment of an ILS approach as beginning at the intersection of the published Glide Slope Intercept Altitude (GSIA) and the Glide Slope. This is the point at which the Jeppesen approach profile view shows the horizontal flight path intercepting the glide slope. An aircraft on the glide slope, descending from a higher altitude, does not start the final approach segment until it passes through the GSIA.

EXAMPLES

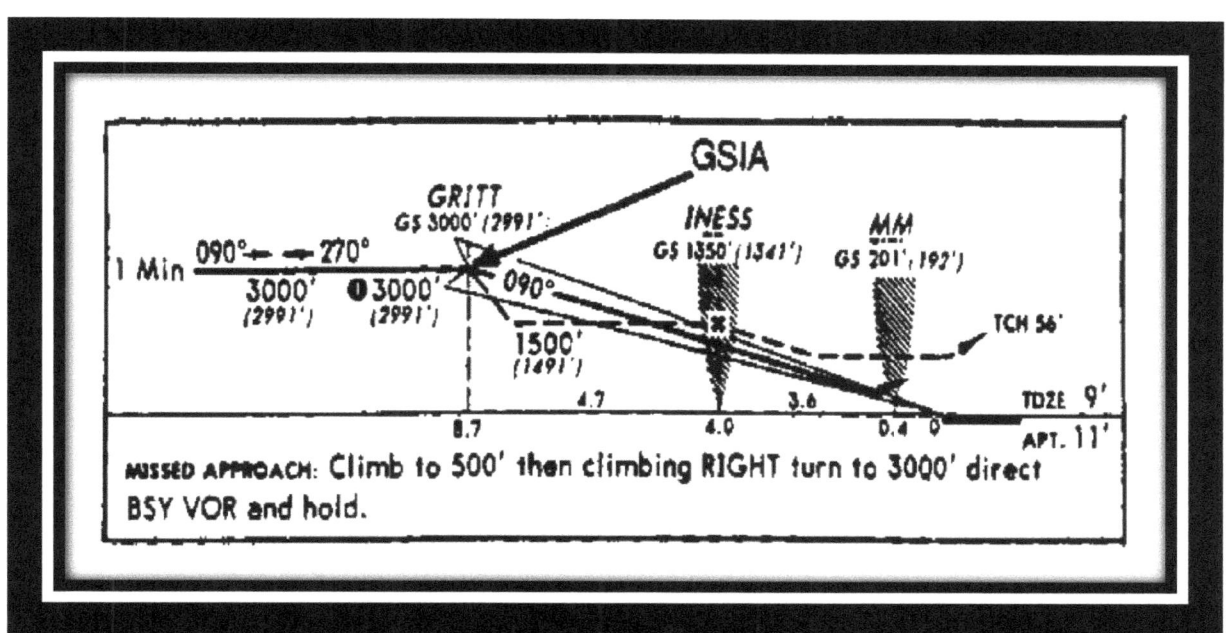

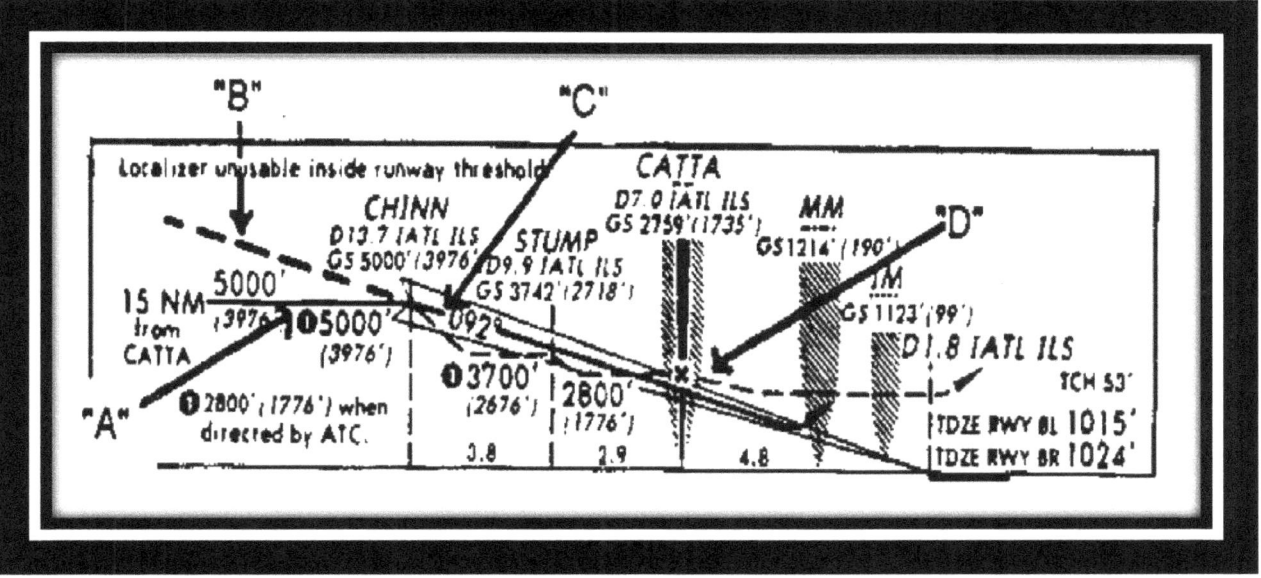

The following examples illustrate the application of these rules:

PRECISION

An aircraft at point "A" conducting a precision approach has not yet entered the final approach segment and could not legally continue past CHINN if the latest weather was reporting below published minimums. The same thing applies to an aircraft at point "B" even though he may be established on localizer and glide slope. NOTE: CHINN is the GSIA point. Under the same condition, an aircraft at point "C" could legally continue the approach even if a below minimum weather report was received.

NOTE: In the event that you are cleared by ATC for a 2800 foot G/S intercept, you are not on final approach segment until on glideslope.

NON-PRECISION

Similarly, an aircraft conducting a non-precision approach could not legally continue the approach past CATTA if the below minimum weather report was received at point "C" but could legally continue if at point "D" when the report was received.

NOTE: CATTA is the FAF for a <u>non-precision approach</u>.

RADIO COMMUNICATIONS FAILURE

It is virtually impossible to provide regulations and procedures applicable to all possible situations associated with two-way radio communications failure. During communications failure, when confronted by a situation not covered in the regulation, pilots are expected to exercise good judgment in whatever action they elect to take. Should the situation so dictate they should not be reluctant to use the emergency action contained in FAR part 91..

Whether radio communications failure constitutes an emergency depends on the circumstances, a determination made by the pilot. FAR Federal aviation regulations authorizes a pilot to deviate from any rule in FAR 91, subparts A and B, to the extent required to meet an emergency. The administrator may request a written report of any deviations to this rule.

In the event of radio communications failure, ATC service will be provided on the basis that the pilot is operating in accordance with FAR A pilot experiencing radio communications failure should, unless exercising emergency authority (FAR 91), comply with the provisions of FAR 91. as quoted below.

A. General - A pilot shall comply with the provisions of PART 91 when in IFR conditions with communications failure.

B. VFR conditions - If the failure occurs in VFR conditions, continue the flight under VFR conditions and land as soon as possible.

C. IFR conditions - If the failure occurs in IFR conditions or if VFR conditions are not available, the pilot shall continue the flight according to the following:

ROUTE - by the route assigned in the last ATC clearance received. If being radar vectored, by the direct route from the point of the radio failure to the fix, route or airway specified in the vector clearance. In the absence of an assigned route, by the route that ATC has advised may be expected in a further clearance; or in the absence of an assigned route or a route that ATC has advised may be expected in a further clearance by the route filed in the flight plan.

ALTITUDE - at the highest altitude or flight levels for the route segment being flown. The appropriate altitude is whichever of these is highest in each phase of flight: (1) the altitude or flight level last assigned; (2) the minimum enroute altitude; or (3) the altitude or flight level the pilot has been advised to expect in a further clearance.

Be advised that the requirement to "land as soon as practicable" should not be misconstrued to mean "as soon as possible". The pilot still retains the prerogative of exercising his best judgment and is not required to land at an unauthorized airport, at an airport unsuitable for his aircraft, or to land only minutes short of destination.

An example of altitude use after a communications failure would go something like this: The assigned altitude was 7,000 feet at the time of the failure and while enroute the pilot comes to a segment which has an MEA of 9,000 feet. The pilot should climb to 9,000 feet at the time or place where it becomes necessary to comply with the 9,000 foot MEA. Subsequently, while still proceeding to his destination, the MEA drops to 5,000 feet; therefore, the pilot should descend to 7,000 feet, which was his last assigned altitude, because it is higher than the MEA. (See FAR 91.

If holding instructions have been received, leave the holding fix at the "expect further clearance" time received or, if an "expected approach clearance" time has been received, leave the holding fix, in order to arrive over the fix from which the approach begins, as close as possible to the expected approach clearance time. The phrase "fix from which the approach begins" means any initial approach fix or the point at which the procedure track symbol begins as depicted in the instrument approach procedure.

Begin your descent from the enroute altitude or flight level upon reaching the fix from which the approach begins, but not before the estimated time of arrival shown on the flight plan as amended with ATC. If holding is necessary at the radio fix to be used for the approach at the destination airport, holding and descent to the initial approach altitude shall be accomplished in a holding pattern in accordance with the pattern on the approach chart. If no holding pattern is depicted, holding and descent will be in a holding pattern on the side of the final approach course in which the procedure turn is described.

If the pilot of an aircraft with a coded radar beacon transponder experiences a loss of two way radio capability, he should adjust his transponder to reply on Mode A/3 Code 7700 (emergency) for a period of one minute, then change to Code 7600 (radio failure) for a period of fifteen minutes or the remainder of the flight, whichever comes first. He should repeat those steps as often as practicable. Also, he should understand that he may not be in an area of radar coverage.

The pilot should attempt to reestablish communications by attempting contact on the previously assigned frequency or with an FSS station or ARINC. This does not preclude the use of 121.5 MHZ. There is no priority on which action should be attempted first. If the capability exists, do them all at the same time. FAR 91. states that the pilot in command of an aircraft operating in controlled airspace under IFR, shall report immediately to ATC the following malfunctions: loss of VOR, TACAN, ADF or low frequency navigation receiver capability, complete or partial loss of ILS receiver capability, or the impairment of air/ground communications capability. In each report the pilot should include the aircraft identification, equipment affected, the degree to which the capability of the pilot to operate under IFR in the ATC system is impaired, and the nature and extent of assistance he desires from ATC.

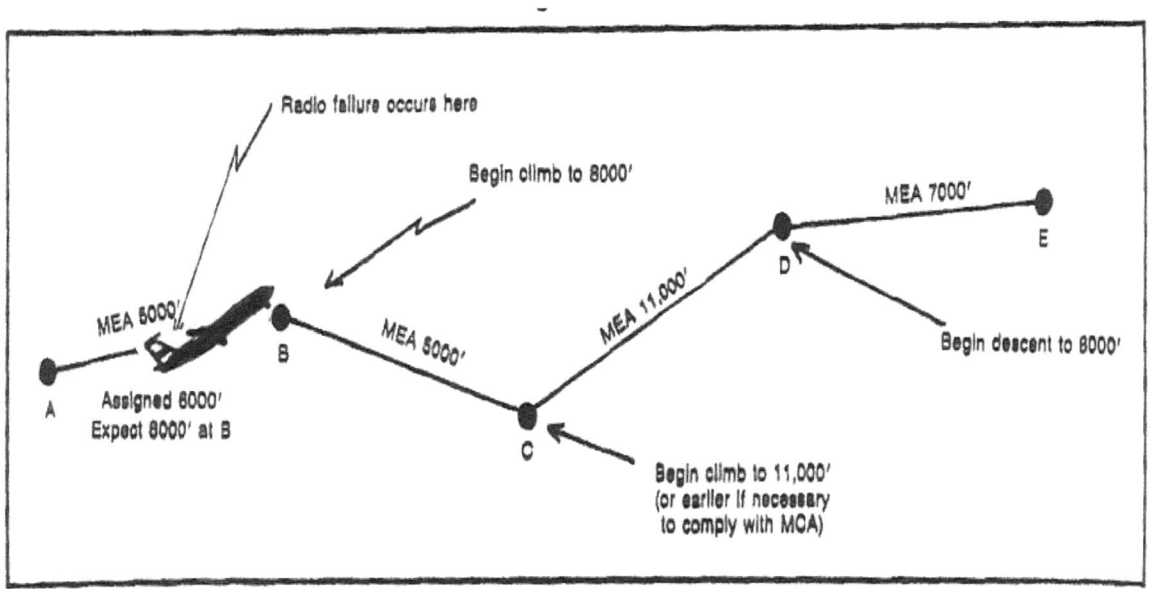

RULES OF THUMB

- Barometric pressure varies approximately 1" for each 1,000' change in altitude.

    Example: Sea level pressure = 29.92 or 1013 mb
    Pressure at 1,000' = 28.92 or 976 mb

- Standard temperature (ISA) decreases 2 degrees Celsius per 1,000' increase in altitude.

ISA = 15 degrees (SL) – 2 degrees (altitude/1000' MSL)
Example: Altitude = 6,000' MSL
   ISA = 15 degrees – (2 degrees x 6) = 3 degrees

- To determine a Visual Descent Point in NM (3 degrees glide path) divide the HAT (in hundreds) by 3.

Example: MDA = 1,200' MSL
            Touchdown elevation = 300' MSL
              1,200 – 300 = 900' HAT
          9 (hundred) /3 = 3 NM VDP

- For each knot of airspeed above Vref over the numbers, the touchdown point will be 100 feet further down the runway.

- A 1,000 ft change in field elevation will cause a 4% change in stopping distance. The greater the altitude, the greater the landing distance.

- A 10 degrees C deviation from standard temperature will cause a 5% change in stopping distance. Higher temperature, longer stopping distance due to increase in TAS.

- ❖ Vref for larger aircraft: Add all the wind and ½ the gust on approach.

- ❖ One dot on the localizer is approximately 300 ft at the outer marker, 100 ft at the middle marker. One dot on the glideslope is approximately 50 ft at the outer marker, 8 ft at the middle marker.

ALTERNATE AIRPORTS WEATHER REQUIREMENTS

To qualify as an alternate airport, the forecast must indicate at the estimated time of arrival the weather to be at least:

- Airports with a precision 600' ceiling and 2 miles visibility approach procedure

- Airports with a non-precision 800' ceiling and 2 miles visibility approach

- Airports without a ceiling and visibility to allow instrument approach and descent from the MEA to landing in VFR conditions.

1-2-3 RULE WHEN ALTERNATE IS NOT REQUIRED

When the destination airport has a published instrument approach procedure and weather report/forecasts indicate:

1 hour before and one hour after of planned ETA;
2,000' ceiling or greater and

3 miles visibility or greater

INSTRUMENT FLIGHT PLAN REQUIRED

No person may operate an aircraft in controlled airspace under IFR unless that person has:

1. Filed an instrument flight plan
2. Received an appropriate ATC clearance

FEEDER ROUTE

- Transition from enroute phase to IAF
- Medium thick lines on plan view with minimum altitudes, distances and directions or headings
- Same obstacle clearance as enroute structure.

OPERATION BELOW DH OR MDA

No pilot may operate below DH or MDA unless:

1. The aircraft is continuously in a position from which a normal descent to landing with normal maneuvers can be made. Part 121 and 135 require the descent allows touchdown within the touchdown zone of the runway.

2. Flight visibility not less than the minimum visibility required for the approach being used.

3. At least one of the following visual references is distinctly visible and identifiable to the pilot:
   a. Approach light system* (ALS)
   b. Threshold, threshold lights, threshold markings
   c. Runway end identifier lights (REIL)
   d. Visual approach slope indicator (VASI)
   e. Touchdown zone (TDZ)
   f. Touchdown zone markings or lights (TDZL)
   g. Runway, runway markings or runway lights

*The pilot may not descend below 100 feet above the touchdown zone unless the red terminating or siderow bars are distinctly visible (ALSF-I and ALSF-II).

INITIAL APPROACH FIX (IAF)

- Identified on approach charts (IAF)
- Found on both enroute and approach charts
- Approach officially begins at IAF.

INTERMEDIATE SEGMENT

- 500' obstacle clearance, maximum descent 300'/NM
- Usually within 30 degrees of final approach course.

FINAL APPROACH FIX (FAF)

- Maltese cross or glideslope interception (FAP)
- PT inbound for on-airport VOR or NDB IAP w/o FAF
- Report FAF inbound to ATC in non-radar environment.

POSITION REPORTS

- Identification
- Position
- Time
- Altitude
- Type of flight plan (FSS only)
- ETA and name of next reporting fix
- Name of succeeding reporting point
- Remarks

STANDARD INSTRUMENT TAKEOFF MINIMUMS (AIRCRAFT FOR HIRE)

- 1 statute mile visibility for aircraft with 1 or 2 engines
- ½ mile visibility for aircraft with more than 2 engines

IFR CRUISING ALTITUDES

- In controlled airspace: Each pilot shall fly the altitude or flight level assigned by ATC. In uncontrolled airspace*:

Below 18,000 MSL:

- Easterly course**   Odd altitudes 3,000', 5,000' etc.
- Westerly course   Even altitudes 4,000', 6,000', etc.

At or above 18,000 MSL and below FL 290:

- Easterly course   Odd flights levels 190, 210, etc.
- Westerly course   Even flight levels 180, 200, etc.

At or above 29,000:

- Easterly course   Flight levels at 4,000' intervals Beginning at 290, 330, 370, etc.
- Westerly course   Flight levels at 4,000' intervals Beginning at 310, 350, 390, etc.

(*Except when holding 2 minutes or less, or while turning.
**Magnetic courses).

REQUIRED IFR REPORTS TO ATC

Non-radar environment:

- Time and altitude passing a designated reporting point

- ❖ Final approach fix or outer marker inbound
- ❖ Change in ETA to next reporting point or ± 3 minutes
- ❖ Over points use to define a direct route

At all times:

- ❖ Any unforecast weather conditions
- ❖ Anything affecting the safety of the flight
- ❖ Loss or impairment of communication or navigational equipment and degree of assistance desired from ATC
- ❖ Missed approach and intentions
- ❖ Vacating an assigned altitude
- ❖ Change in altitude while VFR-on-top
- ❖ Unable to climb or descend 500 fpm
- ❖ Change in airspeed of 10 knots or 5%
- ❖ Time and altitude reaching a clearance limit or holding fix
- ❖ Leaving an assigned holding fix

HOLDING AIRPEED LIMITATIONS	
MHA through 6,000' MSL	200 KIAS
6,001' to 14,000' MSL	230 KIAS
Above 14,000' MSL	265 KIAS
All altitudes when depicted on chart by icon	175 KIAS
6,001' to 14,000' MSL when depicted on chart by icon	210 KIAS

CLEARANCE VOID TIME
- Uncontrolled airports
- Climb through uncontrolled airspace
- Notify ATC within 30 minutes if not airborne
- Do not take off after void time.

CRUISE CLEARANCE
- Assigns block of airspace
- Pilot may climb and descend between the MEA and assigned altitude
- One verbally reporting a descent from an altitude in the block, the pilot may no longer return to that altitude.

CONTACT APPROACH
- Only on request, not assigned by ATC
- Airport must have an Instrument Approach Procedure
- 1 mile visibility, clear of clouds and reasonably expect to continue to the airport
- Separation provided between IFR and VFR traffic.

VISUAL APPROACH
- Still on an IFR flight plan
- VFR minimums apply
- Must have airport or preceding aircraft in sight.

HOLDING (FIVE T'S)

Time	—NOTE TIME (Time Outbound Leg)
Turn	—START A STANDARD RATE TURN CROSSING THE FIX (To/From Indication)

Twist   —SET THE OBS TO THE INBOUND COURSE
Throttle   —REDUCE POWER SETTING
Talk   —REPORT TIME AND ALTITUDE ENTERING HOLD

ATC LIGHT SIGNALS		
Color and type of signal	On the ground	In flight
Steady green	Cleared for takeoff	Cleared to land
Flashing green	Cleared to taxi	Return for landing (to be followed by a steady green)
Steady red	Stop	Give way to other aircraft and continue circling
Flashing red	Taxi clear of runway in use	Airport unsafe – Do Not Land
Flashing white	Return to starting point	Not applicable
Alternating red and green	General warning – Use Extreme Caution	

Atmospheric Pressure decreases at the rate of 1" Hg (1" Mercury) per 1000 feet of altitude above sea level. Therefore, to determine the pressure altitude, find the difference between 29.92 (Standard Sea Level pressure) and the existing pressure; then multiply this value by 1000. This is the number of feet the pressure altitude varies from the field elevation. Now, if the existing pressure is higher than 29.92, subtract the altitude variation from the field elevation. If the existing pressure is lower than 29.92 then add the altitude variation to the field elevation.

EXAMPLE:
Field Elevation = 1230 feet
Existing Pressure = 30.16
Then:
30.16 – 29.92 = .24
.24 x 1000 = 240
30.16 is higher than 29.92
So:
Pressure Altitude = 1230 – 240
Pressure Altitude = 990 feet

❖ **To Determine the Standard Celsius Temperature for Pressure Altitude; double the altitude in thousands of feet and subtract 15 then change the sign.**

EXAMPLE:
Pressure Altitude = 1000
Double Altitude in Thousands = 2

Subtract = 2 – 15 = -13
Change Sign -13 = +13
Standard Temperature C = +13

- **Multiply the Mach number by 5.7 then move the decimal point two places to the right to get TAS.**

  EXAMPLE:
  MACH = .80
  TAS = 5.7 X .80 = 4.56
  TAS = 456 KNOTS

- **To find the approximate Miles Per Minute, use Indicated Mach Number and move the decimal one position right.**

  EXAMPLE:
  Indicated Mach = .80
  Miles per Minute = 8.0

- **To find the approximate Miles Per Minute, round off TAS to nearest ten, drop the zero and divide by 6.**

  EXAMPLE:
  True Airspeed = 238
  Rounding TAS = 240
  Drop Zero and Divide = 24/6 = 4
  Miles Per Minute = 4.0

- A 1% change in airspeed will cause a 2% change in stopping distance.

- A 10 % change in landing weight will cause a 10% change in stopping distance.

- ❖ A 1000 foot change in field elevation will cause a 4% change in stopping distance. The greater the altitude, the greater the distance required due to increase in TAS.

- ❖ A 15 degree F deviation from standard temperature will cause a 4% change in stopping distance. The greater the temperature, the greater the stopping distance due to increase in TAS.

- ❖ A headwind which is 10% of the landing speed will reduce the landing distance approximately 10%, while a tailwind which is 10% of the landing speed will increase the landing distance 21%.

- ❖ Crossing the threshold 50 feet too high increases the landing distance 25%.

- ❖ A 1 degree reduction in glide angle increases the landing distance by 13%.

- ❖ A wet runway can increase the stopping distance 25% to 50%.

- ❖ An icy runway can increase stopping distance by 100% or more.

COMMON CONVERSION FACTORS

The following ratios are provided to set up the slide-rule side of the computer to make the conversions indicated:

LENGTH
Meters: Feet	=	.3048:1
Statute Miles: Nautical miles	=	1.1508:1
Feet: Nautical miles	=	6076.1:1
Feet: Statute miles	=	5280.1
Nautical miles: Kilometers	=	.54:1
Statute miles: Kilometers	=	.621:1
Centimeter: Inches	=	2.54:1

VELOCITY
Miles per hour: Knots	=	1.152:1
Kilometers per hour: Knots	=	1.853:1
Kilometers per hour: Miles per hour	=	1.609:1

PRESSURE
Milibars: inches of mercury	=	1013.2:29.92

WEIGHT
Kilograms: Pounds	=	.45366:1
Grams: Pounds	=	453.6:1
Pounds: Short tons	=	2000:1
Pounds: Long tons	=	2240:1
Pounds: Metric tons	=	2205:1

VOLUME
U.S. gallons: British gallons	=	1.2:1
Liters: U.S. gallons	=	3.785:1

VOLUME AND WEIGHT EQUIVALENTS

Pounds: U.S. gallons of water   =   8.336:1
Kilos: U.S. gallons of water   =   3.781:1
Pounds: U.S. gallons of oil   =   7.5:1

When operating at foreign airports where the metric system is used and the minimums are specified only in meters, the certificate holder shall use the metric operational equivalents in the following tables for both takeoff and landing operations.

METEOROLOGICAL VISIBILITY WHEN RVR IS NOT AVAILABLE		
STATUTE MILES	**METERS**	**NAUTICAL MILES**
¼ sm	400 m	¼ nm
½ sm	800 m	½ nm
¾ sm	1200 m	7/10 nm
1 sm	1600 m	9/10 nm
1 ¼ sm	2000 m	1 1/10 nm
1 ½ sm	2400 m	1 3/10 nm
1 ¾ sm	2800 m	1 ½ nm
2 sm	3200 m	1 ¾ nm
2 ¼ sm	3600 m	2 nm
2 ½ sm	4000 m	2 2/10 nm
2 ¾ sm	4400 m	2 4/10 nm
3 sm	4800 m	2 6/10 nm

RVR	
FEET	**METERS**
300 ft	90m
400 ft	120 m
500 ft	150 m
600 ft	175 m
700 ft	200 m
1000 ft	300 m
1200 ft	350 m
1600 ft	500 m
1800 ft	550 m
2000 ft	600 m
2100 ft	630 m
2400 ft	720 m
4000 ft	1200 m
4500 ft	1400 m
5000 ft	1500 m
6000 ft	1800 m

WEIGHT – KILOS AND POUNDS

Pounds		Kilos	Pounds		Kilos
2.2	1	0.454	1322.8	600	272.2
4.4	2	0.907	1543.2	700	317.5
6.6	3	1.36	1763.7	800	362.9
8.8	4	1.81	1984.1	900	408
11	5	2.27	2205	1000	454
13.2	6	2.72	4409	2000	907
15.4	7	3.18	6614	3000	1361
17.6	8	3.63	8818	4000	1814
19.8	9	4.08	11023	5000	2268
22	10	4.54	13228	6000	2722
44.1	20	9.07	15432	7000	3175
66.1	30	13.6	17637	8000	3629
88.2	40	18.1	19841	9000	4082
110.2	50	22.7	22046	10000	4536
132.2	60	27.2	44092	20000	9072
154.3	70	31.8	66138	30000	13608
176.4	80	36.3	88184	40000	18144
198.4	90	40.8	110230	50000	22680
220.5	100	45.4	132276	60000	27215
440.9	200	90.7	154322	70000	31751
661.4	300	136.1	176368	80000	36287
881.8	400	181.4	198414	90000	40823
1102.3	500	226.8	220460	100000	45359

Example: 260 pounds = 90.7 + 27.2 or 117.9 kilos
40 kilos + 88.2 pounds

METERS/FEET

FEET	↓	METERS	FEET	↓	METERS	FEET	↓	METERS
3.28083	1	0.3048	918.63	280	85.344	2099.7	640	195.07
6.562	2	0.6096	951.44	290	88.392	2132.5	650	198.12
9.842	3	0.9144	984.25	300	91.440	2165.4	660	201.17
13.124	4	1.2192	1017.1	310	94.488	2198.2	670	204.00
16.405	5	1.524	1049.9	320	97.536	2231.0	680	207.26
19.686	6	1.8288	1082.7	330	100.58	2263.8	690	210.31
22.967	7	2.1336	1115.5	340	103.63	2296.6	700	213.36
26.248	8	2.4384	1148.3	350	106.68	2329.4	710	216.41
29.529	9	2.7432	1181.1	360	109.73	2362.2	720	219.46
32.808	10	3.048	1213.9	370	112.78	2395.0	730	222.5
65.617	20	6.096	1246.7	380	115.82	2427.8	740	225.55
98.425	30	9.144	1279.5	390	118.87	2460.6	750	228.6
131.23	40	12.192	1312.3	400	121.92	2493.4	760	231.65
164.04	50	15.240	1345.1	410	124.97	2526.2	770	234.7
196.85	60	18.288	1377.9	420	128.02	2559	780	237.74
229.66	70	21.336	1410.8	430	131.06	2591.9	790	240.79
262.47	80	24.384	1443.6	440	134.11	2624.7	800	243.84
295.27	90	27.432	1476.4	450	137.16	2657.5	810	246.89
328.09	100	30.480	1509.2	460	140.21	2690.3	820	249.94
360.89	110	33.528	1542.0	470	143.26	2723.1	830	252.98
393.70	120	36.576	1574.8	480	146.30	2755.9	840	256.03
426.51	130	39.624	1607.6	490	149.35	2788.7	850	259.08
459.32	140	42.672	1640.4	500	152.40	2821.5	860	262.13
492.12	150	45.720	1673.2	510	155.45	2854.3	870	264.18
524.93	160	48.768	1706.0	520	158.50	2887.1	880	268.22
557.74	170	51.816	1735.8	530	161.54	2919.9	890	271.27
590.55	180	54.864	1771.7	540	164.59	2952.8	900	274.32
623.36	190	57.912	1804.5	550	167.64	2985.6	910	277.37
656.17	200	60.960	1837.3	560	170.69	3018.4	920	280.42
688.97	210	64.008	1870.1	570	173.74	3051.2	930	283.46
721.78	220	67.056	1902.9	580	176.78	3084.0	940	286.51
754.59	230	70.104	1935.7	590	179.83	3116.8	950	289.56
787.40	240	73.152	1968.5	600	182.88	3149.6	960	292.61
820.21	250	76.200	2001.3	610	185.93	3182.4	970	295.66
853.02	260	79.248	2034.1	620	188.98	3215.2	980	298.70
885.82	270	82.296	2066.9	630	192.02	3248.0	990	301.75

Example: 100 meters = 328.08 feet
415 feet = 124.97 ÷1.524 or 126.494 meters

CEILING	FEET	100	200	300	400	500	600	700	800	900	1000	1100	1200	1300	1400	1500
	METERS	30	60	90	120	150	180	210	240	270	300	330	360	390	420	450

METRIC FLIGHT LEVEL & FEET

True track from 000° to 179°						True track from 180° to 359°					
IFR Flights			VFR Flights			IFR Flights			VFR Flights		
Flight Level	Metres	Feet	Flight Level	Metres	Feet	Flight Level	Metres	Feet	Flight Level	Metres	Feet
010	300	1000	-	-	-	020	600	2000	-	-	-
030	900	3000	035	1050	3500	040	1200	4000	045	1350	4500
050	1500	5000	055	1700	5500	060	1850	6000	065	2000	6500
070	2150	7000	075	2300	7500	080	2450	8000	085	2600	8500
090	2750	9000	095	2900	9500	100	3050	10000	105	3200	10500
110	3350	11000	115	3500	11500	120	3650	12000	125	3800	12500
130	3950	13000	135	4100	13500	140	4250	14000	145	4400	14500
150	4550	15000	155	4700	15500	160	4900	16000	165	5050	16500
170	5200	17000	175	5350	17500	180	5500	18000	185	5650	18500
190	5800	19000	195	5950	19500	200	6100	20000	205	6250	20500
210	6400	21000	215	6550	21500	220	6700	22000	225	6850	22500
230	7000	23000	235	7150	23500	240	7300	24000	245	7450	24500
250	7600	25000	255	7750	25500	260	7900	26000	265	8100	26500
270	8250	27000	-	-	-	280	8550	28000	-	-	-
290	8850	29000	-	-	-	300	9150	30000	-	-	-
310	9450	31000	-	-	-	320	9750	32000	-	-	-
330	10050	33000	-	-	-	340	10350	34000	-	-	-
350	10650	35000	-	-	-	360	10950	36000	-	-	-
370	11300	37000	-	-	-	380	11600	38000	-	-	-
390	11900	39000	-	-	-	400	12200	40000	-	-	-
410	12500	41000	-	-	-	430	13100	43000	-	-	-
450	13700	45000	-	-	-	470	14350	47000	-	-	-
490	14950	49000	-	-	-	510	15550	51000	-	-	-
etc.	etc.	etc.	-	-	-	etc.	etc.	etc.	-	-	-

TEMPERATURE (F/C)

C°	↓	F°	C°	↓	F°	C°	↓	F°	C°	↓	F°
-60.0	-76	-104.8	-30.0	-22	-7.6	0.0	32	89.6	30.0	86	186.8
-59.4	-75	-103.0	-29.4	-21	-5.8	0.6	33	91.4	30.6	87	188.6
-58.9	-74	-101.2	-28.9	-20	-4.0	1.1	34	93.2	31.1	88	190.4
-58.3	-73	-99.4	-28.3	-19	-2.2	1.7	35	95.0	31.7	89	192.2
-57.8	-72	-97.6	-27.8	-18	-0.4	2.2	36	96.8	32.2	90	194.0
-57.2	-71	-95.8	-27.2	-17	1.4	2.8	37	98.6	32.8	91	195.8
-56.7	-70	-94.0	-26.7	-16	3.2	3.3	38	100.4	33.3	92	197.6
-56.1	-69	-92.2	-26.1	-15	5.0	3.9	39	102.2	33.9	93	199.4
-55.6	-68	-90.4	25.5	-14	6.8	4.4	40	104.0	34.4	94	201.2
-55.0	-67	-88.6	-25.0	-13	8.6	5.0	41	105.8	35.0	95	203.0
-54.5	-66	-86.8	24.4	-12	10.4	5.6	42	107.6	35.6	96	204.8
-53.9	-65	-85.0	-23.9	-11	12.2	6.1	43	109.4	36.1	97	206.6
-53.4	-64	-83.2	23.3	-10	14.0	6.7	44	111.2	36.7	98	208.4
-52.8	-63	-81.4	-22.8	-9	15.8	7.2	45	113.0	37.2	99	210.2
-52.3	-62	-79.6	22.2	-8	17.6	7.8	46	114.8	37.8	100	212.0
-51.7	-61	-77.8	-21.7	-7	19.4	8.3	47	116.6	38.3	101	213.8
-51.2	-60	-76.0	-21.2	-6	21.2	8.9	48	118.4	38.9	102	215.6
-50.6	-59	-74.2	-20.6	-5	23.0	9.4	49	120.2	39.4	103	217.4
-50.1	-58	-72.4	-20.0	-4	24.8	10.0	50	122.0	40.1	104	219.2
-49.4	-57	-70.6	-19.4	-3	26.6	10.6	51	123.8	40.6	105	221.0
-48.9	-56	-68.8	-18.9	-2	28.4	11.1	52	125.6	41.1	106	222.8
-48.3	-55	-67.0	-18.3	-1	30.2	11.7	53	127.4	41.6	107	224.6
-47.8	-54	-65.2	-17.8	0	32.0	12.2	54	129.2	42.2	108	226.4
-47.2	-53	-63.4	-17.2	1	33.8	12.8	55	131.0	42.7	109	228.2
-46.7	-52	-61.6	-16.7	2	35.6	13.3	56	132.8	43.3	110	230.0
-46.1	-51	-59.8	-16.1	3	37.4	13.9	57	134.6	43.8	111	231.8
-45.6	-50	-58.0	-15.6	4	39.2	14.4	58	136.4	44.4	112	233.6
-45.0	-49	-56.2	-15.0	5	41.0	15.0	59	138.2	45.0	113	235.4
-44.4	-48	-54.4	-14.4	6	42.8	15.6	60	140.0	45.5	114	237.2
-43.9	-47	-52.6	-13.9	7	44.6	16.1	61	141.8	46.1	115	239.0
-43.3	-46	-50.8	-13.3	8	46.4	16.7	62	143.6	46.6	116	240.8
-42.8	-45	-49.0	-12.8	9	48.2	17.2	63	145.4	47.2	117	242.6
-42.2	-44	-47.2	-12.2	10	50.0	17.8	64	147.2	47.7	118	244.4
-41.7	-43	-45.4	-11.7	11	51.8	18.3	65	149.0	48.3	119	246.2
-41.1	-42	-43.6	-11.1	12	53.6	18.9	66	150.8	48.8	120	248.0
-40.6	-41	-41.8	-10.6	13	55.4	19.4	67	152.6	49.4	121	249.8
-40.0	-40	-40.0	-10.0	14	57.2	20.0	68	154.4	50.0	122	251.6
-39.4	-39	-38.2	-9.4	15	59.0	20.6	69	156.2	50.5	123	253.4
-38.9	-38	-36.4	-8.9	16	60.8	21.1	70	158.0	51.1	124	255.2
-38.3	-37	-34.6	-8.3	17	62.6	21.7	71	159.8	51.6	125	257.0
-37.8	-36	-32.8	-7.8	18	64.4	22.2	72	161.6	52.2	126	258.8
-37.2	-35	-31.0	-7.2	19	66.2	22.8	73	163.4	52.7	127	260.6
-36.7	-34	-29.2	-6.7	20	68.0	23.3	74	165.2	53.3	128	262.4
-36.1	-33	-27.4	-6.1	21	69.8	23.9	75	167.0	53.8	129	264.2
-35.6	-32	-25.6	-5.6	22	71.6	24.4	76	168.8	54.4	130	266.0
-35.0	-31	-23.8	-5.0	23	73.4	25.0	77	170.6	54.9	131	267.8
-34.4	-30	-22.0	-4.4	24	75.2	25.6	78	172.4	55.5	132	269.6
-33.9	-29	-20.2	-3.9	25	77.0	26.1	79	174.2	56.1	133	271.4
-33.3	-28	-18.4	-3.3	26	78.8	26.7	80	176.0	56.6	134	273.2
-32.8	-27	-16.6	-2.8	27	80.6	27.2	81	177.8	57.2	135	275.0
-32.2	-26	-14.8	-2.2	28	82.4	27.8	82	179.6	57.7	136	276.8
-31.7	-25	-13.4	-1.7	29	84.2	28.3	83	181.4	58.3	137	278.6
-31.1	-24	-11.2	-1.1	30	86.0	28.9	84	183.2	58.8	138	280.4
-30.6	-23	-9.4	-0.6	31	87.8	29.4	85	185.0	59.4	139	282.2
									60.0	140	284.0

Example: 50°F = 10.0°C
40°C = 104.1°F

CHAPTER THIRTY-FIVE

AIRBUS ABBREVIATIONS

AVIATION ABBREVIATIONS

A

A	Amber
AAC	Airline Administrative Communications
ABCU	Alternate Braking Control Unit
ABD	Airbus Directive and Procedure
ABM	APU Build-up Manual
ABNORM	Abnormal
ABRN	Airborne
ABS	Auto brake System
ABSORB	Absorber
ABV	Above
AC	Airplane Characteristics for Airport Planning
AC	Alternating Current
ACARS	Aircraft Communication Addressing and Reporting System
ACCEL	Acceleration/Accelerate
ACCLRM	Accelerometer
ACCU	Accumulator

ACK	Acknowledge
ACMM	Abbreviated Component Maintenance Manual
ACMP	Airframe Condition Monitoring Procedure
ACMR	Aircraft Configuration Management Rules
ACMS	Aircraft Condition Monitoring System
ACN	Aircraft Classification Number
ACP	Area Call Panel
ACP	Audio Control Panel
ACQ	Acquire
ACQN	Acquisition
ACR	Avionics Communication Router
ACT	Active for Nav/AP signals only
ACT	Additional Center Tank
ACTG	Actuating
ACTR	Actuator
ACTVT	Activate
ADB	Area Distribution Box
ADC	Air Data Computer

ADCN	Avionics Data Communication Network
ADD	Addition, Additional
ADF	Automatic Direction Finder
ADG	Air Driven Generator
ADI	Attitude Director Indicator
ADIRS	Air Data/Inertial Reference System
ADIRU	Air Data/Inertial Reference Unit
ADM	Air Data Module
ADPM	Aircraft Deactivation Procedures Manual
ADPTR	Adapter
ADR	Air Data Reference
ADS	Air Data System
ADS	Automatic Dependent Surveillance
ADV	Advisory
AES	Aircraft Earth Station
AESS	Aircraft Environment Surveillance System
AESU	Aircraft Environment Surveillance Unit
AEVC	Avionics Equipment Ventilation Computer

AF	Audio Frequency
AFDX	Avionics Full Duplex Switched Ethernet
AFMC	Auxiliary Fuel Management Computer
AFN	ATS Facilities Notification
AFS	Automatic Flight System
AGB	Accessory Gearbox
AGC	Automatic Gain Control
AGE	Aircraft Ground Equipment
AGL	above Ground Level
AGW	Actual Gross Weight
AIBU	Advanced Integrated Ballast Unit
AICU	Anti Ice Control Unit
AIDS	Aircraft Integrated Data System
AIL	Aileron
AIM	Aircraft Integrated Maintenance
AINS	Aircraft Information Network System
AIP	Attendant Indication Panel
AIS	Audio Integrated System

ALIGN	Alignment
ALPHA	Angle-of-Attack
ALSCU	Auxiliary Level Sensing Control Unit
ALT	Altitude
ALTM	Altimeter
ALTN	Alternate, Alternative
ALTU	Annunciator Light Test Unit
AM	Amplitude Modulation
AMB	Ambient
AMM	Aircraft Maintenance Manual
AMPL	Amplifier
AMU	Audio Management Unit
ANI	Analog Input
ANLG	Analogic
ANN	Annunciator
ANNCE	Announce
ANNCMT	Announcement
ANO	Analog Output

ANSI	American National Standards Institute
ANSU	Aircraft Network Server Unit
ANT	Antenna
AOA	Angle-Of-Attack
AOC	Airline Operational Control
AOD	Audio on Demand
AOG	Aircraft on Ground
AOM	Aircraft Operating Manual
AP	Autopilot
APLC	Aircraft Power Line Conditioner
APP	Appearance
APP	Approach Control-Approach Control Office
APPR	Approach
APPROX	Approximately
APPU	Asymmetry Position Pick off Unit
APU	Auxiliary Power Unit
AFE	Automatic Fire Extinguishing Control Unit
AP/FD	Autopilot/Flight Director

AR	As Required
ARINC	Aeronautical Radio Incorporated
ARM	Aircraft Recovery Manual
ARP	Aerospace Recommended Practice
ARPT	Airport
ARTF	Artificial
ARU	Audio Reproducer Unit
ASA	All Speed Aileron
ASCII	American Standard Code for Information Interchange
ASD	Accelerate Stop Distance
ASE	Airborne Support Equipment
ASI	Airspeed Indicator
ASIC	Application Specific Integrated Circuits
ASM	Aircraft Schematics Manual
ASN	Aerospatiale Normal (Standard)
ASP	Audio Selector Panel
ASPSU	Autonomous Standby Power Supply Unit
ASSY	Assembly

ASYM	Asymmetric (al)
ATA	Actual Time of Arrival
ATA	Air Transport Association of America
ATC	Air Traffic Control
ATCI	Air Traffic Control and Information
ATCRB	Air Traffic Control Radar Beacon
ATD	Actual Time of Departure
ATE	Automatic Test Equipment
ATI	Air Transport Indicator
ATIMS	Air Traffic and Information Management System
ATLAS	Abbreviated Test Language for Avionics Systems
ATM	Air Traffic Management
ATN	Aeronautical Telecommunications Network
ATR	Austin Trumbull Radio
ATS	Air Traffic Service
ATS	Auto throttle System
ATSU	Air Traffic Service Unit

ATT	Attitude
ATTND	Attendant
AUTO	Automatic
AUTOLAND	Automatic Landing
AUW	All-Up Weight
AUX	Auxiliary
AVAIL	Available
AVNCS	Avionics
AWL	Aircraft Wiring List
AWM	Aircraft Wiring Manual
AWY	Airway
AX	Longitudinal Acceleration
AY	Lateral Acceleration
AZ	Azimuth
AZFW	Actual Zero Fuel Weight Anti-ice, Anti-icing
A/BRK	Auto brake
A/C	Aircraft
A/COLL	Anti-Collision

A/D	Analog/Digital
A/DC	Analog-to-Digital Converter
A/G	Air to Ground
A/N	Alphanumeric
A/S	Airspeed
A/SKID	Anti-Skid
A/STAB	Auto Stabilizer
A/THR	Auto thrust
A/XFMR	Autotransformer

B

B	Blue
BARO	Barometric
BAT	Battery (Electrical)
BCD	Binary Coded Decimal
BCDS	BITE Centralized Data System
BCL	Battery Charge Limiter
BCN	Beacon
BCRC	Bulk Crew Rest Compartment

BCRU	Battery Charge and Rectifier Unit
BCU	Brake Control Unit
BFE	Buyer Furnished Equipment
BFO	Beat Frequency Oscillator
BGM	Boarding Music
BH	Block Hours
BITE	Built-in Test Equipment
BIU	BITE Interface Unit
BK UP	Back Up
BL	Bleed
BLES	Brake Life Extension System
BLG	Body Landing Gear
BLK	Black
BLOW	Blower
BLST	Ballast
BMC	Bleed Monitoring Computer
BNDRY	Boundary
BNR	Binary

BOT	Bottom
BRG	Bearing
BRK	Brake
BRKNG	Braking
BRKR	Breaker
BRKT	Bracket
BRT	Bright, Brightness
BSCU	Braking/Steering Control Unit
BSU	Beam Steering Unit
BTC	Bus Tie Contactor
BTL	Bottle
BTMU	Brake Temperature Monitoring Unit
BTN	Button
BTR	Bus Tie Relay
BU	Battery Unit
BUS	Bus bar
BYDU	Back-Up Yaw Damper Unit
BYP	Bypass

C

C	Celsius, Centigrade
C	Close
C	Cyan
C-MOS	Complementary Metal Oxide Semiconductor
CA	Cable Assembly
CAB	Cabin
CAL	Calibration, Calibrated
CAM	Cabin Assignment Module
CAN	Controller Area Network
CAOA	Corrected Angle Of Attack
CAOM	Cabin Attendant Operating Manual
CAPT	Captain
CAS	Calibrated Air Speed
CAT	Category
CATCH	Complex Anomaly Tracking and Search
CAUT	Caution
CBIT	Continuous BITE

CBMS	Circuit Breaker Monitoring System
CBMU	Circuit Breaker Monitoring Unit
CC	Current Comparator
CCC	Crash Crew Chart
CCG	Cabin Configuration Guide
CCOM	Cabin Crew Operating Manual
CCR	Credit Card Reader
CCRC	Cabin Crew Rest Compartment
CCRM	Cabin Crew Rest Module
CCS	Cabin Communications System
CCW	Counter Clockwise
CD	Control Display
CDAM	Centralized Data Acquisition Module
CDL	Configuration Deviation List
CDP	Compressor Discharge Pressure
CDS	Component Documentation Status
CDS	Control and Display System
CDU	Control and Display Unit

CED	Cooling Effect Detector
CEL	Component Evolution List
CELLI	Ceiling Emergency LED Light
CER	Control Essays Reception
CEV	Centre essays Vol
CFDIU	Centralized Fault Display Interface Unit
CFDS	Centralized Fault Display System
CFM	Cable Fabrication Manual
CFRP	Carbon Fiber Reinforced Plastic
CFS	Cabin File Server
CG	Center of Gravity
CGCS	Center of Gravity Control System
CH	Character
CHAN	Channel
CHG	Change
CHMBR	Chamber
CHRG	Charge
CHRO	Chronometer

CIDS	Cabin Intercommunication Data System
CIN	Change Identification Number
CINS	Cabin Information Network System
CIU	Camera Interface Unit
CK	Check
CKPT	Cockpit
CKT	Circuit
CL	Center Line
CL	Check List
CLB	Climb
CLCTR	Collector
CLG	Centerline Landing Gear
CLK	Clock
CLM	Component Location Manual
CLNG	Ceiling
CLOG	Clogging
CLPR	Clapper
CLR	Clear

CLRD	Cleared
CLS	Cargo Loading System
CLS	Cargo Loading System Manual
CLSD	Closed
CM	Conversion Manual
CMC	Central Maintenance Computer
CMD	Command
CMEU	Cabin Passenger Management Memory Expansion Unit
CML	Consumable Material List
CMM	Calibration Memory Module
CMM	Component Maintenance Manual
CMMV	Component Maintenance Manual Vendor
CMPTR	Computer
CMS	Central Maintenance System
CMS	Code Maître Société
CMS	Component Maintenance Sheet
CMT	Cabin Management Terminal
CMV	Concentrator and Multiplexer for Video

CNCTR	Connector
CNSU	Cabin Network Server Unit
CNTNR	Container
CNTOR	Contactor
CNTRTR	Concentrator
CO RTE	Company Route
COAX	Coaxial
COC	Customer Originated Change
COM	Communication
COMDL	Coding Module
COMP	Compass
COMP	Compensator
COMPSN	Compensation
COMPT	Compartment
COMPTR	Comparator
COND	Conditioned, Conditioning
CONDTR	Conditioner
CONFIG	Configuration

CONT	Continue, Continuous
CONT	Controller
CONV	Converter
COOL	Cooling, Cooler
COUNT	Counter
COWL	Cowling
CPC	Cabin Pressure Controller
CPCS	Cabin Pressure Control System
CPCU	Cabin Pressure Control Unit
CPDLC	Controller-Pilot Data Link Communications
CPIOM	Core Processing Input /Output Module
CPLG	Coupling
CPLR	Coupler
CPMS	Cabin and Passenger Management System
CPMU	Cabin Passenger Management Unit
CPRSR	Compressor
CPU	Central Processing Unit
CRC	Continuous Repetitive Chime

CRC	Cyclic Redundancy Check
CRES	Corrosion-Resistant Steel
CRG	Cargo
CRI	Certification Review Item
CRS	Course
CRT	Cathode Ray Tube
CRU	Card Reader Unit
CS	Center Spar
CSD	Constant Speed Drive
CSK	Countersink
CSL	Console
CSM/G	Constant Speed Motor/Generator
CSTR	Constraint
CSU	Command Sensor Unit
CT	Current Transformer
CTK	Center Tank
CTL	Central
CTL	Control

CTR	Center
CTU	Cabin Telecommunications Unit
CU	Control Unit
CUDU	Current Unbalance Detection Unit
CUR	Current
CVR	Cockpit Voice Recorder
CVT	Center Vent Tube
CVU	Crypto Voice Unit
CW	Clockwise
CWLU	Cabin Wireless LAN Unit
CY	Cycle
CYL	Cylinder
C/B	Circuit Breaker
C/L	Check List
C/O	Change Over
C/S	Call Sign

D

DA	Drift Angle

DAC	Digital to Analog Converter
DAC	Drawing Aperture Card
DADC	Digital Air Data Computer
DAMP	Damping
DAR	Digital AIDS Recorder Used on Single Aisle family
DBLR	Doubler
DC	Direct Current
DCD	Data Control and Display
DCDR	Decoder
DCDU	Datalink Control and Display Unit
DCP	Display Control Panel
DDM	Digital Data Module
DDP	Declaration of Design and Performance
DDRMI	Digital Distance and Radio Magnetic Indicator
DDV	Direct Drive Valve
DECEL	Decelerate
DECR	Decrease

DEDP	Data Entry and Display Panel
DEF	Definition
DEG	Degree
DEL	Delete
DELTA P	Differential Pressure
DEPRESS	Depressurization
DES	Descent
DEST	Destination
DET	Detection, Detector
DEU	Decoder/Encoder Unit
DEV	Deviation
DFDAMU	Digital Flight Data Acquisition and Management Unit
DFDAU	Digital Flight Data Acquisition Unit
DFDR	Digital Flight Data Recorder
DFDRS	Digital Flight Data Recording System
DFIDU	Dual Function Interactive Display Unit
DGI	Digital Input
DGO	Digital Output

DH	Decision Height
DIA	Diameter
DIFF	Differential
DIPLXR	Diplexer
DIR	Direction, Direct, Director
DISC	Disconnect, Disconnected
DISCH	Discharge, Discharged
DIST	Distance
DISTR	Distribute, Distribution, Distributor
DITS	Digital Information Transfer System
DIU	Digital Interface Unit
DLC	Direct Lift Control
DLCS	Data Loading and Configuration System
DLK	Data Link
DLRB	Data Loading Routing Box
DLS	Data Loading Selector
DMA	Direct Memory Access
DMC	Display Management Computer

DMDLTR	Demodulator
DME	Distance Measuring Equipment
DMP	Display Management Processor
DMPR	Damper
DMU	Data Management Unit
DN	Down
DNI	Drawing Numerical Index
DNLK	Down lock
DOLLI	Dome LED Light
DOW	Dry Operating Weight
DPCU	Digital Passenger Control Unit
DPDT	Double Pole/Double Throw
DPI	Differential Pressure Indicator
DR	Dead Reckoning
DR	Door
DRM	Duct Repair Manual
DRMI	Distance Radio Magnetic Indicator
DRVG	Driving

DRVR	Driver
DSDL	Dedicated Serial Data Link
DSEB	Digital Seat Electronic Box
DSI	Discrete Input
DSO	Discrete Output
DSPL	Display
DTD	Document Type Definition
DTG	Distance to Go
DTMF	Dual Tone Multiple Frequency
DTMS	Damage Tolerance Monitoring System
DTMU	Damage Tolerance Monitoring Unit
DU	Display Unit
DWG	Drawing
D/LNA	Diplexer/Low Noise Amplifier

E

E	East
EAROM	Electrically Alterable Read Only Memory
EBCU	Emergency Brake Control Unit

EBHA	Electrical Backup Hydraulic Actuator
ECAM	Electronic Centralized Aircraft Monitoring
ECMS	Electrical Contactor Management System
ECMU	Electrical Contactor Management Unit
ECN	Engineering Change Note
ECON	Economy
ECP	Ecam Control Panel
ECS	Environmental Control System
EEPROM	Electrically erase able Programmable Read Only Memory
EFCC	Electronic Flight Control Computer
EFCS	Electrical Flight Control System
EFCU	Electrical Flight Control Unit
EFF	Effective, Effectivity
EFIS	Electronic Flight Instrument System
EGIU	Electrical Generation Interface Unit
EHA	Electro-Hydrostatic Actuator
EIS	Electronic Instrument System
EIU	Engine Interface Unit

EIVMU	Engine Interface and Vibration Monitoring Unit
ELA	Electrical Load Analysis
ELAC	Elevator Aileron Computer
ELC	Electronic Library Computer
ELEC	Electric, Electrical, Electricity
ELEK	Electronic
ELEV	Elevation, Elevator
ELMS	Electrical Load Management System
ELMU	Electrical Load Management Unit
ELS	Electronic Library System
ELT	Emergency Locator Transmitter
EMC	Electromagnetic Compatibility
EMER	Emergency
EMI	Electromagnetic Interference
EMISN	Emission
ENCDR	Encoder
END	Endurance
ENG	Engine

EO	Engine Out
EOSID	Engine out Standard Instrument Departure
EOT	End of Tape
EP	Entry Panel
EPC	External Power Contactor
EPD	Extended Principle Diagram
EPESC	Enhanced Passenger Entertainment System Controller
EPGS	Electrical Power Generation System
EPLD	Electronically Programmable Logic Device
EPROM	Erasable Programmable Read Only Memory
EPR.D	EPR Descent
EPR.L	EPR Latch
EPSU	Emergency Power Supply Unit
EQPT	Equipment
ER	Extended Range
ERP	Enhanced Runaway Protection
ESDN	Extended System/Structure Description Note
ESLB	ECAM System Logic Book

ESP	Electrical Standard Practices
ESPM	Electrical Standard Practices Manual
ESS	Essential
EST	Estimated
ESU	Ethernet Switch Unit
ET	Elapsed Time
ETA	Estimated Time of Arrival
ETD	Estimated Time of Departure
ETE	Estimated Time Enroute
ETO	Estimated Time Over
ETOPS	Extended Range Twin Engine Aircraft Operations
ETP	Equal Time Point
EVAC	Evacuation
EVMU	Engine Vibration Monitoring Unit
EWD	Engine/Warning Display
EXC	Excitation, Excite
EXCESS	Excessive
EXCHGR	Exchanger

EXH	Exhaust
EXP	Expansion
EXT	Exterior, External
EXTING	Extinguishing, Extinguish
EXTN	Extension
EXTRACT	Extraction, Extractor

F

F	Fahrenheit
FA	Course from a Fixed Waypoint to an Altitude Termination
FAC	Flight Augmentation Computer
FADEC	Full Authority Digital Engine Control
FAF	Final Approach Fix
FAIL	Failed, Failure
FANS	Future Air Navigation System
FAP	Flight Attendant Panel A340-500/600
FAP	Forward Attendant Panel
FAR	Federal Aviation Regulations
FAS	Flight Augmentation System

FAV	Fan Air Valve
FC	Course from a Fixed Waypoint to a Changeover Point
FC	Fully Closed
FCC	Flight Control Computer
FCDC	Flight Control Data Concentrator
FCGU	Flight Control and Guidance Unit A380
FCMC	Fuel Control and Monitoring Computer
FCMS	Fuel Control Monitoring System
FCOM	Flight Crew Operating Manual
FCPC	Flight Control Primary Computer
FCRC	Flight Crew Rest Compartment
FCSC	Flight Control Secondary Computer
FCU	Flight Control Unit
FCV	Flow Control Valve
FD	Course from a Fixed Waypoint to a DME Distance
FD	Flight Director
FD	Fuselage Datum

FDAU	Flight Data Acquisition Unit
FDB	Floor Disconnect Box
FDBK	Feedback
FDC	Fuel Data Concentrator
FDD	Floppy Disk Drive
FDEP	Flight Data Entry Panel
FDIMU	Flight Data Interface and Management Unit
FDIU	Flight Data Interface Unit
FDU	Fire Detection Unit
FE	Flight Envelope
FEDR	Feeder
FF	Fuel Flow
FG	Flight Guidance
FGE	Flight Guidance and Envelope
FGES	Flight Guidance and Envelope System
FH	Flight Hours
FIDS	Fault Isolation and Detection System
FIFO	First Input/First Output

FIG	Figure
FILG	Filling
FIM	Fault Isolation Manual
FIN	Functional Item Number
FIS	Flight Information Services
FIX	Fixed
FL	Flight Level
FLD	Field
FLEX	Flexible
FLP	Flap
FLSCU	Fuel Level Sensing Control Unit
FLT	Flight
FLTR	Filter
FLXTO	Flexible Take-Off
FM	Course from a Fixed Waypoint with a Manual Termination
FM	Flight Management
FM	Flight Manual
FM	Frequency Modulation

FMA	Flight Mode Annunciator
FMC	Flight Management Computer
FMCS	Flight Management Computer System (FMC and CDU)
FMEA	Failure Mode Effect Analysis
FMGC	Flight Management and Guidance Computer
FMGEC	Flight Management Guidance and Envelope Computer
FMGES	Flight Management Guidance and Envelope System
FMGS	Flight Management and Guidance System
FMS	Flight Management System (FMCS and AFS sensors)
FMV	Fuel Metering Valve
FNCP	Flight Navigation Control Panel
FNSG	Flight Navigation Symbol Generator
FO	Fully Open
FOB	Fuel on Board
FOD	Foreign Object Damage
FPA	Flight Path Angle

FPEEPMS	Floor Proximity Emergency Escape Path Marking System
FPMU	Fuel Properties Measurement Unit
FPPU	Feedback Position Pick-off Unit
FPRM	Fuel Pipe Repair Manual
FPT	Flight Path Target
FPV	Flight Path Vector
FQ	Fuel Quantity
FQI	Fuel Quantity Indicating/Indication/ Indicator
FQIC	Fuel Quantity Indication Computer
FQMS	Fuel Quantity and Management System
FR	Frame
FREQ	Frequency
FRM	Fault Reporting Manual
FRU	Frequency Reference Unit
FRV	Fuel Return Valve
FS	Front Spar
FSCM	Federal Supply Code for Manufacturers

FSN	Fleet Serial Number
FTG	Fitting
FTI	Flight Test Installation
FTU	Force Transducer Unit
FU	Fuel Used
FUSLG	Fuselage
FW	Failure Warning
FWC	Flight Warning Computer
FWD	Forward
FWL	Firewall
FWS	Flight Warning System
F/O	First Officer

G

G	Green
GA	Go-Around
GAD	General Assembly Drawing
GAIR	General Assembly Inspection Report
GALY	Galley

GAPCU	Ground and Auxiliary Power Control Unit
GCR	Generator Control Relay
GCU	Generator Control Unit
GDE	Guide
GDNC	Guidance
GEM	Ground Equipment Manual
GEN	Generator
GES	Ground Earth Station
GGPCU	Generator and Ground Power Control Unit
GLC	Generator Line Contactor
GLR	Generator Line Relay
GMT	Greenwich Mean Time
GND	Ground
GNLU	GNSS Navigation and Landing Unit
GNSS	Global Navigation Satellite System
GPCU	Ground Power Control Unit
GPS	Global Positioning System
GPSSU	Global Positioning System Sensor Unit

GPU	Ground Power Unit
GPWC	Ground Proximity Warning Computer
GPWS	Ground Proximity Warning System
GRP	Geographic Reference Point
GRP	Glass-Reinforced Plastic
GRU	Ground Refrigeration Unit
GRVTY	Gravity
GS	Ground Speed
GSE	Ground Support Equipment
GTI	Ground Test Instructions
GW	Gross Weight
GWR	General Working Rules
GYRO	Gyroscope
G/S	Glide Slope

H

HA	Holding Pattern to an Altitude Termination
HARN	Harness
HDDA	Hard Disk Drive Array

HDG	Heading
HDG/S	Heading Selected
HDL	Handle
HDLG	Handling
HDST	Headset
HDWHL	Hand wheel
HEGS	Hydraulic Electrical Generating System
HF	High Frequency
HF	Holding Pattern to a Fixed Waypoint
HFDR	High Frequency Data Radio
HGA	High Gain Antenna
HI	High
HL	High Level
HLD	High Power Amplifier/Low Noise Amplifier/Diplexer
HLD	Hold
HLDR	Holder
HLTY	Healthy
HM	Holding Pattern with a Manual Termination

HMC	Hydro mechanical Control
HMI	Human-Machine Interface
HP	High Pressure
HPA	High Power Amplifier
HPR	High Power Relay
HRP	Horizontal Reference Plane
HS	High Speed
HSI	Horizontal Situation Indicator
HSMU	Hydraulic System Monitoring Unit
HTG	Heating
HTR	Heater
HUD	Head up Display
HUDC	Head up Display Computer
HV	High Voltage
HVPS	High Voltage Power Supply
HYD	Hydraulic
H/W	Hardware

I

IAF	Initial Approach Fix
IAS	Indicated Airspeed
IBIT	Initiated BITE
ICD	Interface Control Document
ICP	Integrated Control Panel
ICY	Interchangeability
ID	Inside Diameter
IDENT	Identification, Identifier, Identify
IDG	Integrated Drive Generator
IDU	Interactive Display Unit
IF	Initial Fix
IFE	In-Flight Entertainment
IFEC	In-Flight Entertainment Center
IFR	Instrument Flight Rules
IGB	Inlet Gear Box
IGN	Ignition
ILLUM	Illumination

ILS	Instrument Landing System (LOC and G/S)
IMA	Integrated Modular Avionics
IMM	Immediate
IMU	Inertial Measurement Unit
INB	Inbound
INBD	Inboard
INCR	Increment
IND	Indicator
INDG	Indicating
INFO	Information
INHIB	Inhibit, Inhibited, Inhibition
INIT	Initial (inaction)
INOP	Inoperative
INR	Inner
INRTL	Inertial
INS	Inertial Navigation System
INST	Instinctive
INST	Instrument

INSTL	Installation
INSUL	Insulate, Insulation, Insulator
INTCP	Intercept
INTEG	Integral
INTERCOM	Intercommunication
INTFC	Interface
INTL	Internal
INTLK	Interlock
INTMD	Intermediate
INTMT	Intermittent
INTPH	Interphone
INTRG	Interrogate, Interrogator
INV	Inverter
IOM	Input /Output Module
IP	Intermediate Pressure
IPC	Illustrated Parts Catalog
IPCU	Ice Protection Control Unit
IPPU	Instrumentation Position Pick-off Unit

IR	Inertial Reference
IRS	Inertial Reference System
ISA	International Standard Atmosphere
ISIS	Integrated Standby Instrument System
ISO	International Standardization Organization
ISOL	Isolation
ISPSS	In-Seat Power Supply System
ISPSU	In-Seat Power Supply Unit
IVASEB	Integrated Video and Audio Seat Electronic Box
IVS	Inertial Vertical Speed
I/O	Input/ Output
I/P	Input
I/P	Intercept Point
I/P	Intercept Profile
JAM	Jammed, Jamming
JAR	Joint Aviation Requirements
JCT	Junction
JTSN	Jettison

K

KCCU	Keyboard and Cursor Control Unit

L

L	Left
L	Length
LA	Linear Accelerometer
LAF	Load Alleviation Function
LAN	Local Area Network
LAT	Lateral
LAT	Latitude
LAV	Lavatory
LBP	Left Bottom Plug
LCD	Liquid Crystal Display
LCH	Latch
LCN	Load Classification Number
LCTR	Locator
LD	Lower Deck
LD CAB	Lower Deck Cabin

LD GALY	Lower Deck Galley
LD LAV	Lower Deck Lavatory
LDCC	Lower Deck Cargo Compartment
LDF	Lower Deck Facilities
LDG	Landing
LDMCR	Lower Deck Mobile Crew Rest
LE	Leading Edge
LED	Light Emitting Diode
LEHGS	Local Electro-Hydraulic Generation System
LER	Leading Edge Rib
LGA	Low Gain Antenna
LGCIU	Landing Gear Control and Interface Unit
LGMS	Landing Gear Management System
LH	Left Hand
LIM	Limit, Limitation, Limiting, Limiter
LIQD	Liquid
LIS	Localizer Inertial Smoothing
LKD	Locked

LKG	Locking
LKSHFT	Lock shaft
LL	Latitude/longitude
LMP	Left Middle Plug
LMS	Leakage Measurement System
LNR	Linear
LO	Low
LOC	Localizer
LONG	Longitude
LONGL	Longitudinal
LONGN	Longer on
LOP	Low Oil Pressure
LP	Low Pressure
LRE	List of Radioactive and Hazardous Elements
LRI	Line Replaceable Item
LRM	Line Replaceable Module
LRU	Line Replaceable Unit
LS	Loudspeaker

LS	Low Speed
LSB	Least Significant Bit
LSI	Large Scale Integrated/Integration/ Integrator
LSR	Load Shedding Relay
LT	Light
LTD	Limited
LTG	Lighting
LTM	Livestock Transportation Manual
LTP	Left Top Plug
LV	Low Voltage
LVDT	Linear Variable Differential Transducer
LVL	Level
LVR	Lever
LW	Landing Weight
LWR	Lower
L/G	Landing Gear

M

M	Maneuvering Speed (EFIS)

MAAP	Members and Associated Partners
MAC	Mean Aerodynamic Chord
MAG	Magnetic
MAG DEC	Magnetic Declination
MAIN MUX	Main Multiplexer
MAINT	Maintenance
MAN	Manual
MAT	Multi-purpose Access Terminal
MAX	Maximum
MCD	Movable Class Divider
MCDU	Multipurpose Control & Display Unit
MCL	Maximum Climb
MCPU	Motor Control and Protection Unit
MCT	Maximum Continuous Thrust
MCU	Modular Concept Unit
MCUR	Mean Cycle between Unscheduled Removals
MD	Main Deck
MDA	Minimum Descent Altitude

MDCC	Main Deck Cargo Compartment Freighters & post-1993 combos
MDDU	Multipurpose Disk Drive Unit
MEAS	Measurement
MECH	Mechanic, Mechanical, Mechanism
MED	Medium
MET	Meteorological
MEW	Manufacturer's Empty Weight
MFA	Memorized Fault Annunciator
MFD	Multifunction Display
MFG	Manufacturing
MFP	Maintenance Facility Planning
MFR	Manufacturer
MI	Magnetic Indicator
MIC	Microphone
MICBAC	Micro-System Bus Access Channel
MID	Middle
MIDU	Multi-Input Interactive Display Unit
MIN	Minimum

MISC	Miscellaneous
MKR	Marker (radio) Beacon
MLA	Maneuver Load Alleviation
MLG	Main Landing Gear
MLI	Magnetic Level Indicator
MLIH	Magnetic Level Indicator Housing
MLS	Microwave Landing System
MLW	Maximum Design Landing Weight
MMEL	Master Minimum Equipment List
MMI	Manual Magnetic Indicator
MMO	Mach Max Operating Speed
MMO	Maximum Operating Mach
MMR	Multi-Mode Receiver
MNFOLD	Manifold
MOD	Modification
MODLTR	Modulator
MON	Monitor, Monitoring, Monitored
MORA	Minimum off Route Altitude

MOS	Metal Oxide Semiconductor
MOT	Motor, Motorized
MP	Modification Proposal
MPD	Maintenance Planning Document
MPU	Modem Processor Unit
MRB	Maintenance Review Board
MRW	Maximum Ramp Weight
MSA	Minimum Safe Altitude
MSB	Most Significant Bit
MSG	Maintenance Steering Group
MSG	Message
MSI	Maintenance Significant Item
MSL	Mean Sea Level
MSN	Manufacturer's Serial Number
MSTR	Master
MSU	Media Server Unit
MSU	Mode Selector Unit (IRS)
MSU	Motor Switching Unit

MSW	Micro switch
MTBD	Mean Time between Defects
MTBF	Mean Time between Failures
MTBR	Mean Time between Removals
MTBUR	Mean Time between Unscheduled Removals
MTG	Mounting
MTI	Multi Tank Indicator
MTO	Maximum Take-Off
MTOGW	Maximum Takeoff Gross Weight
MTOW	Maximum Design Takeoff Weight
MTP	Maintenance and Test Panel (AFS)
MTTF	Mean Time to Failure
MTTR	Mean Time to Repair
MTTUR	Mean Time to Unscheduled Removal
MTW	Maximum Design Taxi Weight
MU	Management Unit
MUX	Multiplex, Multiplexer
MVT	Movement

MXR	Mixer
MZFW	Maximum Design Zero Fuel Weight

N

N	North
N MOS	Negative Metal Oxide Semiconductor
N1	Engine Fan Speed
N1	Low Pressure Rotor Speed
N1.D	N1 Descent
N1.L	N1 Latch
N2	High Pressure Rotor Speed
NAC	Nacelle
NAI	Nacelle Anti-Icing
NAS	Navy and Army Standard
NASA	National Aeronautics and Space Administration Replaces NACA
NATS	North American Telephone System
NAV	Navigation
NAVAID	Navigation Aid
NBPT	No Break Power Transfer

NC	No Computed Data
NCR	NSS Communication Router
ND	Navigation Display
NDB	Non-Directional Beacon
NDM	Noise Definition Manual
NDT	Non-Destructive Test
NEG	Negative
NHA	Next Higher Assembly
NLG	Nose Landing Gear
NMI	Non Mask able Interrupt
NO	Normal Operation
NO	Normally Open
No	Number
NORM	Normal
NOVOLRAM	Non-volatile Random Access Memory
NS	No Smoking
NSA	Norma Sod Aviation
NSCM	NATO Supply Code for Manufacturers

NSDW	Non Specific Design Work
NSS	Network Server System
NTM	Nondestructive Testing Manual
NTWK	Network
NUM	Numerical
NVM	Non-Volatile Memory
N/A	Not Applicable
N/W	Nose Wheel
N/WS	Nose Wheel Steering

O

O	Open
O2	Oxygen (Symbol)
OAT	Outside Air Temperature
OBRM	On Board Replaceable Module
OBS	Omni Bearing Selector
OC	Open Circuit
OC	Over current
OCCPNT	Occupant

OD	Outside Diameter
OEW	Operational Empty Weight
OF	Over frequency
OFST	Offset
OGV	Outlet Guide Vane
OH	Opposite Hand
OHSC	Overhead Stowage Compartment
OHU	Optical Head Unit
OIT	Oil Inlet Temperature Do not use this abbreviation with this meaning for the A380 (risk of confusion with Onboard Information Terminal).
OIT	Onboard Information Terminal
OK	Correct
OMS	Onboard Maintenance System
OMT	Onboard Maintenance Terminal
OOT	Oil Outlet Temperature
OPER	Operative/Operation/Operating
OPP	Opposite
OPS	Operations

OPT	Optimum
OPT	Optional
OPV	Over pressure Valve
ORT	Owner Requirement Table
OU	Outlet Unit
OUT	Outlet
OUTB	Outbound
OUTBD	Outboard
OUTR	Outer
OVBD	Overboard
OVFL	Overflow
OVHD	Overhead
OVHT	Overheat
OVLD	Overload
OVPRESS	Over pressure
OVRD	Override
OVSP	Over speed
OVSTEER	Over steer

OXY	Oxygen
O/P	Output

P

P	Purple
PA	Passenger Address
PARAM	Parameter
PARK	Parking
PAS	Pitch Attitude Sensor
PATS	Passenger Air-to-Ground Telephone System
PAX	Passenger
PBE	Protective Breathing Equipment
PBIT	Power-Up Built-in Test
PBM	Power Plant Build-up Manual
PC	Pack Controller
PC	Personal Computer
PCB	Printed Circuit Board
PCM	Pulse Code Modulation
PCU	Passenger Control Unit

PCU	Power Control Unit
PD	Principle Diagram
PDL	Portable Data Loader
PED	Pedestal
PEF	Pylon Extension Fairing
PEPDC	Primary Electrical Power Distribution Center
PERF	Performance
PERM	Permanent
PES	Passenger Entertainment (System)
PESAR	Passenger Entertainment System Audio Reproducer
PESC	PES Controller
PESMMUX	Passenger Entertainment System Main Mux
PF	Pilot Flying
PF	Power Factor
PFD	Primary Flight Display
PFIS	Passenger Flight Information System
PH	Phase
PHC	Probe Heat Computer

PIN PROG	Pin Programming
PIPC	Power Plant Illustrated Parts Catalog
PIREP	Pilot Report
PIREP	Pilot Reports
PISA	Passenger Interface and Supply Adapter
PIU	Passenger Information Unit
PLCRD	Placard
PMA	Permanent Magnet Alternator
PMC	Power Management Control, controller
PMDB	Production Management Data Base
PMG	Permanent Magnet Generator
PMP	Pump
PMR	Performance Maintenance Recorder
PMS	Process and Material Specification
PMUX	Power Plant Multiplexer
PN	Part Number Airbus preferred abbreviation
PNEU	Pneumatic
PNF	Pilot Non Flying

PNL	Panel
PNR	Part Number Airbus acceptable alternative - use PN where possible.
POB	Pressure-Off Brake
POR	Point of Regulation
POS	Position
POT	Potentiometer
PPU	Position Pickoff Unit
PRAM	Prerecorded Announcement and Music
PRB	Probe
PREAMP	Preamplifier
PRECOOL	Pre-cooler
PRED	Prediction
PREREC	Prerecorded
PRES POS	Present Position
PRESEL	Preselection, Preselect or
PRESS	Pressure, Pressurization, Pressurize
PREV	Previous
PRI	Priority

PRIM	Primary
PROC	Procedure
PROF	Profile PROG Program, Programming
PROJ	Projector
PROM	Programmable Read Only Memory
PROT	Protection
PROX	Proximity
PRPHL	Peripheral
PRR	Power Ready Relay
PRSRZG	Pressurizing
PRV	Pressure Regulating Valve
PSCU	Proximity Switch Control Unit
PSDU	Power Supply Decoupling Unit
PSI	Pound per Square Inch
PSIU	Passenger Service Information Unit
PSS	Passenger Services System
PSU	Passenger Service Unit
PT	Point

PTC	Positive Temperature Coefficient
PTR	Push to Reset
PTT	Push-to-Talk
PTT	Push to Test
PTU	Power Transfer Unit
PU	Parts Usage
PU	Pick Up
PVI	Para visual Indicating
PVIS	Passenger Visual Information System
PWCU	Potable Water Control Unit
PWIP	Potable Water Indication Panel
PWR	Power
PYL	Pylon
P/B	Pushbutton
P/BSW	Pushbutton Switch
P/C	Printed Circuit

Q

Q	Pitch Rate

QAD	Quick-Attach-Detach
QAM	Quadrature Amplitude Modulation
QAR	Quick Access Recorder
QAT	Quadruple ARINC Transmitter
QD	Quick Donning
QFE	Field Elevation Atmospheric Pressure
QFU	Runway Heading
QMU	QAM Modulator Unit
QNE	Sea Level Standard Atmosphere Pressure
QNH	Sea Level Atmospheric Pressure
QTY	Quantity

R

R	Radius
R	Red
R	Right
RA	Radio Altimeter, Radio Altitude
RAD	Radio
RADVR	Random Access Digital Video Reproducer

RAM	Random Access Memory
RAT	Ram Air Turbine
RBP	Right Bottom Plug
RC	Repetitive Chime
RCC	Remote Control Center
RCCB	Remote Control Circuit Breaker
RCDR	Recorder
RCL	Recall
RCP	Reverse Current Protection
RCPT	Receptacle
RCPTN	Reception
RCT	Rear Center Tank
RCVR	Receiver
RCVY	Recovery
RD	Retro Drawing
RDC	Remote Data Concentrator
RECIRC	Recirculate, Recirculation
RECONF	Reconfiguration

RECT	Rectifier
RED	Reduction
REDCR	Reducer
REDUND	Redundancy
REF	Reference
REFUEL	Refueling
REG	Regulator
REGUL	Regulation
REL	Release
REL	Reluctance
RES	Resistance
RET	Retract
RETRD	Retracted
REV	Reverse
REV	Revise, Revision
RF	Radio Frequency
RFC	Request for Change
RFI	Radio Frequency Interference

RFI	Request for Information
RFU	Radio Frequency Unit
RFW	Request for Work
RH	Right Hand
RHEO	Rheostat
RHL	Rudder Hinge Line
RLA	Reverser Lever Angle
RLY	Relay
RMI	Radio Magnetic Indicator
RMO	Retrofit Modification Offer
RMP	Radio Management Panel
RMT	Remote
RNG	Range
ROLR	Roller
ROM	Read Only Memory
ROTG	Rotating
RPDR	Reproducer
RPLNT	Repellent

RPM	Revolution per Minute
RPTG	Repeating
RPTR	Repeater
RQRD	Required
RST	Reset
RSV	Reserve
RSVR	Reservoir
RTE	Route
RTN	Return
RTOLW	Runway Takeoff and Landing Weight
RTOW	Runway Takeoff Weight
RTP	Right Top Plug
RTRY	Rotary
RTU	Radar Transceiver Unit
RUD	Rudder
RVCP	Remote Video Control Panel
RVDT	Rotary Variable Differential Transducer
RVR	Runway Visual Range

RWDS	Rearwards
RWY	Runway
R/C	Rate of Climb
R/D	Rate of Descent
R/I	Radio/Inertial
R/L	Reading Light
R/T	Radio Transmit

S

S	Minimum Slat Retract Speed (EFIS)
S	South
SA	Stress Analysis
SAD	Stress Analysis Data
SAE	Society of Automotive Engineers
SAF	Safety
SAL	System Address Label
SAM	Stress Analysis Manual
SAR	Smart Access Recorder Used on Single Aisle family
SAT	Static Air Temperature

SATCOM	Satellite Communication
SB	Service Bulletin
SC	Single Chime
SCAV	Scavenge
SCE	Source
SCG	System Configuration Guide
SCI	Secured Communications Interface
SCN	Specification Change Notice
SCU	Supplemental Control Unit
SD	System Display
SDAC	System Data Acquisition Concentrator
SDAC	System Data Analog Converter
SDCU	Smoke Detection Control Unit
SDN	System Description Note
SDU	Satellite Data Unit
SDW	Specific Design Work
SE	Simplified English
SEAL	Sealing

SEB	Seat Electronic Box
SEC	Secondary
SEC	Secondary Computer A380
SEC	Spoiler Elevator Computer (SA aircraft only)
SECT	Section
SEL	Select, Selected, Selector, Selection
SELCAL	Selective Calling System
SEPDC	Secondary Electrical Power Distribution Center
SEQ	Sequence, Sequential
SER	Serial
SER	Serial Number Airbus acceptable alternative - use SN where possible.
SES	Support Equipment Summary
SET	Setting
SFC	Specific Fuel Consumption
SFCC	Slat Flap Control Computer
SFE	Seller Furnished Equipment
SGU	Symbol Generator Unit

SH ABS	Shock Absorber
SHED	Shed able, Shedding
SHLD	Shield, Shielding
SHR PN	Shear Pin
SI	Slip Indicator
SIC	System Isolation Contactor
SID	Standard Instrument Departure
SIG	Signal
SIL	Speech Interference Level
SIM	Simulation
SIU	Server Interface Unit
SKT	Socket
SLD	Slide, Sliding
SLT	Slat
SM	Standards Manual
SMK	Smoke
SN	Serial Number Airbus preferred abbreviation
SNGL	Single

SNSG	Sensing
SNSR	Sensor
SO	Shutoff
SOL	Solenoid
SOV	Shut-Off Valve
SPD	Speed
SPDB	Secondary Power Distribution Box
SPEC	Specification
SPKR	Speaker
SPL	Sound Pressure Level
SPLR	Spoiler
SPLY	Supply
SPRDR	Spreader
SPST	Single Pole Single Throw
SQ	Squelch
SRM	Structural Repair Manual
SRPSU	Slide Release Power Supply Unit
SRS	Speed Reference System

SSB	Single Side Band
SSEC	Static Source Error Correction
SSM	Sign Status Matrix
SSMM	Solid State Mass Memory
SSPC	Solid State Power Controller
SSTU	Side Stick Transducer Unit
STA	Station
STAB	Stabilizer
STAR	Standard Terminal Arrival Route
STAT	Static
STBY	Standby
STD	Standard
STGR	Stringer
STRG	Steering
STRK	Stroke
STS	Status
STWG	Stowage
SUCT	Suction

SURF	Surface
SV	Servo valve
SVCE	Service
SVO	Servo
SW	Switch
SWTG	Switching
SYNC	Synchrony, Synchronize
SYNTHR	Synthesizer
SYS	System
S/C	Step Climb
S/D	Step Descent
S/MECH	Shortening Mechanism
S/W	Software

T

T	Trim
T	True
T	Turn
T-R	Transmitter-Receiver

TAC	Taxiing Aid Camera
TACAN	Ultra-high Frequency Tactical Air Navigation Aid
TACH	Tachometer
TACS	Taxiing Aid Camera System
TACT	Tactical
TAS	True Airspeed
TAT	Total Air Temperature
TB	Terminal Block
TBC	to Be Confirmed
TBO	Time between Overhauls
TC	Theoretical Contour
TC	Thermocouple
TCAS	Traffic Alert and Collision Avoidance System
TCC	Thrust Control Computer
TDD	Technical Design Directive
TDS	Technical Data Sheet
TE	Trailing Edge

TED	Tool and Equipment Drawing
TEI	Tool and Equipment Index
TELECOM	Telecommunications
TEM	Illustrated Tool and Equipment Manual
TEMP	Temperature
TER	Trailing Edge Rib
TFTS	Terrestrial Flight Telephone System
TGT	Target
THERAP	Therapeutic
THR	Thrust
THRM	Thermal
THRMST	Thermostat
THROT	Throttle
THROT PUSH	Throttle Pusher
THS	Trim able Horizontal Stabilizer
TK	Tank
TKE	Track Angle Error
TM	Torque Motor

TM	Transportability Manual
TMR	Timer
TO	Takeoff
TOGA	Takeoff/Go Around
TOGW	Takeoff Gross Weight
TOIL	Toilet
TOL	Tolerance
TOT	Total
TOW	Takeoff Weight
TPIC	Tire Pressure Indicating Computer
TPIS	Tire Pressure Indicating System
TR	Transformer Rectifier
TR	Transistor
TRANS	Transition
TRC	Thrust Rating Computer
TRIG	Trigger
TRK	Track (angle)
TRLY	Trolley

TROPO	Tropo pause
TRP	Thrust Rate Panel - Thrust Rating Panel
TRQE	Torque
TRV	Travel
TSM	Trouble Shooting Manual
TT	Trim Tank
TTL	Transistor Transistor Logic
TTS	Trim Tank System
TU	Tapping Unit
TURB	Turbine
TURB	Turbulence, Turbulent
TWLU	Terminal Wireless LAN Unit
TX	Transmission (TCAS to Transponder)
TYP	Typical
T/C	Top of Climb
T/D	Top of Descent
T/F	Track of a Fixed Waypoint

U

UD	Upper Deck
UDCC	Upper Deck Cargo Compartment
UEB	Under seat Electronic Box
UF	Under frequency
UHF	Ultra High Frequency
UICDL	User Interface Configuration Download List
ULD	Unit Load Device
UNBAL	Unbalance, Unbalanced
UND	Under
UNIV	Universal
UNLK	Unlock
UNLKD	Unlocked, Unlocking
UPR	Upper
UTC	Universal Time Coordinated
UV	Ultra-Violet
UV	Under Voltage
U/FLOOR	Underfloor

U/S	Unserviceable
V	
V1	Critical Engine Failure Speed
V1	Decision Speed
V2	Takeoff Safety Speed
V3	Flap Retraction Speed
V4	Slat Retraction Speed
VAC	Voltage Alternating Current
VACU	Vacuum
VAR	Variable, Variation
VC	Ventilation Controller
VCC	Video Control Center
VCM	Video Camera Module
VCO	Voltage Controlled Oscillator
VCP	Video Control Panel
VCU	Video Control Unit
VDC	Voltage Direct Current
VDEV	Vertical Deviation

VDR	VHF Data Radio
VDU	Video Display Unit
VEL	Velocity
VENT	Ventilation
VERT	Vertical
VFG	Variable Frequency Generator
VFR	Visual Flight Rules
VHF	Very High Frequency
VHV	Very High Voltage
VIB	Vibration
VIMU	Video Multiplexer Unit
VLF	Very Low Frequency
VLS	Lower Selectable Speed
VLV	Valve
VM	Voltmeter
VMU	Video Modulator Unit
VOD	Video on Demand
VODDSU	VOD Data Server Unit

VODMU	VOD Modulator Unit
VODSU	VOD Server Unit
VOL	Volume
VOR	VHF Omnidirectional Range
VORTAC	Visual Omni-Range Tactical Air Navigation
VR	Rotation Speed
VREF	Landing Reference Speed
VRMS	Volt Root Mean Square
VRU	Video Reproducer Unit
VSC	Vacuum System Controller
VSCF	Variable Speed Constant Frequency
VSEB	Video Seat Electronic Box
VSI	Vertical Speed Indicator
VSS	Stick Shaker Speed
VSW	Stall Warning Speed
VSWR	Voltage Standing Wave Ratio
VTR	Video Tape Reproducer
V/S	Vertical Speed

W

W	West
W	White
WAI	Wing Anti-Ice
WARN	Warning
WBBC	Weight and Balance Backup Computation
WBC	Weight & Balance Computer
WBM	Weight and Balance Manual
WBS	Weight and Balance System
WD	Warning Display
WD	Wing Datum
WD	Wiring Diagram
WDB	Wall Disconnect Box
WG	Wing
WGD	Windshield Guidance Display
WGDC	Windshield Guidance Display Computer
WGDS	Windshield Guidance Display System
WHC	Window Heat Computer

WHL	Wheel
WIPCU	Water Ice Protection Control Unit
WIPDU	Water Ice Protection Data Unit
WLDP	Warning Light Display Panel
WLG	Wing Landing Gear
WPT	Waypoint
WRG	Wiring
WRK	Work, Working
WSHLD	Windshield
WSSG	Warning System Symbol Generator
WT	Weight
WTB	Wing tip brake
WTR	Water
WX	Weather Mode (ND)
WXR	Weather Radar

X

X	Cross
X	Trans

X-TALK	Cross-talk
X BLEED	Cross bleed
X FEED	Cross feed
X LINE	Cross line
X VALVE	Cross Valve
XBAR	Crossbar
XCVR	Transceiver
XDCR	Transducer
XFMR	Transformer
XFR	Transfer
XLTR	Translator
XMTR	Transmitter
XPDR	Transponder

Y

Y	Yellow

Z

Z	Greenwich Mean Time
Z	Zone

ZC	Zone Controller
ZFCG	Zero Fuel Center of Gravity
ZFW	Zero Fuel Weight
Zp	Pressure Altitude

PILOT'S NOTES

PILOT'S NOTES

PILOT'S NOTES

PILOT'S NOTES

PILOT'S NOTES

PILOT'S NOTES

PILOT'S NOTES

PILOT'S NOTES

PILOT'S NOTES

PILOT'S NOTES

PILOT'S NOTES

PILOT'S NOTES

PILOT'S NOTES

PILOT'S NOTES

PILOT'S NOTES

PILOT'S NOTES

PILOT'S NOTES

PILOT'S NOTES

PILOT'S NOTES